Co-operative – 2025
&
World Economy

Co-operative – 2025 & World Economy

Pratap Chandra Samal

BLACK EAGLE BOOKS
Dublin, USA
Bhubaneswar, India

BLACK EAGLE BOOKS

USA address:
7464 Wisdom Lane
Dublin, OH 43016

India address:
E/312, Trident Galaxy, Kalinga Nagar,
Bhubaneswar-751003, Odisha, India

E-mail: info@blackeaglebooks.org
Website: www.blackeaglebooks.org

First International Edition Published by
BLACK EAGLE BOOKS, 2025

CO-OPERATIVE - 2025 & WORLD ECONOMY
by **Pratap Chandra Samal**
Writer, Senior Co-operator
Cell: 9090325802

Cover : **JM Printer**
Interior Design: Ezy's Publication

ISBN- 978-1-64560-723-6 (Paperback)

Printed in the United States of America

Preface

My late father Madan Samal was a borrowing member of Eranch Service Co-operative Society and was an active participator in Annual General Body Meeting. I was hearing his deliberation regarding Co-operative Society since 1972 at the age of 10 only. My father borrowed 250 rupees from the said society under Cuttack Central Co-operative Bank, to defray my middle school education 1972-1976 and repaid the society with extra 12 rupees which was byforce by the Society Secretary for which I carried some impression of Co-operative activities. In that time due to poor finance which was maximum 500 rupees per farmer but it was insufficient for Agriculture purpose. In that time my father also borrowed 500 rupees to meet the expenditure of my high school education. After completion of my school education I joined in a college. My father sold some agricultural property to meet my college education expenditure. In due course I completed my higher education with M.A.LL.B.degree and joined as a lecturer in a college. By the inspiration of Odisha Chief Minister Mr. Biju Pattanaik, I left the service and joined as a Director in Bank Management. For Co-operative education I was guided and tought by so many eminent Co-operators, Dr. Jogesh Rout, Dr. Arabinda Dhali, Dr. Damodar Rout, Surya Patra, Atanu Sabyasachi Nayak all are (Former Co-operative Ministers), Pradeep Bal Samanta, Minister, Cooperation, Textiles, Handloom & Handicraft, Odisha B.K. Ray (Former MD OSCB & others), The Govt. of Odisha declared me as Senior Co-operator in last National Co-operative weeks 2023.

I think this suggestions through my articles and books which is related to Co-operatives may be the way of reformation in Co-operative institutions for future generations and praised the 'God Lord Jagannath'.

Dedicated and Profound Reference to my Late Father, Mother, Father-in-Law, Mother-in-Law, Teachers & Guides.

Pratap Chandra Samal

SHRI KANAK VARDHAN SINGH DEO

DEPUTY CHIEF MINISTER

Agriculture & Farmers'
Empowerment, Energy

Telephone | 0674-2536962 (O)
| 0674-2390051 (O)
| 0674-2391560 (Res.)

D.O. No. ..../DCMAFE&E.

BHUBANESWAR

Date 28·05·2025

Message

I am delighted to know that on the occasion of The International year of Co-operative -2025 a Co-operative book written by Shri Pratap Chandra Samal on "Co-operative-2025 & World Economy" will be launched.

Co-operatives play a significant role in the world economy, contributing to both economic and social development. Co-operatives are a powerful force, strengthening global economic cooperation by promoting social integration, job creation, and poverty reduction. They are based on values of self-help, self-responsibility, democracy, equality, equity, and solidarity.

I extend my best wishes to the writer in this occasion and publication of the book "Co-operative-2025 & World Economy" a grand success.

(K.V. Singh Deo)

SMT. PRAVATI PARIDA
DEPUTY CHIEF MINISTER
Women & Child Development,
Mission Shakti, Tourism.

Telephone : 0674-2536642
PBX No.   :
Mobile No. :

D.O. No. ....\...............</DCMWCDMST.

BHUBANESWAR

Date ....23|05|2025.......

Message

It gives me immense pleasure to know that a co-operative Book, **"Co-operative–2025 & World Economy"** written by Sri Pratap Chandra Samal will be introduced on the occasion of The International Year of Co-operatives–2025.

This book highlights the vital role of co-operatives in building inclusive and sustainable economies amid global challenges. It explores the link between co-operative values and economic trends, aiming to inspire action toward equitable growth.

On this momentous occasion, I extend my warmest congratulations to all esteemed individuals associated with this initiative. I also wish the publication of the book "Co-operative–2025 & World Economy" every success.

(Pravati Parida)

DR. MUKESH MAHALING

MINISTER

Health & Family Welfare,
Parliamentary Affairs,
Electronics & Information
Technology, Odisha.

Telephone :
PBX No.   :
Mobile No. : 6372051004
Email : m.mahaling@odisha.gov.in

D.O. No. ....910............/MHFWPAE&IT.

BHUBANESWAR

Date ...28 - 05 - 2025

MESSAGE

I am pleased to extend my best wishes to the contributors of "Co-operative – 2025 & World Economy" on the occasion of the International Year of Cooperatives – 2025.

The co-operative sector continues to play a key role in inclusive development and social progress. I appreciate the efforts of Shri Pratap Chandra Samal in highlighting its global and national significance through this publication.

Wishing the initiative great success.

Mukesh Mahaling .
(Dr. Mukesh Mahaling)

BIBHUTI BHUSHAN JENA
MINISTER
Commerce & Transport,
Steel & Mines.

Telephone :
PBX No. :
Mobile No. :

D.O. No. ..../MCTS&M.

BHUBANESWAR

Date ....

Message

  I am pleased to know that Shri Pratap Chandra Samal is launching his book "Co-operative – 2025 and World Economy" during the observance of the International Year of Co-operatives – 2025.

  This insightful work reflects the importance of co-operatives in building a just, inclusive, and sustainable economic future. At a time when the world is focusing on collective growth models, this book offers valuable perspectives aligned with our national vision.

  I extend my best wishes to the author and congratulate him on this timely contribution. May the book reach a wide audience and inspire thought and action in the co-operative movement.

(Bibhuti Bhushan Jena)

SHRI RABI NARAYAN NAIK

MINISTER

Rural Development, Panchayati Raj &
Drinking Water

Telephone :
PBX No. :
Mobile No. :

D.O. No. ....8.7.8...../MRDPRDW

BHUBANESWAR

Date ....31.|5.|25

MESSAGE

The book **"Cooperatives-2025 & World Economy"** written by Pratap Chandra Samal; documents the success story of Cooperative Organisation.

I complement the effort for book **"Cooperatives-2025 & World Economy"** and wish the endeavour all success.

(Rabi Narayan Naik)

DR. KRUSHNA CHANDRA MAHAPATRA
MINISTER
Housing & Urban Development
Public Enterprises, Odisha

Telephone : 0674-2536952 (O)
PBX No.   : 0674-2390525 (A)
Mobile No. : +91 7008251870
              9437960752

D.O. No. ..../MH&UDPE.

BHUBANESWAR
Date 28·05·2025

MESSAGE

I have the pleasure to know that a cooperative Book, **"Cooperative-2025 & World Economy"** will be introduced on the occasion of The International Year of Cooperatives-2025.

The Book underlines the Cooperative concept. It also highlights the vital role of cooperatives in building inclusive and sustainable economies amid global challenges. It explores the link between cooperative values and economic trends, aiming to inspire action toward equitable growth.

I hope this book provides a comprehensive idea on economic benefits for the society. I wish the publication of the book **"Cooperative- 2025 & World Economy"** every success.

28/05/2025

(Dr. Krushna Chandra Mahapatra)

SHRI NITYANANDA GOND

MINISTER

School & Mass Education, S.T. & S.C.
Development, Minorities & Backward
Classes Welfare and Social Security &
Empowerment of Persons with
Disabilities, Odisha

Office Tel. No. : 0674-2536910

D.O.L. No. ..../ M

BHUBANESWAR

Date 15-05-2025

MESSAGE

I am happy to know that the book 'Co-operative-2025 & World Economy', written by senior cooperator Sri Pratap Chandra Samal, is being launched on the occasion of The International Year of Co-operative 2025.

Many Cooperatives have made a mark of their own in their areas of work and achieved exemplary results. It is a matter of pride and privilege that it has been highlighted in sector-wise that Co-operative Societies have shown excellence strewn all over the State. I hope this will inspire Cooperative Societies to achieve excellence in their field of activities and all those who are staunch believers in the Ideology, Values and Principles of Cooperatives.

I extend my warmest greetings on the occasion of publication of the book 'Co-operative-2025 & World Economy'.

(Nityananda Gond)

SHRI KRUSHNA CHANDRA PATRA
MINISTER
Food Supplies & Consumer Welfare,
Science & Technology, Odisha

Phone
Office : (0674) 2536975
Assembly : (0674) 2539027
EPABX : 2322182
Residence : (0674)
Mobile No. : 9437332200

D.O. No. ..../MFSCWS&T.

BHUBANESWAR
Date 27/05/2025

MESSAGE

The book "Cooperatives-2025 & World Economy" written by Pratap Chandra Samal, Senior Cooperator speaks the successful journey of Cooperative Organisation in the country. The book underlines the cooperative concept in a nutshell. The Co-operatives are the vital instrument of economic progress and uplifting of downtrodden population in our society. Through co-operative organisations, a self-reliant nation can be achieved.

I hope, this book "Cooperatives-2025 & World Economy" provides a comprehensive idea on economic benefits for the Society. The book also says evolution of Cooperative Society in Odisha.

I convey my heartfelt congratulations & wish the writer and release of book all success.

(Krushna Chandra Patra)

SHRI PRADEEP BAL SAMANTA
Minister of State
(Independent Charge)
Co-operation, Handlooms, Textiles &
Handicrafts

Telephone: 0674-2536948
PBX No. : 2193
E-mail Id : pradeepbal.samanta@
odisha.gov.in

D.O No.: ..../MSCHT&H.

BHUBANESWAR

Date: 23.05.2025

MESSAGE

The book **"Cooperatives-2025 & World Economy"** written by Pratap Chandra Samal; Senior Cooperator speaks the success story of Cooperative Organisation for the progress of downtrodden & development of Society. The book deals with the cooperative concept in a very convincing manner & style.

Co-operatives are the vital instrument of economic prosperity. It ensures advantages for poorly-equipped citizens who were unable to achieve their goal by their own resources & efforts. Through co-operative organisation a self-reliant and a just economic and social order can be built. This book **"Cooperatives-2025 & World Economy"** provides a comprehensive account of the economic benefits of co-operative Society. The book takes us down the memory lane to the evolution of Cooperative Society in Odisha.

I convey my heartfelt congratulations & wish the endeavour of Mr. Pratap Chandra Samal all success.

(Pradeep Bal Samanta)

SHRI SAMPAD CHANDRA SWAIN
MINISTER OF STATE (Ind. Charge)
Industries, Skill Development &
Technical Education, Odisha

Phone
Office : (0674)-2530650
EPABX : 2322197
Res. : (0674)-
Assembly : (0674)-
Email: minind2024@gmail.com

D. O. No. ..../MoS(I)ISD&TE.

BHUBANESWAR

Date 29.05.2025

MESSAGE

It is with great pleasure that I extend my best wishes to the writer of "Co-operative- 2025 & World Economy" on the esteemed occasion of the International Year of Cooperatives -2025.

The co-operative sector remains a powerful catalyst for inclusive development and social advancement across the globe, particularly in India. I sincerely appreciate the dedicated efforts of Shri Pratap Chandra Samal in illuminating the profound impact and enduring significance of cooperatives at both the national and international levels through this insightful publication.

May this book inspire greater awareness and achieve resounding success.

(Sampad Chandra Swain)

GANESH RAM SINGKHUNTIA

MINISTER OF STATE (IND.)

Forest, Environment &
Climate Change, Labour &
Employees' State Insurance, Odisha

Phone:
Office : (0674) 2536930
Res. Off. : (0674) 2536795
Mob. No. : 9438829870
6372036830

e-mail : min.fecc@gov.in

D.O. No. ..../MFL

BHUBANESWAR

Dated ....30|05|2025

MESSAGE

I am happy to know that Shri Pratap Chandra Samal, a senior co-operator of our state has written a book entitled "Cooperative – 2025 and World Economy" which will be launched by Hon'ble Union Minister, Home & Cooperation Shri Amit Saha at New Delhi.

India's cooperative movement, deeply rooted in its cultural and socio-economic landscape, has evolved into a powerful vehicle for inclusive growth, community empowerment, and rural development. United Nations General Assembly proclaimed 2025 as the International Year of Cooperatives, underscoring the crucial role of cooperatives in achieving the UN's Sustainable Development Goals particularly in areas like poverty alleviation, gender equality and sustainable economic growth. The theme, "Cooperatives Build a Better World," emphasizes the enduring global impact of cooperatives in addressing various challenges and promoting inclusive growth by strengthening communities by providing local solutions and ensuring that economic benefits stay within the local area, empowering marginalized communities and promoting social inclusion, creating jobs and opportunities. These are instrumental in providing financial services to individuals and communities who may not have access to traditional banking services.

I congratulate Shri Samal for his book and hope that it will showcase our innovative strides in the cooperative sector.

I wish him all success in his endeavour.

(Ganesh Ram Singkhuntia)

SURYABANSHI SURAJ
MINISTER OF STATE (IND.)
Higher Education, Sports & Youth Services
Odia Language, Literature & Culture, Odisha

Phone Office : 0674-2536916
D.O. No.............../ MoSHES&YSOLL&C
Bhubaneswar

Message

I am happy to know that the International Year of Cooperatives-2025 is being celebrated, recognizing the vital role that cooperative institutions play in fostering inclusive growth and sustainable development. On this significant occasion, I extend my heartfelt congratulations to Sri Pratap Chandra Samal for his insightful contribution through the book "Cooperative 2025 & World Economy". This publication is both timely and relevant, offering a thoughtful perspective on how cooperatives can act as dynamic drivers of economic resilience and inclusive growth in the evolving global economy.

Cooperatives are not merely economic units; they are instruments of social transformation, rooted in democratic values and community empowerment. By bridging local aspirations with global objectives, cooperatives can redefine the contours of the world economy with inclusivity, participation and shared prosperity. I am confident that this book will inspire thoughtful engagement among policymakers, scholars and leaders while contributing meaningfully to the collective progress.

I commend the author for his vision and dedication, hoping the publication achieves great success in reaching a wide and thoughtful readership.

ଶ୍ରୀକୃଷ୍ଣ ଶୁଭ
(Suryabanshi Suraj)

Address. : Res. Office: QR No-6R-2, Unit-VI, Bhubaneswar-751001
Office: Room No.MB-I-006 & 007, Lok Seva Bhawan, Bhubaneswar, Odisha-751001
e-Mail id.: suryabanshi.suraj@gov.in

CONTENTS

Sl. No.	Topic	Page
1.	Environment for Co-operative in 2025	21
2.	Socio-Economic Implications	29
3.	Economic Thoughts	37
4.	Message of the ICA - 2013	46
5.	Housing - Dream to Reality	49
6.	Three Pivot of Co-operative	62
7.	Service Tax in Co-operative	69
8.	Constitutional Amendments A Milestone	77
9.	National Policy on Co-operatives	87
10.	Major Pillars of Co-operative	100
11.	Taskforce on Rural Co-operative Bank	104
12.	Architecture of Co-operative Movement	112
13.	B.R. Amendment Act. - 2012	117
14.	Co-operative in Gram Swaraj	126
15.	Agriculture Labourer in India	131
16.	Co-operatives as Economic Enterprises	141
17.	Co-operative in Villages	151
18.	Constitution guarantee to Co-operative	158
19.	Rural Employment Guarantee Scheme	162
20.	Panchayat Raj Administration in India	169
21.	Agricultural Marketing	175
22.	H.R. Development and Co-operative	183
23.	Future of Co-operative Bank in India	188
24.	Proper management is the key to success	197
25.	Strengthening Credit Institutions	199
26.	The Labour Co-operative Society	203

27.	A Duty of a Public Servant	207
28.	Management of Milk Producers Co-op. Society	216
29.	Balance Sheet in Co-operatives	220
30.	97th Constitution Amendment	226
31.	Second Green Revolution	232
32.	Rural Development through Co-operative	244
33.	Women in Management	249
34.	Co-operative in Post "Kalia"	254
35.	The Indian Co-operative Society's Law	260
36.	Miracles in Co-operative	262
37.	Crisis on Co-operatives	265
38.	Woman A Perennial Source of love	268
39.	Co-operatives : Alignment to Agility	270
40.	"Kaizen", Japanese - work culture	275
41.	Benefit of Co-operative credit	281
42.	Liberalisation of indian economy	284
43.	Report of Kapoor Committee	287
44.	Role of Micro Credit	293
45.	Farmers Suicide in India	303
46.	Mainsteaming Gender	308
47.	NPA Management	315
48.	Co-operative Education	321
49.	Co-operative Education Fund	327
50.	Deprived Children - A New Horizon	336
51.	Co-operative in Tamilnadu	343
52.	The Connotation 'Representative'	350
53.	Govt of Odisha Co-op. Dept. Circular	353
54.	Policy on Co-operative in Odisha	356
55.	O.C.S. Act 1962 and Rules for Performance	366
56.	Housing Movement	374
57.	The Odisha S.H. Co-op. Ordinance-2013 (Repeal)	380
58.	Quality Programme in Co-operatives	385

Environment for
Co-operative in 2025

The year 2025 is expected to be strategically important in many ways and will be remembered as a landmark in the history of Indian Cooperative Movement. Firstly, the recognition of cooperative as a conducive vehicle for eradication of poverty, financial inclusion for the people of small means, food security of the nation social services and promoting entrepreneur development are some of the significant contribution made by them globally. Secondly, the declaration by United Nation to celebrate Year 2012 as International Year of Cooperatives is another feather in its cap. The government of India and state governments are also showing the commitment and support for the growth and development of cooperatives in the country.

Recently, the Indian Parliament passed the Constitutional Amendment Bill giving a autonomous and independent role to the cooperative societies and promoting democratic functioning, professionalization and members participation in the affair of cooperative. society. This amendment to the constitution also grants every citizen a fundamental right to form cooperative society. We all know that cooperative is a state subject and they operate in a different environment due to different cooperative laws in the states. Despite stunning achievements and large scale success they have faced problems which are consequences of operating in extremely challenging legal environment. The amendment in the constitution bill has enabled uniformity in the states cooperative laws and empower the institution in a significant manner. Now, the cooperative institution in the states should come forward to urges their respective government to sensitize on the constitutional provisions made in the Parliament and removal of all the restrictive provision of their respective state act and amend the bills in the line of provisions of constitutional amendment of cooperatives.

Recently, the Standing Committee on Agriculture of Parliament has sought the suggestions and views of various cooperative organization with regard to amendment of Multi-State Cooperative Societies Act, Union Of India New Delhi 2002. It is a duty of the cooperative members to communicate to the standing committee regarding the difficulties they come across in the area of governance, management, and resource mobilization and also running of the societies. The apex level cooperative organization may also urge the said committee for removal of all the restrictive provisions of the existing MSCS Act and also demand the restoration of democratic character of the cooperatives necessary for and autonomous, democratic functioning professionalization of cooperative in the country.

Co-operatives are dedicated to democratic and accountable governance and service to their members. The ownership and controlled by member i.e. one vote per member is a key aspect of the cooperative society. They raise their equity or savings from their members and are designed to provide services to their users as their priority. Because of these characteristics, cooperative enterprise build a better world. When the whole world struggle to find the most effective ways to alleviate extreme poverty and sufferings, the role of cooperative institutions is more vital than ever since they offer grass root solution to their members and owner and also nurture their capabilities and capacity building as imbibed in the cooperative values and principles and their concern for communities.

Amending Cooperative Act-Need of the Hour :

The State Governments to amend their State Cooperative Acts to ensure compliance with the 97th Constitutional (Amendment) Act-2011. It may be mentioned that Central Government has enacted the Constitutional Amendment Act on February 15, 2012 through Gazette Notification. The objective of the Act is to ensure democratic, autonomous and professional functioning of the cooperatives in the country. The said amendment in the Constitution, seeks to empower the Parliament in respect of Multi-State Cooperative Societies and the State Legislatures in case of other Cooperative Societies to make appropriate law. The Central Government has taken a number of initiatives for laying strong foundation for the development of cooperatives. The Government has enunciated National Policy on Cooperatives and Multi-State Cooperative Societies Act, 2002 with a view to provide enabling legal and policy environment for the growth and development of the cooperatives. It has been experienced that inspite of considerable numerical expansion of cooperatives in different sectors of the national economy, their performance in qualitative terms has not been up to the desired level. These institutions suffer dependency syndrome and heavily depend on financial support from the Government which has led to intervention in their day-to-day functioning. There are also instances of political interference in working of these institutions.

Unless cooperatives developed their own internal strength and run an organization on professional lines by the enlightened and active membership with innovation and vision it will be difficult for the cooperatives to protect and preserve their identity and values in the present economic scenario. The issue of good governance is also vital for the cooperatives who are suffering from serious problems. The lack of governance prevents the cooperative to function in a democratic manner and becomes hindrance to survive in the competitive environment. The Constitution Amendment of Cooperatives will go a long way in protecting and insulating the cooperatives from avoidable political and bureaucratic interference in the State.

In this regard, the role of the State Government is very important to amend their State Cooperative Acts in the tune with the provision of amendments in the cooperative law which will not only ensure democratic functioning of the cooperatives in the State, but also ensure accountability of management to the members and other stakeholders and also enhance public faith in these institutions. Since the constitutional amendment provides for a maximum period of one year from the date of its commencement to amend the state laws relating to cooperative societies, it is the duty of the State Governments to initiate necessary action to amend their Cooperative Act at the earliest to create an enabling legal and policy environment for the development of cooperatives in the States.

The role of apex organizations is also very important to sensitize their membership base and also organize various training and education programmes to highlight the features of 97th Constitutional (Amendment) Act so that the members also put an effort for an early amendment in the State Act.

It is also advisable to form a National Committee on Cooperatives at the centre and state level to work on various modalities for early amendment of State and Central Act.

Co-operative Business-A Model to Equitable Economic Growth :

The Indian Cooperative Movement have shown notable accomplishment at an impressive scale that can be described with 6 lakh cooperative societies, 25 crore members, 100 per cent rural network and significant presence in diverse fields of agriculture credit marketing, fertilizer, housing, sugar, dairy, labour fisheries etc. It has been realized that cooperative business model is more relevant today because it has helped the economy and individuals by improving income, creating values, investment opportunities in product supply chain in today's competitive world. The cooperatives are a school of democracy and provided firsthand experience with democratic governance, members participation, transparency and also trust and solidarity leading to stability in the face of conflict and adversity. The cooperatives empower the poor people to participate in socio-economic development and integrating the need of the rural poor and other stakeholders of our rural economy. They are also recognised as important institutions to contribute to country's food security through their participation in natural resource management for rural development.

Today, co-operatives in the country are dedicated to democratic and accountable governance and service to their members and also contribute to rebuild the socio-economic fabric of their communities that are being served. Economically, cooperative effectively reduce market barrier and allow entrepreneur to generate economies of scale and also increase income through volume sale, increase efficiency along the value chain to have greater access to information and networks and increase access to capital through joint pooling of resources.

Demand for food is manifold. The increasing demand. A country of over a billion population to feed the will be fulfilled through the rapid agriculture growth in the country which will required substantial public investment in the agriculture and rural development sector. Another important fact is two-third of the population in India live in rural areas and derive their livelihoods from agriculture or related activities and lifting people out of poverty is highly dependent on what happened in agriculture sector in the years to come. The successful agriculture growth to large extent will depend upon the development of strong PACS in the country to help small and marginal farmers to achieve better access to agri-inputs equipments and markets. It will have a positive impact for the country's food security in both rural and urban areas and also enable to raise income of the farmers and ultimately enhance the economic growth. There are several kinds of agriculture cooperatives including marketing cooperatives, credit cooperatives and processing cooperatives for the benefits of the farmer members.

The time has come when we create enabling legal environment for the cooperatives in the country to have inclusive growth of economy through cooperative business model and also simultaneously increasing the visibility and awareness of cooperative business model among the masses for which NCUI in collaboration with National and state level cooperative organizations may chalk out ambitious programme and activities to strengthen the cooperative base in the country.

Need to Revamp Cooperatives through Good Governance :

Co-operatives an institution aimed at growth with equity and are useful institutions for inclusive growth as they provide the livelihood, employment and other essential services in rural India. Cooperatives can also be an institutional mechanism for billions of people in the country who depend upon the informal sector of Indian economy to participate in the economic activities. Promoting women cooperatives will be useful in many ways since these institutions would be better acquainted with the requirements of women and can become instrument of their socio-economic betterment. Educational institutions should hold courses on cooperatives so that youth can develop an understanding and appreciation of the cooperative movement. The government has taken several legislative and policy initiatives to create an enabling environment for cooperatives to facilitate their functioning as autonomous, self-reliant and democratically managed institutions. A land mark step in this direction in the recent amendment of constitution under which the Right to form cooperative societies was made a fundamental right and reservation for the women and weaker section representatives on the board of cooperative has been included in the constitutional amendment. The various challenges faced by cooperative today are lack of human resource development, inadequate resource of modemization, lack of facilities of education and training etc. were highlighted in her speech. She called upon the cooperators to improve their performance to meet the expectation of their stakeholders and also explore the immense possibilities of networking among themselves to boost and rejuvenate the cooperatives in the country so that these institutions remains relevant in this fast globalised world order.

Ensure good governance in India's cooperative sector there is an urgent need to revamp cooperatives as autonomous, democratic and professional bodies to achieve inclusive economic development. The Central Government has enacted the Constitutional Amendment Act to ensure democratic, autonomous functioning of the cooperatives in the country. The centre has taken a number of initiatives for laying a strong foundation for development of cooperative movement. Unless cooperative has developed their internal strengths in the form of professional management, active membership and inspiring leadership it will be difficult for them to protect and preserve their identity in the present competitive world.

There is a need for restoring the confidence of the people in the cooperative sector in which good governance assumes importance and need to change the cooperative governance structure through both internal and external reforms. There are serious inadequacies in governance preventing the cooperatives to function on professional lines in the country. Now, time has come for the cooperatives to survive in this competitive market by adding values to their services. The survival and growth of the cooperative sector will depend upon their ability to change and rise up to the occasion by becoming more relevant and sustainable for the members and other stakeholders.

Socio-economic Implications

Though a lot of economic development has taken place in the country since independence, it has created a number of distortions which have destroyed the social and cultural values of the society. Economics does not mean only creation of wealth; it has to improve the economic and social well being of the people and maintain and promote ecological balance of the nature. Even great economists like Alfred Marshall and A.C. Pigou admit that the main motive of economic study is to help social improvement. Paul A. Samuelson points out that 'political economy shows people, how, if they really wish to, they can trade off quantity of goods for quality of life'.

Gandhi's coverage of economics is much wider, because he is just not an economist, but a great humanist with a mechanism of social action to improve the quality of human life. His economics is not, therefore, just a science of wealth, but it has a moral and spiritual purpose and is designed to serve the moral and spiritual needs of the society. He did not accept economics from the point of view of increasing only the material standard of living of the individuals, but as a means to establish higher social values. As he himself said, "I do not draw any sharp distinction between economics and ethics. Economics that hurts the moral well being of any individual or a nation are immoral and therefore, harmful. His economics aimed at betterment and elevation of human life, both individual and social, in the broadest and most comprehensive sense. It is based upon truth, non-violence and simplicity. When economists discuss development on the basis of GDP growth, capital intensive technology, centralized planning, urbanization, energy consumption etc., they cannot find an answer in the Gandhian system. According to Gandhiji, India needs an economic system based on self-reliance and self-respect which must fulfil certain basic human values. And these human values imply simple rules of conduct and action for living together, social living and mutual benefit.

In the light of these rules of conduct, let us examine the distortions of economic development and find out how Gandhian concepts and values help us to escape from the maladies that engulf us.

1. (i) Even though there has been considerable increase in the rate of growth of income since the beginning of plan period, unemployment, underemployment and poverty continue to be the major maladies of the country. Even increase in the rate of income did not reduce unemployment. For example, the rate of growth of Indian economy was about 3.5% per annum during the 1960's and 1970's and the rate of growth of employment came to about 2% per year. In the eighties, the economy grew at a higher rate, about 5.4 to 5.5% per year, but the growth rate of employment was about 1.8% per year, inspite of additional allocation of funds to reduce unemployment through special programmes to create self employment and short term wage employment. And during the period 1983 to 1987-88, the growth of employment was even lower, 1.55% per year.

(ii) It is not only unemployment which is staggering,

absolute poverty is also colossal. The Planning Commission defines poverty in terms of calorific value amounting to per capita daily consumption of 2400 calories in rural and 2100 calories in urban areas. Even on the same calorific value, the poverty ratio comes to more than 40% of the total population. According to the Indian Council of Medical Research, the consumption standard of an average Indian adult is very low in relation to nutritional requirements. In particular, the protein intake is about one-third of requirement. If we consider the position of India from the point of view of HDI (Human Development Index) as formulated by United Nations Development Programme which includes literacy, longevity and purchasing power of money, India's position comes to about 135 in a list of 173 countries (for the year 1994).

(iii) Further, though economic growth has substantially increased the production of steel, cement, consumer durables etc., economic development has succeeded in driving a large wedge between different segments of Indian society. What is most distressing is that the gap between the urban and rural areas has increased in recent years. Early in the 1950s, when the rural population was more than 80% of the total population of the country, the share of the rural sector was less than 70% of the national income. Consequently per capita income in the rural sector was a little over one-half of its level in the urban sector. By the middle of 1980s, a rough estimate suggests that the percentage share of the rural sector was perhaps only a little over one-half of the national income (due to the fact that agriculture has not grown much faster than population while industry and services have grown at much higher rates). Since the share of the rural sector has remained close to four fifths of the total population, per capita income in this sector appears to have declined to less than one third of the level in the urban sector. The per capita income in the rural sector has risen by less than 30% over this entire period while per capita income in the urban sector has risen by more than 135%. There are also glaring disparities between different groups of people in the country. Only about 10% of people may claim to be in a privileged position.

(iv) Apart from the economic disparities, the deficiency in social amenities is also staggering According to recent estimates, 61% of females, and 36% of males are still illiterate,97% in rural areas and 52% in urban areas do not have any access to sanitation facilities and per capita state government expenditure on medical, family planning, public health, etc. comes to about Rs. 50 per year. The child mortality rate is 80 per thousand live births. All this implies that economic growth has not been able to bring about any improvement in the economic condition of the poor nor any significant social transformation.

(v) Again the pattern of development is gradually destroying the life support system, both for the present and future generation. The economic development is pursued which leads to reckless exploitation of natural resources. For example, indiscriminate industrialization has given rise to emission of toxic gases, depletion of ozone layer, threat of acid rain, pollution of air, water and land surfaces, etc., in fact, nothing is spared resulting in total pollution. Take the case of agriculture which is a part and parcel of nature. Indiscriminate use of pesticides, improper use of land, excessive use of ground water, etc., have caused severe damage to livelihood and health of people.The use of pesticides leaves behind residues in food and produces ill effects on health. India's land area is rapidly turning barren and it is estimated that about one million hectares of crop lands and grazing lands are badly affected due to lack of proper maintenance. In many parts of India, arsenic contamination in ground water has assumed alarming proportions due to intensive digging of tube wells. And forests which provide us with basic needs of the like food and shelter and influence environment through the supply of clean air by absorbing carbon dioxide and other harmful gases, are being rapidly destroyed on account of irrigation projects, industries, power projects and so on. And the effect of industrialization and urbanization can be seen just by visiting Delhi, the capital of India. It is ;now called a gas chamber. According to WHO, Delhi is the fourth most polluted city in the world.

(vi) Ganjhiji's preference to village industries has both economic, political and sociological aspects. We can mention a few of the basic propositions which justify the development of small and village industries.

2. (i) It is sometimes argued that since growth depends mainly on the rate of savings depends on profits, it follows that to maximize profits, capital-intensive production is superior to small scale industries. But as Bauer and Yamey have pointed out, there is a confusion between standards of technical efficiency with that of economic efficiency.

There is no justification in recommending techniques which may be efficient technically but are wasteful in terms of resources and inappropriate at the level of technical achievement of local population. It may be mentioned here that since incomes generated in small scale industries will go mostly to poor people, the health and efficiency of those will also improve, thus increasing the human capital which is as important as and perhaps more important than physical capital.

(ii) Gandhiji's Khadi has evoked derision from economists, technologists and scientists. Modern men wedded to advanced technology and higher standard of living have derided Gandhiji's old and primitive techniques to solve new and growing demands of the people. Yes, Gandhiji was no economist or technologist. He did not believe in the multiplication of wants and their solution. He wanted to simplify life, and follow a simple technique to meet the needs of people and avoid exploitation that has been the key note of industrial civilization.

Khadi may not have any economies of scale but is necessary to provide some livelihood to those who are otherwise idle. According to Gandhiji, "A starving man or woman who has the time hanging on his or her hands will be glad to earn an honest anna during the time." The pity is even an additional anna makes the difference in the condition of the poor in India, In explaining the importance of hand spinning in the Khadi industry Gandhiji further said,"No body has ever suggested that spinning can be a means of livelihood, except to the very poor. It is intended to restore spinning to its ancient position as a universal industry, auxiliary to agriculture, resorted to by the agriculturist during those months, when agricultural oerations are suspended as a matter of course.....". Again he says,"No body has suggested that spinning should replace any wage earing occupation. It has always been regarded as a subsidiary industry".

According to Gandhiji, one cannot reach a non-violent society by violence. Violence breeds violence. One cannot reach truth by untruthfulness. Truthful conduct alone can reach truth. Similarly there can be no freedom, no equal opportunity, no social justice in an environment of mob rule and lawless behavior. We guess it is reasonable to expect that in an era of violence, where truth suffers, hate triumps and love is a waif, socialists would, particularly after the debacle of communist empire, change their doctrine and accept what is good and decent even though in the process, they have to deviate quite a great deal from the orthodox Marxism.

The above analysis shows the economic structure of Gandhian system.gandhiji wants a non-violent society which proposes a cooperative economy which could be established through a process of give and take between the rich and poor. Neither is there unlimited individual ownership nor the ownership of productive resources by the state, Both are equally harmful from the point of view of community interest. Gandhiji tries to evolve a non-exploitative and participatory economy based on mutual cooperation and consent of the entire economy.

Some people think that Gandhiji was a friend of the rich. Yes, he was a friend of the rich, but his love for the poor was no less for that. He had love for everybody. He once wrote to a friend,' I do not believe in the doctrine of the greatest good for the greatest number. It means in its nakedness that in order to achieve the supposed good of fifty one per cent, the interest of forty nine per cent may be, or rather should be, sascrificed. It is a heartless doctrine and has done harm to humanity. The only real, dignified, human doctrine is the greatest good of all, and this can be achieved by uttermost self-sacrifice.

Gandhiji's programme has the following Important components :

(i) Economic development should not be construed as an improvement only in the material standard of living of the individuals, but as a means to establish higher social vlues. Industrialisation may increase GNP of a country, but may not bring about any social change.

(ii) Gandhiji's prescription of compulsory bread labour for all was meant to shake the artificial division of society into different groups and castes. He wanted to bestow dignity to those who earn their livelihood through physical labour. That is why he suggested that all wages should be according to needs. The wages of a barber and the wages of a professor should be equal in a welfare society.

(iii) Gandhiji did not advocate the reckless replacement of the old or blind acceptance of the new. His approach to social reconstruction was informed of the most modern quest for quality of life which can ensure full employment, abolish poverty and create a more equal society.

We can conclude by quoting what Prof. Dantwala has said about Gandhian economic system. According to him Marx supplied an antidote to the 19th Century capitalism; Gandhiji, possessing the advantage of having witnessed the 20th Century, prescribes a remedy for a later disease, capitalism plus totalitarianism. Socialism alone may not be able to restore democracy to the pedestal of a great ideal; it will require the aid of a New Man, who resists evil activity but nonviolently.

*"Gold medals are not really made or gold,
They are made of sweat, determination,
and a hard to find alloy called guts"*

– Dan Gable

Economic Thoughts

The social reformer and the politician in Gandhi had clearly taken the better of him as an economic thinker. He wanted to create a society based on canons of equality - economic, religious and social. In the environment and in the age that he lived, and with his education and experience of the world, he must have considered his ideal to be almost an impossibility. Probably because of the height of the target that he had fixed he had imposed upon himself the impossible task of correcting industrial civilization with his own ideas of economic thought.

He had his own code for the value of money, ideas of trusteeship, the nature of industrial civilization and the place of the charkha in our economy. In the issue of Harijan dated December 26, 1936 there is a coverage of an interview of one Dr Mott with Gandhi about the place of money. Dr. Mott had asked Gandhi, If money is to be given to India, in whatways can it be wisely used without causing any harm? Mott's question was whether money will be any value to India or not. To this question Gandhi's categorical reply was:" No. When money is given it can only do harm. It has got to be earned when it is required. I am convinced that the American and British money which has been voted for Missionary Societies has done more harm than good.

You cannot serve God and Mammon, And my fear is

that Mammon has been sent to serve India and God has remained behind, with the result that He will one day have His vengeance. When the American says, 'I will serve you through money,' I dread him. I simply say to him:'Send us your engineers not to earn money but to give us the benefit of their scientific knowledge;"" But Mott did not agree with the answer. His reply was that money can be badly used as well as used. He said it makes possible the good as well as the bad use of money. Kagawa of Japan admitted the use of money and machinery is attended with peril, but insisted, and Mott agreed with him, that Christ is able to dominate both the money and the machine. Gandhi's reply to this was rather involved and it cannot be said that it was very convincing either, Gandhi answered, "I have made the distinction between money given and money earned, If an American says he wants to serve India, and you packed him off here, I should say we had not earned his services. But take Pierre Ceresole who came at his own expense, but after our consent, to earthquake-stricken Bihar.

We would love to have as many Ceresoles as could possibly come to ourhelp. No. It is my certain conviction based on experience that money plays the least part in matters of spirit." The argument was not concluded. Dr. Mott and Gandhi ultimately agreed to differ. Gandhi's favourite doctrine of Trusteeship is another controversial economic thought. Professor Nirmal Kumar Bose had an interview with Gandhi on November 9 and 10, 1934, a report of which was corrected by Gandhi and was published in the Modern Review of October, 1935. The questions and answers will show that no very definite conclusions were arrived at and the arguments were also rather complicated.

When Gandhi was asked although he thought private possession was incompatible with non-violence why was he putting up with it, the reply was: "That is a temporary measure. No one should have property who would not voluntarily use his earnings for the benefit of mankind." He was then asked in that case why should not there be State Ownership in place of private property and thus minimize violence. To this the reply was as follows: "It is better than private ownership. But that, too, is objectionable on the ground of violence. It is my firm conviction that if the State suppressed capitalsm by violence, in a concentrated and organized form.

The individual has a soul, but as the State is a soulless machine, it can never be weaned from violence to which it owes its very existence. Hence I prefer the doctrine of trusteeship."

It is doubtful if this reply was convincing and Professor Bose went on putting other questions. Another question was: "Then, sir, shall we take it that the fundamental difference between you and the Socialists is that you believe than men live more by self-direction or will than by habit, and they believe that men live more by habit than by will; that is the reason why you strive for self-correction while they try to build up a system under which men will find it impossible to exercise their desire for exploiting others? Gandhi replied: "While admitting that man actually lives by habit, I hold that it is better for him to live by the exercise of will. I also believe that men are capable of developing their will to an extent that will reduce exploitation to a minimum, I look upon an increase of the power of the State with the greatest fear, because although while apparently doing good by minimizing exploitation, it does the greatest harm to mankind by destroying individuality, which lies at the root of all progress.

We know of so many cases where men have adopted

trusteeship, but none where the State has really lived for the poor." Obviously Professor Bose was not satisfied and his next question was: "But have not those cases of trusteeship which you sometimes cite been due to your personal influence rather than to anything else? Teachers like you come infrequently. Would it not be better, therefore, to trust to some organization to effect the necessary changes in man, rather than depend upon the casual advent of men like yourself?"

This was a very personal question but the reply of Gandhi shows that he short-circuited the question and gave the following roundabout reply:"Leaving me aside, you must remember that the influence of all great teachers of mankind has outlived their lives. In the teachings of each prophet like Mohammad, Buddha or Jeses, there was a permanent portion and there was another which was suited to the needs and reuirements of the times. It is only because we trybto keep up the permanent with the impermanent aspects of their teaching that there is so muchbdistortion in religious practice today. But that apart you can see that the influence of these men has been sustained after they have passed away. Moreover, what I disapprove of is an organization based on force, which a State is. Voluntary organization there must be," At another place, in Young India, October 7, 1926, Gandhi had written: I do not fight shy of capital. I fight apitalism..

The West teaches one to avoid concentration of capital, to avoid a racial war in another and deadlier form, Capital and labour need not be antagonistic to each other.I can not picture to myself a time when no man shall be richer than another. But I do picture to myself a time when the rich will spurn to enrich themselves at the expense of the poor and the poor will cease to envy the rich. Even in a mst perfect world, we shall fail to avoid inequalities, but we can and must avoid strife and bitterness.

There are numerous examples extant of the rich and the poor living in perfect friendliness. We have but to multiply such instances.... Apparently Gandhi thought that capitalism could be separated from capital. In his own time he had seen how industrialism and capitalism had flourished in India. At one place he would say:"Industrialise and perish" but at another place he would encourage machinery within limits and these limits were to be interpreted according to his varying mood.

For resisting the wave of industrialism which Gandhi could clearly observe, he only suggested the reinstatement of the ancient cottage industry of hand-spinning. His message of hand-spinning has clearly fallen flat as the present trends show. One feels that if Gandhi as a political strategist had not given the slogan of the charkha to impoverish Lancashire and to stop the economic drain of India through the import of factory-made goods, but had insisted on the importance of agriculture and had required the hands of every available Indian to be employed for growing two blades instead of one, Indian to be employed for growing two blades instead of one, India would have been much better off today.

The campaign against "foreign" cloth was political expediency. His real objection was to all machine-made cloth. Some of Gandhi's own followers who were capitalists and industrialists flourished fully with Gandhi's knowledge and he must have felt a forlorn man as to how his cult of no-capitalism, no-industrialism and trusteeship had failed miserably. One feels that Gandhi as an economist was unrealistic and he allowed dubious economic thought to get the better of him as an idealist and a social reformer and then as a political strategist.

But it is clear that Gandhi was rather dogmatic in his viewpoint. Hind Swaraj or Indian Home Rule was first published in 1908. In a republication in 1921, he says, "I withdraw nothing except one word of it and that in deference to a lady friend." The reason for changing the word is the indelicacy of it. Now in this book Gandhi has made certain observations about the railways which could be quoted.Although he was extensively using the railways and knew very well what an important role railways play in the integration of a vast country like India, he made the following remarks: Man is so made by nature as to require him to restrict his movements as far as his hands and feet will take him.

If we did not rush about from place to place by means of railways and suc other maddening conveniences, much of the confusion that arises would be obviated, Our difficulties are of our own creaton. God set a limit to man's locomotive ambition in the construction of his body.

Man immediately proceeded to discover means of overriding the limit. God gifted man with intellect so that he might know his Maker. Man abused it so that he might forget his maker. I am so constructed that I can only serve my immediate neighbours, but in my conceit, I pretend to have discovered that I must with my body serve every individual in the Universe.

In thus attempting the impossible, man comes in contact with different religions and is utterly confounded. According to this reasoning. It must be apparent to you that railways are a most dangerous institution. Man has gone further away from his Maker. This quotation is obviously much off the mark and yet in 1921 Gandhi stuct to these observations when he was himself a constant user of the railways. In this book and in many of his later publications and speeches, Gandhi made it clear that he would not have mills and factories, as the machine as a chief symbol of modern civilization has created havoc in the West. According to him, India does not need manufactured goods; he observes:"What did India do before these articles were introduced: Precisely the same should be done today. As long as we cannot make pins without machinery, so long will we do without them.

The tinsel splendor of glassware we will have nothing to do with, and we will make wicks, as of old, with home-grown cotton, and use hand-made earthen saucers for lamps." He finally adds," I cannot recall a single good point in connection with machinery" Before we pass on to some of his other economic thoughts it may be mentioned that one would like to know what Gandhi would have thought of our present Parliament as the Centre and the State Legislatures in different States, as he had made the following observations in that book regarding Parliament:

The condition of England at present is pitiable. I pray to God that India may never be in that plight. That which you consider to be Mother of Parliaments is like a sterile woman and a prostitute. Both these are harsh terms, but exactly fit the case. That Parliament has not yet of its own accord done a single good thing; hence I have compared it to a sterile woman. The natural condition of that Parliament is such that without outside pressure it can do nothing. It is like a prostitute because it is under the control of ministers with change from time to time. Today it is under Mr. Asquith; tomorrow it may be under Mr Balfour. If the money and the time wasted by Parliament were entrusted to a few good men, the English nation would be occupying today a much higher platform. The Parliament is simply a costly toy of the nation. These views are by no means peculiar to me. Some great English thinkers have expressed them. That you cannot accept my views at once is only right. If you will read the literature on this subject, you will have some idea of it.

The Parliament is without a real master; under the Prime Minister, its movement is not steady, but it is buffeted about like a prostitute. The Prime Minister is more concerned about his power than about the welfare of the Parliament. His energy is concentrated upon securing the success of his party. His care is not always that the Parliament shall do right. Prime Ministers are known to have made the Parliament do things merely for party advantage. All this is worth thinking over.

Gandhi was not an economist but a social reformer trying to rebuild human society. He envisaged a society where economic motives are kept in check to stop moral decay and achieve social integration. In Hind Swaraj he observed:"Those who are intoxicated by modern civilization are not likely to write against it. Later he wrote:" My conviction is deeper today,than ever. I feel that if India will discard 'modern civilization.' She can only gain by doing so. In 1926 in Young India he wrote:"The fact is that this industrial civilization is a disease because it is all evil. Let us not be deceived by catchwords and phrases....Our concern is, therefore, to destroy industrialism at any cost." He was deeply convinced and reiterated frequently that Industrialism is a curse for manking. But was this not like trying to sent the sea- waves back from the sea-shore? While condemning industrial civilization Gandhi drew up a picture of real civilization in Hind Swaraj which will justify a lengthy quotation to show how he thought.

PROVERB OF MAHATMA GANDHI ON COOPERATIVE

(1) We will not measure the success of the movement by the number of Cooperative Societies formed but by the normal condition of the cooperative.

(2) The Secret of successful Cooperative effort is that the members must be honest & know the great merit of cooperation & it must have a definite progressive goal.

(3) My outlook at present is not the out look of spreading the Cooperative movement gradually progressively as it has done. My outlook is to converse India with cooperative movement or rather with cooperation.

(4) Whatever steps we take in regard to cooperation have to be in the democratic contest i.e. it has to get the good will of the people.

(5) Education in relation to the cooperative means imparting of knowledge about the principles, methods, aims & practice of Cooperation among people & developing them in Cooperative spirit & abilities to work together.

Message of the Ica - 2013

This year's International Co-operative Day celebrated July 6, 2013 has the theme "Co-operative enterprise remains strong in times of crisis".

It is an apt theme when one considers how other forms of business measure up when faced with current global economic struggles.

Investor owned business models currently suffer from a crisis of unsustainability in economic and social and environmental terms while the co-operative model has demonstrated time and again that it is resilient in times of crisis.

The financial crisis was an epic example of the perils of valuing short term gain over longer term viability. The global crises we have faced derive from a business model that puts financial return ahead of human need; a model that seeks to privatise gains and yet socialise loses. There is considerable evidence that a diversity of ownership models contributes to a more stable financial sector as a whole. By placing human need at their core, co-operatives respond to today's crises of sustainability and deliver a distinctive form of "shared value." Furthermore the co-operative model does not fall victim to the lure that has afflicted capitalism for more than twenty years in which financial performance is the central indicator of good business. Quite simply a cooperative is a collective pursuit of sustainability for it seeks to "optimise" outcomes for a range of stakeholders without seeking to maximize the benefit for any one stakeholder.

This also means that as times become more difficult the entire work force is viewed as vital to the well-being of the co-operative, not just a few people at the top.

Certainly another area in which the global public has been buffeted is in the practices and ultimately the closing of many big banks. What were considered venerable institutions safe for investment and deposits too often have been shown to be weak and poorly run. Financial co-operatives however have often fared far better.

Savings and credit co-operatives, co-operative banks and credit unions have grown; kept credit flowing especially to small and medium sized enterprises and remained stable across regions while indirectly creating employment. It is their unique combination of member ownership, control and benefit that is at the heart of their resilience and that provides a series of advantages over its competitors. With financial co-operatives representing an astonishingly large slice of the global banking market, it is important to better understand the model.

A recent report distributed by the International Labour Organization (ILO) and written by Professor Johnston, Birchall, examines financial co-operatives from their origins in Germany in the 1850s to the global movement they represent today.

Birchall explained in an interview with ILO how before the crisis, economists said financial co-operatives were bound to be less efficient than investor - owned banks because they did not reward their managers with shares. However, the crisis has proved that financial co-operatives were less likely to risk as much as PLC banks, particularly because their managers did not receive a share of the profits.

"Stability and the aversion to risk are built into the DNA of financial co-operatives. They make surpluses and they need to, otherwise they wouldn't be businesses. But what they do with those surpluses is put them into the reserves, which means they are very strong financially and they don't tend to have problems with the capital requirements of the regulators.

"In credit unions in other parts of the world you can see that they didn't even face a drop in 2008. They didnot notice the banking crisis; they just kept on growing slowly, regularly not dramatically".

Another benefit of co-operative in times of crisis should also not be overlooked: Its social dimension. As economic shrink and pressure is put on governments to reduce social benefits, co-operatives often provide an invaluable lifeline. In short co-operatives contribute to the social capital in ways that investor owned businesses do not. Co-operatives may also be critical in delivering services such as health care centres that would otherwise come from private insurance or the state or may not be provided at all as state budgets shrink. And of course one should not overlook a key benefit of consumer co-operatives: the ability to offer the public lower costs for food and other essentials - so vital when consumer's paychecks are shrinking or they have none.

This International Day of Co-operatives July 6, 2013 gives us an opportunity to reflect on all that co-operatives have done in hard times and in good times and to redouble our resolve to ensure that this values based business model continues to draw more attention and support globally. It is a model that works time and again.

Housing - Dream to Reality

FOOD, CLOTHING AND SHELTHER are the three basic human needs. Food gets priority attention of every Government whether capitalist or socialist, whether developed,developing or under developed In India, after Independence, Five Year Plans have been formulated for fostering planned economic development. From the status of a country highly dependent on import of food grains (under PL-480) from foreign countries, India presently has achieved Self-sufficiency in production of food grains on account of sincere endeavour and concerted effort in implementing series of schemes and programmes.

Indian Housing Scenario:-

The issues relating to relating to Shelter (housing) deserves to get due priority keeping in view its enormity and magnitude. One study reveals that one fifth of the world's Population lives in Slum. Repaid industrialisation and urbanisation brings in mass exodus of rural people to Urban areas in search of employment and livelihood opportunity. The housing shortage scenario, coupled with the need for safe drinking water, sanitation, health and education gets aggravated contributing to pitiable living conditions of people in Urban areas including the metros.

Housing in India varies significantly and reflects the

Socio-economic mix of its vast population. In the last decade, ere has been tremendous growth in the housing Sector in India-along with demographic charges, use in income, growth in number of nuclear families and urbanisation. Despite, this growth, the housing shortages has reached a staggering level at about six crores units. The housing / Real Estate Sector contributes 6% to the Gross Domestic product of India.

Next to agriculture, housing Sector is the largest Sector providing direct and indirect employment with annual investment of Rs. 7,20,000 crores. The average annual growth of housing sector is 5% between the period from 2008 to 2014. The Government of India has set the vision. "Housing For All by 2022". To achieve the vision there is requirement of about 11 crore housing units. For creation of such huge housing stocks, total investment of Rs. 120,00,000 crores is required with annual investment of about Rs.15,60,000 crores. Growth rate required is about 70% to 80% as compared to present annual average growth of 6%. About 1.7 to 2.0 lakh hectares of land is required for construction of housing units. The task is herculean indeed.

No doubt, initiatives have been taken at the Government level, both Central as well as states to mitigate the housing problems. State Housing Boards, Development Authties, Regional Improvement Trusts have been established with a view to formulating Long Term Shelter / housing development Plans and Projects. The Private Builders and Real Estate Developers have achieved significant strides in providing housing units to the people. But their contributions are confined to the metro, semi Metro and few Urban areas addressing mostly to the housing needs of HIG/MIG category.

People belonging to Economically Weaker Section

(EWS) and Lower Income Group (LIG) and Lower Middle Income Group (LMIG) have made significant contribution in the growth of any Urban Centre. But they are still vulnerable as far as housing is concerned. Their plight still remains unresolved. Investment or expenditure for purchase of land and construction of houses or for purchase of house or appartment by a Low or Middle Income House hold is perhaps the single largest and the most important expenditure. They make investment of their entire life time saving for realising their dream of having their "Home, Sweet Home". It constitutes prime asset of their families. With unabated increase in cost of land and cost of construction, the miseries of LIG and EWS households gets multiplied. Their dream for a house of their own still remain miles away away from reality therefore. "Affordable Housing" deserves to get the Priority attention of Policy makers and Urban administration.

Affordable Housing Re-Defined :

A comparative study of the cost of house vis-à-vis gross income of household presents a startling picture. In developed countries, housing cost normally does not exceed 30 % of a house hold's gross income. In India, however, an average household spend around 40% to 50% of their gross income for construction / Purchase of a house. Besides, with scanty income and rising cost of construction of house they are over -burdened with debt services and trapped in the vicious circle. Over and above the cost of construction," there is stamp duty, holding tax, cost for approval of building Plan etc. The incidence of all these factors including the processing fees for housing loan, other hidden cost fall on the household. Besides, the borrowing capacity coupled with loan repaying of capacity of a person constitute an important factor of Affordable Housing. As per the definition out lined by the Deepak Parekh Committee, the monthly Income of EWS/LIG house hold ranges between Rs. 8000/- to Rs. 14,000/-. However, on the basis of the definition advanced by the Reserve Bank of India(based in 2008 prices) which have been adopted by the Ministry of Housing and Urban Poverty Alleviation, Government of India, the monthly Income of EWS is confined to Rs. 5000/-, of LIG is between Rs. 5001/- to Rs. 10,000/-. Depending upon the subsistence level of income and standard of living, the borrowing capacity of EWS may be maximum 3.5 time of annual income, in case of EWS households 4 times of annual income and in case of MIG, it is 5 time of annual income. Accordingly, the borrowing capacity and repaying capacity of F EWS category of house hold is limited to Rs. 3.50 lakhs, LIG- between Rs. 3.50 lakhs Rs. 7.5 lakhs, LMIG between Rs. 7.5 lakhs to 'Rs. 9.5 lakhs and for MIG between Rs. 12 lakhs to Rs. 15.00 lakhs.

The Ministry of Housing and Urban Poverty Alleviation has declared Interest subsidy @ 5% under the Interest Subsidy Scheme for Housing the Urban Poor. Under this Scheme, the maximum loan amount is likely to be raised an additional limit of Rs. 1.00 lakh to Rs.5.00 lakh. The capability of making upfront payment toward borrower's contribution is an important factor. In both EWS and LIG category of house hold, the maximum capacity is likely to be within 20% of total loan eligibility or purchase price of house. Linking the Interest Subsidy for Housing Urban Poor (ISHUP), the ceiling on loan eligibility and unit cost of house which is the essence of Affordable Housing, may be clubbed as follow :

Category	Loan Eligibility
EWS	Rs. 3.00 lakh to Rs. 5.00 lakh

LIG	Rs. 5.01 lakh to Rs. 8.00 lakh
LMIG	Rs. 8.01 lakh to Rs. 10.00 lakh
MIG	Rs. 10.00 lakh to Rs. 15.00 lakh

Challenges :

For successful implementation of Affordable Housing Scheme, it is imperative to formulate strategies to overcome three challenges: (i) availability of land at concessional rates (ii) adoption of technology to drastically reduce the cost of construction and (iii) minimum profit margin.

(i) Availability of land :-

Availability of land is a major constraint. Rising cost of land, land, litigation litigation and involvement of multiple middle-men and the Benchmark price fixed by the Government make the matter most complicated. The only viable alternative is identification of land in the outskirt of cities. Of course, it would have an implication on cost of development of infrastructure like, road, provision for drinking water, sanitation sewerage and drainage, power supply etc.

(ii) Adoption of technology :-

Adoption of technology for reduction of cost of construction can play a vital role in implementation of Affordable Housing. Optimum use of building of building materials, establishment of prefabricated roof, columns manufacturing centres and nanufacture of these aterials adopting economics of scales lead to substantial reduction of cost of construction.

It is quite relevant to mention here that ate Builders and Developers are the now acquiring cheap land and technology for low-cost housing after the Government have announced incentive for affordable Housing.

To commensurate with the initiative of the Government, the Reserve Bank of India has also announced cheaper loan to the developers and buyers specifically under this affordable Housing segment. There is unlimited demand for houses under this segment. There is a large market for such homes. Yet there is supply constraints. The Challenge for the Builders and Developers is to find cheaper land and make the project economically viable. In most cases, such lands are available only at places away from cities. And these places do not have transport facilities, sanitation, supply of drinking water and sewerage. For development of these infrastructure, there is also a cost implication.

Another challenge that Builders do encounter is to adopt technology to manufacture building materials by scales and speed up construction. The leading Real Estate Houses like Tata Housing, ATS Infrastructure, Bharatiya Group have taken initiatives to addressee to these challenges with a view to capitalising the huge market potentiality and bridge the demands supply mismatch. Strategy is volume game-low cost, low margin and high volume. In countries like Korea, South Africa and Mexico", Mass housing Scheme with low cost have been very successful.

(iii)   Minimum Profit Margin:

Keeping minimum profit margin is quite a sensitive issue. The Development Authorities, State Housing Boards and private Developers do take up CSR (Corporate Social Responsibility). Activities. The Affordable Housing for EWS LIG and LMIG has a huge demand. There is glarring mismatch between demand and market supply in this segment. The volume of business in this segment has the potentiality to generate profit to the desired extent.

Pro-active Initiatives of the RBI :

The Reserve Bank of India has announced recently a series of measures that encourage bank lending rates to the affordable housing. It has broaden the scope of affordable housing in as much as both the small value loans and home loans to individuals up to Rs. 50.00 lakh (for houses of value upto Rs. 65.00 lakh in metros and loans up to Rs. 40.00 lakh (home value of Rs.50.00 lakh) in other centres will be considered under affordable housing. Extending these loans will entitle the Banks to float infrastructures bonds upto seven years. Money raised under these bonds will not be subject to Reserve Requirements such as Cash Reserve Ratio (CCR) and Statutory Liquidity Reserve (SLR). Eligible bonds will also get exemption in calculation of priority Sector lending targets. These measures will definitely make home loan portfolio more attractive. These measures are sequels to the vision and Road map set by the Hon'ble Finance Minister in his Budget allowing banks to float long term bond for lending to infrastructures.

The RBI reiterated that apart from what is technically defined as infrastructure, affordable housing is another segment of the economy which both requires long-term funding and is of critical importance. It has taken initiatives to ease the way for banks to raise long-term resources to finance their long-term loans to infrastructure as well as affordable housing. This will help promote both growth and stability, as well as improve the supply side.

These initiative and exemptions will mitigate the Asset-Liability Management (ALM) problems faced by banks in extending project loans to infrastructure and core industries sectors. "A collateral benefit in shape of bond is expected to boost the development of the domestic corporate bond market and constraints.

BRIDGING THE GAP :-

It is imperative that all the stake holders need to address the issues of affordable housing and to formulate Action Plan to bridge the gap persisting in the demand and supply of affordable housing. The stake holders include the Government of India. State Governments, Bankers, Development Authorities, Corporate houses including Real Estate Developers and housing Cooperatives.

A Role of Government of India :-

Soon after Independence, the Government of India has been taking series of initiatives to address the shortages of housing units- in general and for EWS and LIG categories in particular.

In the past five years, there has been renewed thrust on affordable housing. The Government of India has formulated and adopted the National Urban Housing and Habitat Policy, 2007 with a view to providing fiscal incentives and developing innovative financial instruments like mortgage used as securities, to augment flow of finance to the housing market and reform in Rent Control Act. It also seeks to assist the poor and EWS category of people to have access to subsidized housing on rental and ownership basis. It also envisages for setting up of a National for providing Fund for subsidies to EWS and LIG housing.

This Policy also aims at housing for Urban poor and has also the benefit of cost Shelter subsidisation and higher tax exemption/ Slum concessions. The Jawarlala Nehru National Urban Renewal Mission (Jn NURM), provides for a scheme namely Basic Services for Urban Poor (BSUP). Now Jn NURM Cities are covered by Integrated Housing and Development Programme (IHSDP). The Rajiv Awas Yojna (RAY) envisages for sum-free cities. Under the Interest

Subsidies Scheme for Housing the Urban Poor (ISHUP), the EWS get access to concessional housing loans. The Affordable Housing Scheme gets Income Tax Relate under Section 81/A. of the Act. The Union Budget for 2012-13 also provided for exemption from service tax in respect of mass housing upto an area of 60 Sq. mt. per unit. Besides formulation of policies, it is imperative that Government of India need to ensure effective coordination, monitoring and funding for effective implementation of these schemes within a timeline.

Role of the State Governments :-

Since housing is a State subject, state need to take a proactive role in addressing housing shortage and providing infrastructure for affordable housing. More dependence on the Government of India or shifting responsibilities to the Centre by the State Government does not help solve the problem. Many State Governments have adopted appropriate policy support to promote affordable housing like single-window clearances of housing projects, reservation, allocation and alienation of land for exclusive affordable housing, liberalization of Development and Regulation Act for EWS and LIG housing, additional FAR/FSI exemption and concession in stamp duty etc. The Government of Odisha has taken initiative creating an enabling environment with appropriate policy support for implementation of affordable housing for EWS and LIG. Households keeping in line with various on-going schemes of the Government of India.

The Scheme for Affordable Urban Housing in Odisha, 2012 was formulated in 2012 with an objective (i) to address shortage of EWS, LIG, LMIG and MIG housing in a time bound manner, (ii) prescribe unit cost and size of EWS and

LIG housing (iii) to promote affordable housing through multiple cost reduction measures and (iv) to provide linkages with slum redevelopment rehabilitation programmes. The scheme envisages four model (a) earmarking 60% of total built up area for EWS, LIG MIG housing developed by Odisha State Housing Housing Board on Government land (b) Voluntary development on private land with reservation of 65% of built up area for EWS /LIG category and additional FAR for HIG and Commercial purpose (c) Private and Developer on Government land with reservation of 50% of built up area for EWS /LIG and (d) Voluntary social housing Scheme with 50% of built up area for EWS /LIG category and over all price cap of Rs. 15.00 lakh. With a view to making the scheme more effective in delivering its objective the Government of Odisha has revised the provisioning of the scheme by virtue of a Notification published in Gazette dated 26th September, 2013.

Role of Real Estate Developers :-

The Corporate Houses, and Real Estate Developers command a greater role in mitigating the plight of EWS, LIG and LMIG households for a dream house within their range of affordability. Like Tata Housing, ATS Infrastructures, Bhartiya Group and Anantaram Industries other developers should come forward in an aggressive way to capitalise the vast opportunity in this segment of affordable housing. High demand vis-a vis low supply syndrome, economic scale operation and high volume the command the strengths and opportunity. The Real Estate of this segment. Developers need to take the call and strive hard with appropriate marketing strategy to usher in a new era of affordable housing. They should harness the potentiality in all 'B' and 'C' category of cities and Urban Centres in providing affordable housing for EWS and LIG households. This would pave the path for sustainable solution to the problem of affordable housing.

Role of Banks :-

The Commercial Banks including Private Sectors Banks and housing financing institutions can play a vital role in addressing the issue of affordable housing. The initiatives of the Reserve Bank of India as declared recently would definitely help the Commercial Banks to give a renewed thrust on sanction of loan under affordable housing in an aggressive way. The Bankers are now preparing for a pick up in home loans in the light of the increase in tax breaks from Rs. 1.5 lakhs to Rs. 2 lakhs. The infrastructure status to affordable housing projects would make it easier for developers to get finance. Banks also prefer home loans because housing are less risking as the lending is diversified and also provide them an opportunity to cross-sell other services to borrowers. The measures make home loans more attractive. The Interest Subsidy for Housing Urban Poor (ISHUP) will definitely help in leveraging loans for affordable housing to the individual buyers as well as developers. This would also boost the loan port-folio to a substantial extent.

Role of Housing Cooperatives :-

The Housing Cooperatives comprising of the NCHFI, 25 State Apex Cooperative Housing Societies and 35000 Housing Cooperative Societies. Constitute the third biggest networks next to credit and milk Cooperatives having their presence in subdivisions taluks. Housing Cooperative are friendly towards members belonging to EWS and LIG category and strive hard to mitigate their plight for a dream house. They command a niche market as they are committed to the concern of LIG & EWS category of members. About 75% of the houses constructed with the financial assistance of Apex Cooperative Housing Federations, are meant for EWS and LIG LIG category households. In the states like TamilNandu, Meghalaya and Maharashtra the ratio of houses constructed for EWS/LIG category is 89%, 73% and 63% respectively. The housing cooperatives need to take up the challenge of Affordable Housing as this Sector commands a niche market and accomplish the objectives.

Housing cooperatives are not profit maximisation institutions. They have a committement and concern for the basic housing needs for the poor, the EWS/LIG households. With its vet networks, infrastructure and resource base, housing Cooperative can present a meaningful solution to the problems of affordable housing. An Action Plan need to be formulated on a sustainable mode for affordable housing in every city. The NCHFIS and leading ACHFS may take the leadership in formulation of Action Plan, acquisition of land, mobilization of resources and implementation of programme. This would not only boost the credibility of housing Cooperative but also brings smiles of happiness in the millions of needy families belonging to EWS/LIG categories. The housing Cooperative must take the call.

Conclusion :-

India is the land of unity amidst diversity. Innovation is the hallmark of its Plans and Programmes formulated for bringing Socio-economic about development. As housing is one of the basic needs, convergence of all stake-holders in mobilisation of resources, implementation of plan and programmes for afordable housing would go a long way in accomplishment of the objective, "Housing for all" Let us strive to achieve the goal by putting in sincere endeavours of all the stake holders. The goal is achievable and must be achieved at any cost.

"Look forward and see Hope"
- Dr. Abdul Kalam

Three Pivot of Co-operative

No doubt cooperatives are by and large economic and business organizations or enterprises. They are not similar with other types of business organizations in public and private sectors like corporations, companies, partnership firms and chit fund organizations including societies or associations incorporated under different statutes like the cooperative societies.

The cooperative societies therefore occupy a distinct sector alongwith private and public sectors in the national economy. Cooperative Societies have only unique and special characteristics being based on ethical values of seven cardinal principles of cooperation as declared by the International Cooperative Alliance (ICA) which is world body of all cooperatives of the world at the international level and followed by al cooperatives in all countries whether capitalistic, socialistic or socialistic pattern of society like India as a golden mean between capitalism and socialism which are enumerated below-

    i) Voluntary and open membership.

    ii) Democratic member control

    iii) Member economic participation

    iv) Autonomy and independence.

    v) Education, Training and information.

vi) Cooperation among cooperatives.

vii) Concern for community.

The cooperatives are not charitable organizations but service oriented towards their members. They do not have profit motive like other types of business organizations. In course of their business transactions they derive some surplus which cannot be termed as profit but surplus for their own survival to meet their both ends so as to enable them to provide service. In such scenario let us focus our discussion on three pivots on which the cooperative infrastructure is build up and moves namely:- (1) Membership (2) Management and (3) Managerial Carders

1. Membership :

The most vital and primary pivot on which the cooperative structure or edifice rests is the membership in whose interest the cooperative aims at is their "Common Economic felt-need" which is to be fulfilled as the main objective being the fore most right of membership and duty of the cooperative as mentioned in the constutional document called the "Bye-laws" without which the cooperative becomes defunct and non-existent. The cooperative beneficiaries are primarily its membership and the cooperative is a "member-driven organization unlike other types of economic and business organizations and as such the membership of cooperative can never afford to be inactive passive, and non-involved in its business operations to achieve the common economic objective as "felt-need" behind organization of the cooperative which is first test or yard stick to measure the intrinsic worth/value of cooperative in true sense of the term and without such active participation, the cooperative cannot afford to be vibrant and retain its true character Hence the geniuses of promoter membership at the time of formation and registration of cooperative is to be tested very carefully with reference to their "Common economic felt - need" so as to distinguish real and faqhe/ ghost membership.

The rights of members are the duties of cooperative comprising of all members and so also the duties of the membership is the right of cooperative as the rights implies duties and are corollary to each other. The entire membership of cooperative constitute the General Body of member which is the final authority in the affairs of the cooperative each and every member is part of General Body of members. Each and every member is part of General Body of Members and they are indivisible. The General Body of members constituted of all members is therefore supreme body in the cooperative which elect all the members of the Committee Management democratically through the system of election or select them unanimously including members of other sub committees like Executive Committee, Appointment Committee and other committees as psi provisions embodied in the byelaws of the cooperative to look after management of cooperative at periodical internal as it is not possible on the part of the General Body of members very often at short interests say monthly, quarterly or half yearly basis unless such need arises except meeting annually once in a year as per the statute and the byelaws governing the cooperative.

The General Body of members also delegates powers to the committee of management to elect the President, Vice-President and other office bearers to look after the day-to-day management of the cooperative as per permission contained in the Byelaws. The inherent powers to re-elect the members of the Committee of Management after expiry of the term of office as per the statute and byelaws also remain with the General Body of members. The emergent meeting of the General Body of members can also be convened by minimum members of the cooperative as provided in the statute and the Byelaws. It is therefore rightly said that "the cooperatives are owned, controlled and managed by the members to whom they serve"

2. Management : The secondary pivot of the cooperative is Management. The day to day Management of the cooperative stand on the second pivot called the Board of Directors" leaded by the President who are elected by the General Body of members which is subservient to the General Body of members which is final ultimate authority in the affairs of the cooperative The decision taken by the Committee of Management of the Board of Directors can be modified or reversed by the General Body of members as the Committee of Management is the creation of the General Body It is worth pointing out here that elections are held in cooperative to fulfill the second cardinal principle of cooperation as set up by the I.C.A. namely "Democratic member control" so as to elect the representatives of the members of the General Body of members to the Committee of Management of the Board of Directors as a tool of democracy by resorting to system of election as a method or a tool or means of democracy but not as an end in itself to elect representatives on partisan character because politics is the greatest enemy of cooperative and encouragement on entry of politics into cooperative on political partisan character divides or foragments the cooperatives and cuts the very root of cooperative which is rocted and biased on the generally recited saying "united we stand, divided we fall" and "unity is strength"

3. Managerial cadre: The third and tartiary pivot on which cooperative edifice stands is the managerial cadre of

employees who run the business the cooperative or day to day basis since the management of cooperative IS "absentee management" unlike other proprietorship of business enterprises partnership firms where the owners look after the day to day business. In cooperative, General Body members sit once in a year or more as per necessity whereas the committee of Management or Board of Director sits once in a quarter or more as required. Hence the business of any cooperative is actually run by the managerial cadre of employees readed by Chief Executive, Secretary or Managing Director as variously called who is assisted by other employees who belong to various Managerial carder or grades like Top executive, middle level executive and base level executive variously called as Chief General Manager, General Manager Executive Director / Deputy, Asst. General Manager, Deputy Manager, Asst. Manager etc. The selection procedure of managerial cadre of employees should be transparent based on requisite qualification, experience and professionalisation to ensure their competency and efficiency as the employees are both assets and liabilities for any organization according to their worth. So it should be the goal to employ right person in right place and in right time.

The job requirements of the employees should be specific and pin pointed with reference to their job specifications so as to make them squarely accountable for any lapses and fraud committed in discharging their codified job requirements as per their of job charts giving no chance for escaping job accountability. Further four eyed principle of supervision of work of one by another higher up is essential for detecting of errors and fraud immediately for remedial measures system of job rotation at periodical internally say quarterly / half yearly or yearly basis should be mandatory to ensure detecting fraud/lapses if any at the time of charge of seats and also avoid bed fligs System of concient audit of accounts on day to day basis is also very much essential in banking and financing cooperatives for detection of errors & fraud immediately.

Last but not the least word of oaktion in recruitment and selection of employees to various managing cadres should be made very impartial, transparent in entire process by keeping the management away from the entire procedure of selection from advertisement to appointment except deciding the broad principles of appointment like number of vacant posts to be filled up in different Managerial cadres but their qualification, experience, professionalision and examination with written and viva-voce should be conducted by reputed firms of panelists covering the areas for which reicruitment is made so as to avoid repotism influence interference in recruitment beyond all reasonable doubts which spoil. The cooperatives to a very great extent in many cases giving ample scope for fraud and malpractices for appointment of kith and kin of management as well as persons having full loyalty and allegiance to the Management of do and undo anything as per their dictates being their hand-maids in making the cooperatives loosing the confidence of general public and their harte hardeness towards cooperatives for such haenone misdeeds of few handful so called promoter cooperators forming and registering cooperatives to give vent to their evil designs, vested interest law malafide intentions complying with the legal requirement of minimum members by any means with illiterate, fague and forged primary members who are ghost and nonexistent and vanishing from scene by removing the sign board of cooperative all in a sudden after pocketing the hard earned money of customers giving them allowing high hopes either to provide high rate of return interest by multiplying their capital or by providing land to them at very nominal/cheep rate besides giving costly presentations of gold / silver coins or simple lunch/dinner in a ceremony organized in star hotels.

This has to be guarded with strict I vigilance by all level. At present times it is now red signal for the registering and administrative authority of cooperatives to take all precautionary meassures by acid test of all promoter members about their geniuses and actual felt economic common need of genuine for taking their photographs and signatory before registering any cooperatives and for the audit to detect faguet forged back sheep of cooperatives abinding registered for winding them up as earlier as possible Lastly before concluding it is worth pointing out that cooperative has been rightly compared with sacred cow "Kamadhunu" for rawling it with much care and caution with all fairness.

Authorities said that cooperatives run well in fair weather but not in rough weather which means it looses its inherent character by foul play in absence of confidence unitary team spirit, transparency, honesty and integrity which are greatest evils for cooperatives. It will suffice to say cooperative can do wonders to provide service in all walks of human life in the society like AMUL, IFFCO etc which are pride of cooperatives in India if the seven golden cardinal principles which is unusually accepted declaration of the International Cooperative Alliance (ICA). They should be very strictly adhered to at all times in letter and spirit as prime check points. To end it will suffice to say that eternal vigilance is the price of cooperative like the golden saying "eternal vigilance is the price of liberty."

Service Tax in Co-operative

With the expansion of the service sector, successive Finance Ministers in the Union Government have found it expedient to bring more and more services under the tax net. First introduced in the Finance bill of 1994 (sections 64 to 96, Chapter V), the scope of service tax has expanded, covering a mere three services in 1994 to encompass 109 services in 2008. Expectedly, service tax collection has increased substantively from Rs. 407 crores in 1994-95 to Rs.52,000 crores in 2007-08. Initially, the Union Government levied service tax (S T) invoking their residuary power in Entry 97 of List I under the Seventh Schedule of the Constitution. Entry 92C is now inserted in List I, empowering the Union Government to tax services under the 95th Constitutional Amendment Act 2003.

In recent months, cooperators in Kerala in particular and those in the country in general are agitated as they fear that services provided by cooperatives are covered under the ST net.

Their apprehension is two fold; one, imposition of ST will increase burden on cooperative members as cost of services will increase, and two, cooperatives will be subject to harassment by the taxman. The present paper makes an attempt to critically examine the apprehensions raised by cooperators with a view to allay their fears. Further, this author would feel gratified, if cooperators and experts in large numbers read this article and come up with their suggestions and comments, so that more clarity emerges on the issue, in particular on taxing the services offered by cooperative banks (under the BR Act)

Apprehension of cooperative :

Fears are being expressed that services/items like entrance fee, locker facilities, commission on issue of demand draft, money transfer and pay orders, fee for account maintenance, processing and legal fees, chitty income, mantap services. godown and storage services etc. covered under ST. However, in reality all the above mentioned services/items provided by cooperatives do not fall under ST net, the only exception being "mantap service". Out of the 109 services covered under the ST net, five services, namely banking and other financial services, mantap services, godown and warehousing services, club and association services and auctioning services are most relevant to cooperatives. The provisions relating to each of these services under Finance Act (FA) 1994 is reproduced in the annexure separately. The applicability of these provisions to cooperatives is examined in detail in the paragraphs that follow.

Banking and other financial services :

The institutions covered under this service include a banking company, a financial institution including a non banking financial company, any other body corporate commercial concern. The relevant definition of these terms under S.65 of the Finance Act 1994 are reproduced below :

(11) "banking company" shall have the meanings

assigned to it in clauses (a) of section 45 A of the Reserve Bank of India Act, 1934 (2 of 1934);

(Under S.45) (a) of RBI Act, a "banking company" means a banking company as defined in S.5 of the BR Act 1949, and includes the SBI, any subsidiary bank, as defined under the SBI (subsidiary banks) Act 1959, any corresponding New Bank New constituted by S.3 of the Banking Companies (Acquisition and Transfer of Undertakings) Act 1970 and any other financial institution notified by the Central Government in this behalf).

(14) "Body corporate' shall have the meaning assigned to it in clause (7) of section 2 of the Companies Act, 1956(1 of 1956);

(clause (7) of section 2 of the Companies Act, 1956 - "body corporate" or "corporation" includes a company incorporated outside India, but does not include - (a) a corporate sole; (b) a cooperative society registered under any law relating to cooperative societies; and (c) any other body corporate (not being a company as defined under this Act) which the Central Government may, by Notification in the official Gazette specify in this behalf).

While the term "financial institution' is are assigned the meaning given to it in S.451-c of the RBI Act (S.65-45 of FA 1994) and the term 'non banking financial company' is assigned the meaning given to it in S/45 (1) f of the RBI Act (S 65-74 of FA 1994), the term "commercial concern" is not defined by the FA 1994. Since cooperatives, which include cooperative banks, primary agricultural credit societies and primary credit societies are specifically excluded under S.45H of the RBI Act from the purview of Chapter 3B of the said Act (S 451 forms part of Chp 3B), PACS conducting "Chitty business" automatically excluded from the definition of "a financial institution".

In the other hand, if one insists on a narrower interpretation of the law and argue that what is referred to in S.65-45 of FA 1994, confines to S.451 c of the RBI Act and therefore does not give immunity to cooperatives from the said clause (65-4) of the FA 1994., Still, cooperatives are not affected by S.451-c-v of the RBI Act. For, the said clause of the RBI Act covers" managing, conducting or supervising, as foreman, agent or in any other capacity, of chits or Kuries as defined in any law which is for the time being in force in any state or any business, which is similar thereto. Since the Monthly Deposit Scheme (MDS) run by PACS in Kerala is not registered under the Chitty Act of the state, these cooperatives are not covered under the ST even under this narrow interpretation of the law.

The clear conclusion that emerges from the above discussions in this section is that cooperatives whether PACS or cooperative banks (including State Cooperative Banks and District Cooperative Central Banks) do not come under the ST net, as the term cooperative society, is explicitly excluded from the definition of a body corporate under S2(7) of the companies Act 1956.

Mantap services :

Taxable service under this head means any service provided or to be provided to any person by a mantap keeper in relation to the use of a mantap in any manner including the facilities provided or to be provided to the client in relation to such use and also the services, if any, provided or to be provided as a caterer (S.65-1 05-m). Several PACS in Kerala are providing mantap services and every item ancillary or supplemental to renting out the mantap are covered under ST. These services could include electricity, lighting and decoration, floor coverings, furniture, crockery, cutlery etc. The term "man tap keeper" is defined in S.65(67) of the FA 1994 as "a person who allows temporary occupation of a Mantap for consideration for organising any official, social or business function". In the explanation given to the said clause social function includes marriage.

While issuing the bill, the mantap keeper may show the above mentioned above mentioned ancillary/ supplemental services separately or he may club them along with the mantap rent. It shall be collected at the prevailing rates from the customer for the entire billed amount. If t catering service is provided along with the man tap service and the same is not mentioned separately in the bill, then ST shall be collected on only 60% of the total billed amount. Apart from marriage halls, the term "mantap" cover banquet halls, conference halls etc. Hotels and Restaurants providing such facility within their premises are covered under the ST net. The definition also includes mantaps, which are situated within the premises of any public place of worship like temple, church etc., and let out on charges. A man tap booked and subsequently cancelled does not attract ST, as no service is provided. The amounts of statutory charges included in the bill like sales tax and expenditure tax are to be excluded before arriving at the value of taxable service for calculating ST.

The renting of banquent halls for conducting seminars or conferences would fall within the ambit of ST. Since the law does not distinguish between providers of mantap services, cooperatives are duty bound to collect ST from customers and remit the same to Central Government. However, cooperatives can avail the general exemption available to any service provider under the Act, if the annual value of the taxable service/services put together provided by them does not exceed RS.10 lakhs. But, it shall be the duty of a cooperative society to apply for registration before the ST authorities, as soon as the value of the taxable service/ services exceed Rs.9 lakhs. Storage and ware housing services:

Under this service, taxable service include the service provided or to be provided by a storage or a warehouse keeper in relation to storage and warehousing of goods (S.65-105-zza). Service provided in relation to agricultural produce and service provided by cold storage is outside the ambit of ST. The term "agricultural produce" would cover all cereals, pulses, fruits, nuts and vegetable, fibres such as cotton, flax, jute etc., indigo, unmanufactured tobacco, beetle leaves, tendu leaves and similar products. However, manufactured products such as sugar, edible oils, processed foods etc. will not come under the term "agricultural produce". It is clear from the above explanation that godown/cold storage services provided by PACS, cooperative marketing societies (at all levels), dairy societies, poultry societies and fisheries societies to their members do not fall under the ST net when the service provided is related to agricultural produce.

Taxable service under this head means any service provided or to be provided to the members by a club or Association in relation to provision of services, facilities or advantages for a subscription or any other amount (S 65-105-zzze). Club or Association is a place where people get together to pass their time playing cards, billiards and other games, all for a membership fees which is generally paid for life time plus small amount which is contributed on an yearly basis. Any body formed and registered as a company or a society which provides services, facilities or advantages for a subscription or any other amount to its members is liable to pay ST. In an notification of exemption no.8/2007 service tax, dated dated 1.3.2007, the ST department has clarified that a resident welfare cooperative society is eligible to get the exemption under the said notification if the following three conditions are fulfilled, the exemption is available for the services specified under S.65 (105) (zzze) and provided or to be provided by the cooperative society to its members, the sole criterion for membership is the residential complex or locality and the value of total consideration received by an individual member by the association for providing the services does not exceed Rs.3000 per month.

The rather longish explanation given in para 6.1 above is to show that membership fees/entrance fees charged by a PACS or any other cooperative society is not subject to ST. For, membership in any cooperative society is necessarily confined to those living within its area of operation and the membership fees/ entrance fees charged by a mainstream cooperative society does not exceed Rs.3000 per month. Taxable service include any service provided or to be provided by any other person, in relation to auction of property, moveable or immoveable, or immoveable, tangible or intangible, in any manner, but does not include auction of property under the directions or orders of a court of law or auction by the government (S.65-105-zzzr). Auction is done by the Sale Officer in execution of the decree issued by the Registrar of Cooperative Societies/ Cooperative Arbitration Court, who are conferred the powers of a civil court under the cooperative law. Besides, the Sale Officer is also deemed to be a civil court for the purpose of Art 136 of the Limitations Act when he is passing orders in connection with execution of a decree/ order under the Cooperative Act. As such, auctions made in pursuance of the awards/

decrees issued under the provisions of the cooperative law are outside the ambit of ST.

Cooperative societies like other organisations, operate under the overall legal framework of the country, including the legal framework pertaining to taxation. Given the special nature of a cooperative organisation and its operations, the tax regime has exemptions to cooperatives. Even the law relating to taxation of services, has extended this special consideration to certain services extended by cooperatives and has fully exempted them from collection and payment of service tax, as in the case of banking and financial services. In certain other cases, ST exemption is given to certain operations, like storage and warehousing services related to agricultural produce and since cooperatives are also engaged in these services, they are exempted from ST. As regards auctioning service, auctions done for government or under the orders of a court are exempted from ST. Since the latter case holds true for auctions made by cooperatives, they can claim exemption from ST. As is clear from the explanation given in section 6, cooperatives are not clubs and associations and hence the entrance fees/membership fees collected by them is outside the ambit of ST. Only man tap services provided by cooperatives, attract ST, provided the annual value of this service exceeds Rs.10 lakhs.

Constitutional Amendments a Milestone

BACKDROP :

The century old fine-tuning of the Co-operative statutes is the resultant progressively draconian elements in the Co-operative statutes. It is a reflection of economic, social and political circumstances. The existence of Cooperative law is necessary, though not a sufficient condition for getting a Co-operative policy to work. Co-operatives in India, from colonial times to date grew essentially as a result of state action.

The Government during the British period was gravely concerned with the rising unrest and discontent in the vast stretches of the country side. But it was perceived largely to be a result of the chronic indebtedness of the farmers having been victims of usury at the hands of private money lenders. The answer of this question given rise to creation of an institutional mechanism for providing rural credit and the co-operative mechanism came as an ideal choice, With this backdrop, in this paper an attempt has been made to throw light on co-operative legislation and its progress under ever changing socio-economic environment.

The evolution of co-operatives in India would be better appreciated by studying it together with the evolution of

Raiffeisen Model of co-operatives hundred years ago, Even before formal co-operative structures came into being through the passing of a law, the practice of the concept of co-operation and co-operative activities were prevalent in several parts of 'India. Village communities collectively creating permanent assets like village tanks or village forests called Devarai or vanarai was fairly common. Similarly, instances of pooling resources by groups, like food grains after harvest to lend to needy members of the group before the next harvest or collecting small contributions in cash at regular intervals to lend to members of the group viz., Chit Funds, in the erstwhile madras presidency, "Kuries" in Travancore, "Bhishies" in Kolhapur etc. were to be found. The "Phads" of Kolhapur where farmers impounded water by putting up bunds and agreed to ensure equitable distribution of water, as well as harvesting and transporting of produce of members to the market, and the "Lanas" which were yearly partnership of peasants to cultivate jointly and distribute the harvested produce in proportion to labour and bullock power contributed by their partners were similar instances of co-operation.

The agricultural conditions and absence of institutional arrangements to provide finance to agricuiturists during the latter part of the Nineteenth century led to mounting distress and discontent. The famine commission 1880 and 20 years later, the famine commission 1901 both highlighted the deep indebtedness of the Indian farmer, resulting in many cases in his land passing into the possession of the money lending classes. The Deccan Riots and the prevailing environment of discontent resulted in the Government taking various initiatives but the legislative measures did not substantially improve the situation.

The proposal for agricultural banks was first mooted

in 1858 and again in 1881 by William Wedder burn, the district judge of Ahmed Nagar, in consultation with justice Ranade, but was not accepted. In March 1892, Mr. Frederick Nicholson was placed by the Governor of Madras presidency (For enquiring in to the possibility) of introducing in this presidency, a system of agricultural or other land banks and submitted his report in two volumes in 1895 and 1897.

In 1901 the Famine commission recommended the establishment of Rural Agricultural Banks through the establishment of Mutual Credit Associations, and such steps were taken by the Government of North Western provinces and Oudh. The underlying idea of a number of persons coming together was the voluntary creation of a new valuable security. A strong association competent to offer guarantees and advnntages of lending groups instead of individuals were major advantages. The commission also suggested the principles underlying Agricultural Banks.

Taking cognizances of developments and to provide a legal basis for co-operative societies, the Edward Law Committee with Mr. Nicholson as one of the members, was appointed by the Government to examine and recommend a course of action. The co-operative societies Bill, based on the recommendations of this committee was compiled by Devzililieleetson and the sources were taken from (1) English friendly societies Act-1793. (2) Industrial provident societies Act- 1883 and (3) English companies Act & Societies Registration Act of 1862 and 1860 respectively. Thus the co-operative societies Act was enacted on 25th March, 1904. This is the first legislative attempt to give a legal back up for the co-operative movement was simultaneously started with the enactment of cooperative legislation in 1904. Its objective is to combat the problem of usury and indebtedness of farmers (short-term structure) and to redeem the old debts of farmers (Long term structure) to rejuvenate the stagnant rural economy.

The Act gave general outline of co-operative fabric best suited to the country as a whole. It enabled for registration of credit society and encourage thrift and self-help among the members. The Act of 1904 was very restrictive in nature with limited in its application and scope. It was rigidly in vogue from 1904 to 1912.

In order to provide wide scope to overcome the short comings of 1904 Act, a new Act was passed in 1912. With the development in terms of growth in the number of co-operatives, Co-operative societies Act of 1912 became a necessity and cooperative could be organized for organizing non-credit services to their members. The Act also provided for Federation of Cooperatives. The hope of co-operators were fulfilled by the enactment of the co-operative societies Act II of 1912 with 50 sections. This Act, aims that a society which has as its object, the promotion of theeconomic interests of its members in accordance with co-operative principles and a society established with the object of facilitating the operations of such society could be registered under the Act with or without limited liability. After two years working of the co-operative movement, in October, 1914 a committee on co-operation under Sir Edward Maclagen was appointed by the Government,. The committee recommended for building up a strong threetier structure in every province with primaries at the base, the Central co-operative Banks at the middle -tier and the provincial co-operative Banks at the apex basically to provide short-term and medium-term finance.

In 1919, with the passing of the reforms Act, co-operation as a subject was transferred to the provinces, and

Provincial Government began taking active interest in it. The subject came under discussion of various committee and..ecessity of provincial Act was keenly felt because Act-II of 1912 could not cope up with the many sided development of co-operative movement.

The provincial Acts are more comprehensive than the 1912 Act. The Bombay co-operative societies Act of 1925, the first provincial Act was passed followed by the Madras co-operative societies Act, 1932; Bihar and Odisha co-operative societies Act, 1935, Bengal Co-operative societies Act, 1940; Mysore co-operative societies Act 1948; M.P co-operative societies Act 1949, Assam Act, 1949; Odisha cooperative societies Act 1951; Hyderabad co-operative societies Act, 1952; UP co-operative societies Act 1965; Rajasthan co-operative societies Act, 1965 and Delhi co-operative societies Act, 1972 etc.

The Multi Unit Co-operative Societies Act 1942 : After struggling from the experimental stage, co-operative practice developed further. The business expansion of some well entrenched societies recorded measurable growth and the state boundaries started shifting. Need arose for new instruments of law. The multi-unit co-operative societies Act of 1942 was born with six provisions namely title, co-operative societies to which this Act applies before commencement this Act. Co-operative societies to which this Act applies after the commencement of this Act, appointment and power of the central Registrar, penalties and power of the Government to make rules. It was enacted to provide for incorporation, regulation and winding up of co-operative societies with objects not confined to one state.

Multi-State Co-operative Societies Act, 1984:

With the object of introducing a comprehensive

central legislation to facilitate the organization and functioning of genuine multi-state societies and to bring uniformity in their administration and management, the MSCS of 1984 was enacted and the earlier Multi-unit co-operative societies Act of 1942 was repealed. This is the improved version of the Act of 1984 which gave legal recognition to such units up to 18 years. As a treatise on law it gave both light and shade as till then, cooperation had permeated in to new sectors of Indian economy.

With actualities starting in the face to the farmers of central law, the major deficiencies of the Act of 1984 were located and removed in 2002 Act. This Act weaved in to its texture the four major co-operative principles which conferred cooperative character to the societies. Presumably, some of the important provisions were added which were highlighted by the model Act of 1991, drafted by the planning commission under the overall guidance of Ch. Brahm Parkash.

Multi State Co-operative Societies Act 2002 :

The multi-state co-operative societies (MSCS) Act, enacted in 1984 was modified in 2002, in keeping with the spirit of the Model Co-operatives Act. Unlike the state laws, which remained as a parallel legislation to co-exist with earlier laws, the MSCS Act 2002 replaced the earlier Act 1984.

The multi-state co-operative societies Act 2002 is an Act to consolidate and amend the laws relating cooperative societies, with objectsnot confined one state and serving the interest of members in more than one state, to facilitate the voluntary formation and democratic functioning of co-operatives as peoples institutions based on self help and mutual aid and to enable them to promote their economic and social betterment and to provide functional autonomy for matters connected there with or incidental there.

Enacted by parliament in the fifty-third year of the Republic of India. The multi-state co-operative societies act, 2002 is having XV chapters, 126 sections and two schedules.

97th Constitutional Amendment Act 2011:

The year 2011 was a golden year for the co-operative movement in India. 97th constitutional Amendment Act (2011) has now come as a guiding star and a miracle for co-operatives. The bill was introduced on 30-11-2009 as 111th bill and referred to standing committee on 29-12-2009. The standing committee report on 21-12-2010 after consulting all states and Union Territories Loksabha passed the bill on 22-12-2011 and Rajya sabha passed it on 28-12-2011. The 97th constitutional Amendment Act got presidents assent on 12th January 2012 and Gazette notification came on 15th February 2012.

It is stated that the 97th Constitutional Amendment aims at bringing about uniformity across the Indian'states / Union territories and across all co-operative sectors. It is expected not only to ensure autonomous and democratic functioning of co-operatives but also the accountability of the management to the members and other stakeholders. As per the amendment the changes done to constitution are :- In part III of the constitution, after words "or Unions" the words "Co-operative societies" was added.

The amendment inserts a newdirective principle in to part IV of the constitution. In part IV a new Article 43B was inserted which says, The state shall Endeavour to promote voluntary formation, autonomous functioning, democratic control control and professional management of the co-operative societies. After part IX A of the constitution a part IX B was inserted to accommodate state vs centre roles.

Salient features of part IXB :

It makes right to form co-operative is a fundamental right. The salient features are as follows:

1. Provision for incorporation, regulation, winding up co-operative societies based on the principles of voluntary formation, democratic member control. member economic participation and autonomous functioning;
2. Specifying the maximum number of directors of a co-operative society to be as twenty one;
3. Providing for a fixed term of five years from the date of election in respect of the elected members of the board and its office bearers;
4. Providing for a maximum time limit of six months during which a board of directors of co-operative societies could be kept under supersession or suspension;
5. Providing for an independent professional audit;
6. Providing for right of information to the members of the co-operative societies;
7. Empowering the state Governments to obtain periodic reports of activities and accounts of co-operative societies; which have individuals as members from such categories.
8. Reservation of one seat for SC and the ST and two seats for women on the board of every co-operative society which have individuals as members from such categories.
9. Providing for offences relating to co- operative societies and penalties in respect of such offences.

10. The constitution 97th Act, 2011 which is inconsistent with the provisions of this part shall continue to be in force until amended or repealed by a competent legislature or other competent authority or until expiration of one year from commencement of the amendment whichever is less. In other words the state Acts are to be consistent with the 9th Amendment with a maximum period of one year from 15th February 2012.

Implications :

The amendment of the constitution to make.it obligatory for the states to ensure autonomy of cooperatives makes it binding for the state Governments to facilitate voluntary formation, independent decision-making and democratic control and functioning of co-operatives. It also ensures holding regular elections under the supervision of autonomous authorities, five year term for functionaries and independent audit. Significantly, it also mandates that in case the board is dissolved, the new one is constituted withi"! six months. Such constitutional provision was urgently required as the woes of the cooperative sector are far too many, long-lasting and deep rooted to be to be addressed under the present tax legal frame work. However, it fails to establish what constitutional amendment can't do in reviving institutions and may be victim of rival political institutions at state level as happened in case of 73rd amendments.

It is feared that state-level politicians will do this amendment on co-operatives what they did to the one on panchayats. Barring exceptions in a few sectors and states, the cooperative sector, particularly cooperative credit societies numbering over 120 million, has for a long time been in a shambles with all kinds of vested interests using them as personal freedoms and ladders to political power and means of personal aggrandizement.

Conclusion :

In fine co-operative legislation since 1904 to the 9Th constitutional Amendment Act have played a pivotal role and seen as a way of speeding up the development process. India's first Prime minister. Jawaharlal Nehru spoke of "Convulsing India" with the co-operative movement making it a way of life. None the less, from time to time changes in legislation as per the need of the hours were inserted in the existing law taking in to consideration to make cooperatives more vibrant. The amendment objectives is to encourage economic activities of cooperatives which is in turn help progress of rural India and to ensure autonomous democratic functioning of cooperatives with the spirit of accountability of the management to the members and other stake holders.

"The idea of co-operation is something much more than merely an efficient and economic way of doing thins.
It is economic, It is fair, It equalizes and prevents disparities from growing. But it is something even before than that. It is realy a way of life".
– Jawaharlal Nehru

National Policy on Co-operatives

1. **INTRODUCTORY**

    1.1. The cooperative movement in India traces its origin to the agriculture and allied sector and was originally evolved as a mechanism for pooling the people's meager resources with a view to providing to them the advantages of the economies of scales. The first attempt to institutionalize cooperatives began with the enactment of the Cooperative Credit Societies Act, 1904, the scope of which was subsequently enlarged by the more comprehensive Cooperative Societies Act of 1912.

    Under the Government of India Act, 1919, the subject of Cooperation was transferred to the then Provinces, which were authorized to enact their own cooperative laws. Under the Government of India Act, 1935, cooperatives remained a provincial subject. Presently, the item "Cooperative Societies" is a State subject under entry 32 of the State list of the Constitution of India. Cooperative Societies Acts enacted by State Governments are now in place in the respective states.

    1.2. In order to administer the operations of cooperative societies where membership was from more than one province, the Government of India enacted the Multi-Unit Cooperative Societies Act, 1942, which was subsequently replaced by the Multi-State Cooperative Societies Act, 1984, under entry 44 of the Union List.

2. REVIEW SINCE INDEPENDENCE

2.1. In the pre-independence era, the policy of the Government, by and large, was one of laissez-faire towards the cooperative and Government did not play an active role for their promotion and development. After independence, the advent of planned economic development ushered in a new era for the cooperatives Cooperation came to be regarded as a preferred instrument of planned economic development and emerged as a distinct sector of the National Economy. It was specifically stated in the first Five Year Plan document that the success of the Plan should be judged, among other things, by the extent to which it was implemented through cooperative organizations.

In the sixties, special importance was attached to achieving increased agricultural production as well as rural development through cooperatives. A significant development on the agricultural front, during during 1966-71, was the implementation of the new agricultural strategy, aimed at the achievement of self- sufficiency in food. The introduction of high-yielding and hybrid varieties of seeds and the allocation of large outlays for the provision of irrigation facilities and adequate application of farm inputs led to a manifold increase in the role of cooperatives.

Thus, the Green Revolution gave a big boost to the activities of the cooperatives; increased agricultural production and enhanced productivity necessitated an emphasis on value-addition in agricultural produce, marketing and storage and the development of allied sectors. As a result, specialized cooperative societies in the fields of milk, oil seeds, sugarcane, cotton, agro-processing, etc. were set up. Many large cooperatives emerged in the fields of fertilizer manufacture and marketing of agricultural produce. The role of cooperatives, thus, no longer remained confined to their traditional activities and expanded to new economic ventures as in the case of other such enterprises in the public or the private sector.

2.2. The past few decades have witnessed substantial growth of the sector in diverse areas of the economy. The number of all types of cooperatives increased from 1.81 lakh in 1950-51 to 5.04 lakh in 1998-99. The total membership of cooperative societies increased from 1.55 crore to 20.91 crore during the same period covering about 67% rural households and about 99% villages. Cooperatives advanced agricultural credit to the tune of Rs. 16987.00 crore during the year 1998-99 and had 44.6% share in institutional agricultural credit. The share of cooperatives in fertilizer distribution is of the order of 30.35% while the fertilizer produced by the cooperatives accounts for 18.64% of the total fertilizer production in the country. 56.8% of the sugar production in the country is from the cooperative sector.

There are 84,289 village dairy cooperative societies in the country procuring 157.80 lakh kg. milk per day. These village level dairy cooperative societies are having membership of 106.28 lakh out of which 21.19 per cent are women members. Besides procurement and marketing of milk, dairy cooperatives are actively engaged in the field of superior cattle breeding, product diversification, nutrition, animal health and high quality animal feed.

The number of urban cooperative banks rose from 1106 as on 30th June 1967 to 1936 as at the end of March 1999 and deposit increased from Rs. 153 crore to Rs. 50,544 crore. The average deposits per bank, which stood at Rs.13.83 lakh in March 1967, rose to Rs. 26.11 crore by March 1999.

3. EXISTING CONSTRAINTS

Inspite of the quantitative growth, the cooperative sector is best with several constraints related to legislative and policy support, resource availability, infrastructure-development, institutional inadequacies, lack of awareness among the members,erosion of the democratic content in management, excessive bureaucratic and governmental controls and needless political interference in the operations of the societies.

3.1. LEGISLATIVE AND POLICY CONSTRAINTS

Operatives are basically economic enterprises requiring proper legislative and policy support aimed at the creation of an environment conducive to their healthy development. Provisions continue to remain in the cooperative laws which hinder and hamper the development of these institutions. The restrictive regulatory regime has also restricted the autonomy of the cooperatives.

3.2 RESOURCE CONSTRAINT

The cooperative sector in general and cooperative societies in the agricultural credit sector in particular are facing severe resource-crunch. Mounting over dues in cooperative credit institutions and lack of recycling of funds together with inability to mobilize internal resources, have made a large number of cooperatives sick and defunct.

3.3 INFRASTRUCTURE CONSTRAINT

The cooperative sector in still predominated by poor infrastructure, particularly, in the field of post harvest technology, storage, marketing and processing apart from lack of basic rural infrastructural support such as roads, electricity, communications, etc.

3.4 INSTITUTIONAL CONSTRAINT

There have been instances of cooperative institutions in some cases working at variance. Some federal cooperatives which were supposed to guide and nurse their affiliate organizations are competing with them resulting in deterioration of the health of the primary and grass root level cooperatives. Lack of professional management and human resource development are also some of the traditional institutional constraints. Cooperatives in the financial sector and particularly in the banking sector are facing the problems of

(i) dual controls;

(ii) increasing incidence of sickness; and

(iii) low level of professionalism, which have been adversely affecting the depositors' interest.

3.5   CONSTRAINT RELATING TO MEMBER Awareness

A successful cooperative requires enlightened and informed membership. Although the membership of cooperatives in terms of numbers has increased manifold, dormant membership and the absence of active participation of members in their management have not only resulted in sickness but also encouraged the dominance of vested interests causing blockages in the percolation of benefits to the members. In a large number of cases, elections and general body meetings in cooperatives are not held regularly. The non-conduct of elections and general body meetings regularly has been creating apathy among members towards the management.

3.6   CONSTRAINT ARISING OUT OF Excessive Government Controls and Needless Political Interference

Unjustified supersession of elected managements by the Government and bureaucratic controls over the management of cooperatives have rendered these institutions as Government driven bodies rather than the member driven. There are institutions where the administrators continue for unduly long periods and members are not allowed to exercise their right to elect their own management. This situation leads to a regulatory regime and excessive governmental control and political interference in the day-to-day management of cooperatives.

4.1 The ideology of cooperatives is based on the principles of self-help, self-responsibility, democracy, equality, equity and solidarity. Members of cooperatives should believe and imbibe the values of honesty, openness, social responsibility and concern for one another.

4.2 BASIC COOPERATIVE PRINCIPLES

As pronounced in the Declaration of the Machester International Cooperative Alliance (ICA) congress 1995, the basic Cooperative Principles are as follows:

4.2.(1) VOLUNTARY AND OPEN MEMBERSHIP

Cooperatives are voluntary organizations, open to all persons capable of using their services and willing to accept the responsibilities of membership, without discrimination on basis of gender, social status, racial, political ideologies or religious consideration.

4.2.(2) DEMOCRATIC MEMBER CONTROL

Cooperatives are democratic organizations controlled by their members, who actively participate in setting their policies and decision making. Elected representatives of these cooperatives are responsible and accountable to their members.

4.2.(3) MEMBER'S ECONOMIC PARTICIPATION

Members contribute equitably and control the capital of their cooperatives democratically. At least a part of the surplus arising out of the economic activity would be the common property of the cooperatives. The remaining surplus could be utilized benefiting the members in proportion to their shares in the cooperative.

4.2.(4) AUTONOMY AND INDEPENDENCE

Cooperatives are autonomous self-help organizations controlled by their members. If cooperatives enter into agreement with other organizations including government or raise capital from external sources, they do so on the terms that ensure democratic control by members and maintenance of cooperative autonomy.

4.2.(5) EDUCATION, TRAINING AND INFORMATION

Cooperatives provide education and training to their members, elected representatives and employees so that they can contribute effectively to the development of these institutions. They also make the general public, particularly young people and leaders, aware of the nature and benefits of cooperation.

4.2.(6) COOPERATION AMONG COOPERATIVES

Cooperatives serve their members most effectively and strengthen the cooperative movement by working together through the available local, regional, national and international structure.

4.2.(7) CONCERN FOR COMMUNITY

While focusing on the needs of their members, cooperatives work for the sustainable development of communities through policies accepted by the members.

5. THE NEED FOR A NATIONAL POLICY

The role of cooperatives has acquired a new dimension in the changing scenario of globalization and liberalization of Nation's economy. Internal and structural weaknesses of these institutions combined with lack of proper policy support have neutralized their positive impact. There are wide regional imbalances in the development of the cooperatives in the country.

This has necessitated the need for a clear-cut national

policy on cooperatives to enable sustained development and growth of healthy and self-reliant cooperatives for meeting the sectoral /regional aspirations of the people in consonance with the principles of cooperation. In this connection, it is also imperative to address the issues which require to be attended to by evolving a suitable legislative and policy support to these institutions.

The proposed National Policy on Cooperatives, as follows, is a part of the concerted efforts of the government to provide appropriate policy and legislative support to cooperatives with a view to revitalizing them.

6. OBJECTIVE

The objective of the National Policy is to facilitate all round development provided necessary support, encouragement and assistane, so as to ensure that they work and self-reliant as utonomous, democratically managed institutions accountable to their members and make a significant contribution to the national economy, particularly in areas which require people's participation and community efforts. This is all the more important in view of the fact that still a sizeable segment of the population in the country is below poverty line and the cooperatives are the only appropriate mechanism to lend support to this section of the people.

The National Policy on Cooperatives to this end would seek to achieve : Ensuring functioning o the cooperatives based on basic cooperative values and principles as enshrined in the declaration of the International Cooperative Alliance Congress, 1995;

Revitalization of the cooperative structure particularly in the sector of agricultural credit;

Reduction of regional imbalances through provision of support measures by the Central Government/State

Government, particularly in the under-developed and cooperatively undeveloped States/regions;

Strengthening of the Cooperative Education and Training and Human Resource Development for professionalization of the management of the Cooperatives;

Greater participation of members in the management of cooperativesand promoting the concept of user members;

Amendment/removal of provisions in cooperatives laws providing for the restrictive regulatory regime;

Evolving a system of integrated cooperative structure by entrusting the federations predominantly the role o promotion, guidance, information system, etc. towards their affiliate members and potential members;

Evolving a system of inbuilt mechanism in Cooperative legislation to ensure timely conduct of general body meetings, elections and audit of cooperative societies;

Ensuring that the benefits of the cooperatives Endeavour reach the poorer sections of the society and encouraging the participation of such sections and women in management of cooperatives.

7. POLICY

The Government of India in consultation and collaboration with the State Governments hereby enunciates the following:

(i) While upholding the values and principles of cooperation, it recognizes the cooperatives as autonomous associations of persons, united voluntarily to meet their common economic, social and cultural needs and aspirations through jointly owned and democratically controlled enterprises.

(ii) Upholds the preservation of the distinct identity of cooperatives, its values and principles by providing an appropriate environment and taking the required administrative and legislative measures;

(iii) Recognizes cooperatives as a distinct economic sector and an integral component of the socio-economic system of the country and an effective and potential instrument of socio-economic development. It considers them as essentially community initiatives for harnessing people's creative power, autonomous, democratically managed, decentralized, need-based and sustainable economic enterprises. Cooperatives will, however, remain the preferred instrument of execution of the public policy especially in the rural area;

(iv) The regulatory role of the Government will be mainly limited to the conduct of timely elections, audit of the cooperative societies, and measures to safeguard the interest of the members and other stake holders in the cooperatives. There shall, however, be no interference in the management and working of the cooperatives. The Government recognizes the a political nature of cooperatives;

(v) Reiterates and reinforces its commitment to the cause of the SC/ST, women and other weaker sections of the Society and their development through the cooperatives. Wherever members belonging to women or Scheduled Castes/Scheduled Tribes and other backward castes want to have their exclusive societies provided they find a socio-economic reason to form such a society, encouragement and assistance will be provided by the Government. Cooperative Societies, if they so decide, can provide for the representation of such category of persons in their bye-laws which they are competent to frame;

(vi) Accepts the need to phase out its share holdings/equity participation in the cooperatives. It shall, however, endeavour and eaxtend appropriate support for improving financial viability and resource mobilizationby harnessing local savings and adequate refinance facility, and to the possible extent providing policy framework ensure that there is no discrimination against the cooperatives in the matter relating to resource mobilization to attain financial viability. The cooperatives shall be enabled to set up holding companies/sub-sidiaries, enter into strategic partnership, venture into futuristic areas like insurance, food processing and information technology etc., and shall be independent to take the financial decisions in the interest of the members and in furtherance of their stated objects.

(vii) Recognizes the role of the Government in ensuring that the benefits of liberalization and globalization in the emerging economic environment are extended to the cooperatives in equal measure through suitable fiscal policies and pledges to provide support and protection to the cooperative movement through suitably designed investment programmes with a view to providing the cooperatives a level playing field vis-à-vis other competing enterprises especially in the field of agro-processing and marketing;

(viii) Recognizes the need for more effective regulation of cooperatives operating in the financial sector and accepting public deposits;

(ix) Also recognises the need for incorporating special provision in the Cooperative Societies Acts with regard to banking, housing, real estate development, processing, manufactures' co-operatives, infrastructure development, etc;

(x) Recognizes the need to provide preferential treatment, as far as possible, to the cooperatives engaged in areas such as credit, labour, consumer, services, housing development of SC/ST and women and development of emerging areas as well as sectors requiring people's participation especially in rural areas;

(xi) Undertakes to devise and execute suitable programmes and schemes to build and develop cooperative institutions in the cooperatively under-developed States/ regions with particular reference to the North Eastern Sates including Sikkim.

(xii) Recognizes the need to support the cooperative movement to develop human resources, cooperative education and training, appropriate technologies and infrastructural facilities so as to promote professional management in cooperatives particularly at the primary level, for their greater functional and operational efficiency. It may also include the introduction of cooperatives as a curriculum vitae at school level;

(xiii) Undertakes to initiate structural reforms in order to improve the functioning of the cooperatives at various levels to ensure greater efficiency and viability. These may include steps to activate idle membership, enhance member participation and involvement, provision of multi cooperatives approach, ensure timely conduct of general body meetings and elections, provide for effective audit, devise suitable mechanism for rehabilitation of the sick societies particularly in the processing sector, expedite winding up of defunct societies; and providing legal framework for voluntary winding up of cooperatives.

(xiv) Undertakes to bestow autonomy to cooperatives to follow appropriate personnel policies including those relating to recruitment, promotions and other such matters with due emphasis on quality and transparency;

(xv) Undertakes to introduce the required electoral reforms through legislative measures. Elections to the cooperative societies should be held through an independent authority like the State Election Commission; and

(xvi) Also undertakes to take other such measures as would be required for

8. PLAN OF ACTION –

A plan of action for implimentation of the policy shall be formulated and persued with adiqueat budgetary support by the Govt. of India, State Government and other concerned agencies including federal / national level co-operative organisation in a time bound manner.

9. CONCLUSION

The Govt. of India trusts that the enuciation of this statement of policy on co-operatives aimed at professionalisation and democratization of their operations will faciliated the development of co-operatives and self reliant and economically viable organisations, providing their members improved assets to the economics of scale, offsetting various risk elements, safeguarding them against market inporfections and bestoving the advantages of collective action.

And further trust that the above statement of policy would ensure enduring autonomy and lasting viability to them as democratically owned, self reliant enterprises, responsible and accountable to their members and a larger public interest.

"Co-operation is non violence. The Co-operative society should therefore the organise with the willing concent of the constituents ends and fellow feeling should be the binding force. Their should be no rooms for compulsion in any forms."

– Mahatma Gandhi

Major Pillars Of Co-operative

The Cooperative movement is the movement of the people. There are three major pillars of Cooperatives, which play pivotal role. Without their positive Contribution any Society can not be Successful: Those pillars are members, leaders and employees.

MEMBER :

The Member of the Cooperative Societies have three distinct roles. They are owner as well as custodian of the Societies, they are customers of the Societies and they are Producer of the Societies. Member's Participation in business and managerial affairs are essential. They are both second line leaders and main decision makers of the Societies. They take part in Annual General Body Meeting of Societies and take policy decisions for the Societies. But unfortunately most of the member are neither vigilant nor aware of their rights and duties towards Societies of course most of them do not even attend A.G.M. Many a time they neither deal any type of business nor they take services from the Societies. This they remain indifferent towards the activities of the Societies.

LEADER :

Second major pillar of the Co-operative Societies is

Leaders: They have very significant role in the Societies. Leaders are also custodian and main decision makers of the Societies. Without competent leadership cooperative Societies can not run successfully. It is observed that a number of successful Cooperative Societies have emerged in the last one decade because of Competent Leadership. Leaders should have some qualities for successful leadership. Viz, personal contact, character, Vision, dedication, sacrifice, Courage, Conviction, personal Values, boldness, punctuality etc. Though most of our leaders have such qualities, yet some do not exploit their Competence for the development of their organization. Some leaders lack competence and even they remain imposed on the Societies. They have no knowledge about the basic theme of Cooperative concept and ideology. Some of our leaders are interested only in their personal benefits and they try to get it by any means. Most of such leaders have the feeling of casteisem, racialism and nepotism. They are even narrow minded. All their activities are politically motivated. These are the reasons that in some cases the members of the societies do not openly support their leaders. A few leaders have to the feeling of monopoly and they try to change their societies as a one-man society. Leaders should to avoid such type of situation and maintain their dignity because all the members look towards their Leaders with hopeful eyes.

EMPLOYEE :

Another most important element of the cooperatives is employees. They are considered third pillar of the Societies. They are the permanent element of the Societies. Some employees are not only worthy but also honest and dedicated to their work as well as societies. They have knowledge of rules and regulations of the Cooperative societies, which are neces sary for the smooth functioning of business of the Societies. Therefore their role for the success of societies is very important. But some employees do not play their role effectively, due to some reasons best known to them. Some employees do not have proficiency in their work because some times their selections is not fair. Such employees mostly remain interested in their personal benefits. Most of the employees are associated with some or the other leaders for their self interest. In some cases a nexus between employees and leaders is also observed. Both work as a team for their mutual.

Benefits Patronage and in return give them various tricks for back door benefits. Such sycophant type of employees are in fact the liabilities on the Societies. They never think in interest of Societies. We can say that such type of employees are stigma on their profession. If the Cooperative movement Collapses the employees will be the worth sufferers whereas the leaders and the members will be the least effected. The leaders can get assocated with some other organization and members can get services from other societies or organizations. But where the employees will go ? if the activity of Cooperative movement comes to a halt, the future of the employees will be ruined Therefore I will have pleasure to give my message to employees of Cooperative Societles.

My message is as follows :

"We can neither become the moon, nor the Sun, but we can bum ourselves to spread the light in our Vicinity it is the only indispensable way to save the future of our societies and ourselves, otherwise the day is not far away when the Cooperatives will come to an end. Hence it is the only basic duty of every employee of the Cooperative sector to think and work in the larger interest of Cooperative Societies and themselves.

"The Idea of Co-operation is something largen then merely an efficient and economic way for doing things, It is economics, It is fair, It equalizes and presents disparities from going. But it is something even deeper than that, It is really away of life."

– Jawaharlal Nehru

Task Force On Rural Co-operative Bank

Credit Co-operative Societies and Banks were organized with Govt. aid first in India. At Banki, Orissa since 1903. The Banks are collecting deposit to advance farm loan. The Cooperative Banks were collecting deposit equal to loan advances to avoid interest burden on excess deposit. The RBI was established in 1935 and started farm refinance to Central Cooperative Banks since 1940. The members were used to repay loan regularly as they were believing that they will go to hell if they will fail to repay their loan. But sometimes, they were unable to repay the crop loan in case of crop loss in natural calamities and were selling land to repay the loan as there was no Crop Insurance to compensate their damaged Crop. PACS and Cooperative Banks were managed by Managing Committee without Government participation in the said Committee. But only 3 percent of Indian Agricultural Family were members till 1950-51 in spite of Cooperation is State Subject since 1919.

Governments contributed share capital to augment resource base for Credit Cooperative Societies and Banks in order to borrow more and Govt. participated in Managing Committee for efficient management. Registrar, Cooperative Societies (RCS), is empowered in State Cooperative

Societies Acts in different States to supervise, hold election of Managing Committee of Cooperative Credit Structure, to audit the account, to take legal action against defaulters,bto supersede mismanagement of Coop. Socieites, to liquidate defunct Credt Cooperative Societies and Banks. The Secretary of PACS was a part time employee and was getting commission on the basis of 10% of collection and quantum of investment for which the farm loan collection was always above 80%. The political parties with their short sighted policies and to gain cheap popularity dissuaded farm borrowers for non repayment of the loan since 1952 for which collection percentage became very low and decreased day by day. PACS and CC Banks lost their eligibility to borrow from higher financial agencies. Imbalance and accoumulated loss mounted at their level at the end of the financial year. The numbers of defaulters are many and they are denied fresh credit raise new crop.

Small PACS were merged to form large sized credit Cooperative Societies as per 1964 Action Programme of RBI for appointment of whole time permanent Secretary to raise investment. Only 30% farmers were members of Credit Cooperative Societies for which Govt. of India had nationalized 14 Commercial Banks in 1969 with instruction to supplement Farm Credit needs for which Credit Cooperative Societies and Banks lost their monopoly of Farm finance and are facing competence with multi credit agencies.

Both Central and State Govts. on sharing basis provided aid to weak Central Co-operative Banks against their irrecoverable loan during 5th Plan for their reviability and eligibility for RBI refinance and also Central and State Govts. both provided risk fund to PACS and CC Banks for advancing Crop loan to small and marginal farmers. The

Secretary of PACS were caderised and transferable to remove their vested interest. To raise their salary with the aid of State Govt. and C.C. Banks they got scope for agitation to fulfil their demands neglecting collection for which the Cooperative Societies and Banks were weakened. Some nonviable PACS were ceded to nationalized commercial banks in case of weak Central Cooperative Banks but they were again receded to their parent Central Cooperative Banks for non-remunerative margin. So, the recommendation of Task Force to amend the bye-laws of PACS to borrow from any financial institution is not acceptable.

Govt. of India established Gramya Banks in 1975 to advance loan only to weaker section of the societies for which Govt. of India is bearing extra financial burden as Credit Cooperative Structures are for weaker section. Crop Insurance was introduced for Crop loan borrowers by Govt. of India in 1985 to compensate their crop loss in natural calamities to step up collection and to make the borrowers eligible for fresh finance in order to raise next crop.

But some State Govts. and Govt. of India started policy of waiving farm loan of chronic willful defaulters since 1989 for which honest farmers did not repay their loan which lead to low collection again as a result of which many Central Cooperative Banks lost their viability for refinance.

Govt. of India had introduced liberal economic policy in 1991 Govt. of India set up Narsigham Committee for recommending to contribute capital of Rs. 24,934 crores to weak commercial Banks for their revitalization under Capital Adequacy Scheme in spite of their professional Management. But the said Committee did not recommend any capital contribution for revitalization of Coop. Credit Structure on the plea of Cooperation is a State subject in spite of their 62% farm fiancé out of the total in our country during during 1992. Politicalisation and officialisation of Managing Committee of PACS and CCBs, loan recovery, mismanagement, misappropriation, disproportionate establishment cost to their income led to heavy imbalance at their level. Cooperative Credit Structure are still major player in advancing farm credit against all commercial Banks and Gramya Banks together for which Govt. of India had set up Vikhe Patil, Vyas and Kapoor Committee from time to time to revitalize the PACS, CCBS and SCBs. But their recommendation was not given effect. The present Govt. under the Prime Minister Dr. Man Mohan Singh, has decided to double farm credit within three years since 2003-04 for raising farm productivity. Govt. of India realized the credit cooperative structures are major player in advancing farm credit and unless they are strengthened, the target of farm credit advancebcan not be achieved. So, Govt. of India again set up another Baidyanathan Committee to recommend the following steps for improving managerial efficiency, re-structuring reengineering these Credit Cooperative Structure. The PACS are grass root organization at village level to approach each farm borrowers easily than other financial institutions.

(i) To restore pre-independence self-reliant democratic management, Credit Cooperative Societies without Govt. participation is to hold regular free and fair election. Many present day electing Managing Committee have no dedicated members and Presidents for managerial efficiency. Rather, they have got vested and political interest to weaken Coop. societies and Banks. Unless proper screening of defaulters and otherwise disqualifying candidates are identified, efficient Managing Committee can not be realized. Such eligible candidates should be allowed to contest for Presidents or members of Managing Committee. Presiding and Election Officers should identify eligible candidate on their own initiation and on allegation of contesting candidate to eliminate disqualified persons.

User members at least with 3 years membership and having member education training will be allowed to contest management election Committee. He should not be defaulter to Coop. Society, Central and State Govt., local bodies or to any corporate loan. RBI or NABARD should supervise the election as the RCS is a Govt. officer. He can no conduct free and fair election under influence of State Govt. RCS is only to supersede mismanagement Committee with prior approval of RBI or NABARD to avoid politicalization.

(ii) RBI or NABARD can also supersede the mismanagement societies on its own initiation. It will be mandatory for RBI, NABARD and RCS to hold election within three months of supersession of PACS, CCB and SCB to maintain their democratic character. Once election process is started, it can not be stopped or withheld by any authorities. The Managing Committee members and Presidents of Credit Coop. Structure having no interest for attending two consecutive Board meeting and General Bodies will be ineligible to contest the election again. Accordingly, Central and State Coop. Act, B.R. Act of RBI and NABARD Act should be amended.

(iii) Abolition of duality control in matters of financial regulation will vest with RBI. But still then, many commercial banks and Gramya banks managed by professionals, RBI and NABARD control were weak due to indiscriminate finance under external influence, for which they needed capital under Capital Adequacy Scheme.

(iv) Gramya Bank and Commercial Banks are always

managed by trained and experienced professionals. But many of them were weak and received capital of Rs. 24,934 crores under capital adequacy scheme. The reason must be analyzed and appropriate action should be taken to eliminate these employees. They should step up collection, proper appraisal of investment. Coercive action should be taken for recovery by Banks.

(v) The Task Force has properly analyzed and justifying financial assistance of Rs. 10,835 crores for three-tiers of Credit Cooperative Structures on sharing basis by Govt. of India of Rs. 5793 crores as grant, by State Governments Rs. 3402 crores as State share and Rs. 1,644 crores by Cooperative Credit Structures i.e. share of liability 53%, 31%, and 16% respectively. latter it has been changed. The share of liability is 72%, 24% and 4% respectively. If the State Govt. and Credit Cooperative Structures can not arrange their share they can borrow soft loan from Govt. of India. But there should not be 50% viability norm for PACS and CC Banks as the Task Force recommended to wipe out their imbalance PACS and CCBanks can be again rejuventated to meet their credit needs. Nonviable PACS can again be viable for efficient management.

There is no such norm viable or non-viable PACS I have observed many weak PACS affiliated to Banki CC Bank are agin viable by taking step for collection and investment. So, there is no such norm to define viable and non-viable PACS and Banks. It depends essentially on managerial efficiency. Credit Cooperative Societies and Banks are federal structure. PACS should not be exploited by CCBanks and CC Bank can not be exploited by State Cooperative banks in case of recovery of loan and adjustment of interest first for which theirnimbalance and accumulated loss are mounting very fast for which Task

Force isrecommending option of PACS to borrow from any financial institutions which I opposed because the CC Bank and SSB will suffer as they are getting lucrative amount of deposits in shape of their own fund, share capital, deposit etc.

Loan recovery climate by both Central and State Governments is vitiated for frequent subsidies since 1990 for which honest borrowers are not repaying loan in anticipation of waiving of their loan. In this context, it is encouraging for credit cooperative societies registered under SelfHelp Cooperative Act as collection is always about 80% and above should be taken against willful defaulters. Crop Insurance should be implemented properly to compensate each affected insured farm borrowers and Crop cutting procedure simplified for the said purpose.

(vi) Staff salary and other establishment cost should be within income generation. Employees should be surcharged and should be taken to task if they will eaten up share capital loan and loan collection for which credit cooperative societies and Banks are losing their viability.

(vii) NABARD and RBI should be empowered with legal action for irregularities, misappropriation, revealed during their inspection instead of they are thinking their job is over after reporting the matter waiting action by RCS.

(viii) Reserve Bank of India should not withhold election of Managing Committee of Credit Coop. structures upto 5 years. Elections should be held within three months after it is superseded for up-keeping democratic tradition of Cooperative movement.

(ix) There is paucity of Govt. auditors due to non-appointment for financial stringencyof State Governments. Every Coop. Soci-ety and Bank should complete audit by Chartered Accountant within three months of closing of financial year. The responsi bility should be fixed on Committee members and employees after discussing with them before presentation of audit report.

(x) Arbitrary section like 123 of OCS Act, 1962 should be deleted. Such section is giving handle State Govts. For interferingin Management and superseding managing committee for political reasons.

(xi) Cooperative Bank should appoint only trained professionals and Govt. should recruit such person as Departmental Officers and employees.

(xii) Govt. will get back their share money of Rs. 1243 Crores from Credit Structure which will ease its financial burden to share 31%. Orissa Govt. should accept Task Force recommendation as Central Government is giving grant and soft loan to strengthen coop. credit societies and Banks for their viability to borrow more to meet the farm credit need.

It is mania with many State Governments to supersede Managing Committee and to post Collectors and other Govt. Officers who have no knowledge in credit advances for which they are not sanctioning credit limit in time.

(xiii) The report of Task Force are very ex- haustive, informative and suggestive. If they are effectively implemented, it will certainly meet the farm investment as targeted by Govt. of India to increase productivity. In my conclusion, if there will be dedicated management with managerial efficiency including Committee Members and professionals the Credit Coop. Structure will not need any subsidies or grants and can be self-reliant to meet the credit needs of our farmers.

Architecture of Co-operative Movement

Co-operation as a thought and concept is perhaps the best of its kind on this plant. One can not find a more simple and easier way to attain betterment of mankind. Irrespective of caste and creed, culture and gender, the idea of Co-operation endeavours for common benifit of all concerned on joing venture basis without any self-interest. "One for all and all for one" is the guiding spirit behind the idea of co-operation. While implementing the above spirit, importance is focussed on majorit virous and thus the democratic process is upheld. Common interst, free access to all and democratic process are in fact the pillars of Co-operative thought. Can any body find a better concept than that of Co-operatives on the earth?

Like that of Co-operation, truth adn non-violence is also a thought process which can definitely be acclaimed as best way of life on earth. Mahatma Gandhi in his philosophy of life has put immense importance on Co-operation, truth and non-violence. During the course of independence movement of the country, he adopted the thought of Co-operation, truth and non-violence. But he cused the idea of Co-operation in a different way for achieving independence of the country. By using the thought of co-operation in opposite manner he launched non-Cooperation movement throught out the country to remove British Raj. Ultimately India tasted the fruit of indepent due to the non-co-operation movement of Mahatma Gandhi. If non-co-operation movement was responsible for end of British Raj, co-operation thought was definitely a road to the upliftment of rural people in India under the guidance of Mahatma Gandhi.

Gandhi had inclination towards Co-operation principles can be traced back to his stay at South Africa. He was very much influenced by socialistic views of leo Tolstoy. During his stay at south Africa he formed "phoenix settlement" a type of Co-operative based on socialistic principles. The landless members of the "Settlement" were provided with three acres of land each for callivation in close coordination with other members. This way of helping each other members. This way of helping each other proved fruitful and led to improvement of financial condition of the members. Another settlement know as "Tolstoy Farm" was established and experimented by Gandhiji at Lawley, near Johannessburg based on Co-operative ideas comprising of 77 members. The members were employed in virious type of activities of the Fary leading to their economic development. Both above experiment had a lot similarity with that of Robert Owen's Cooperative Community" which had earlier emboldened Gandhiji to persue Co-operation thought and ideas.

After return from South Africa, Gandhi extnively travelled through out India in connection with independence movement and was very muchmoved after seeing the miserable financial conditions of rural folk. Basing onthe expenience of South Africa Gandhiji vowed for "Gramya Swarajya" in India in which Co-operative would play a pivotal role in emeliorating the economic conditions of rural poor whether they are engaged in cottage industries or agricuture. He believed that the co-operative societies are very much suitable to the Indian conditions for upliflment of rural poor.

According to Gandhi co-operation must be voluntary. He was very cautious about the utility of co-operatives which was to be adopted according to the local conditions. According to him co-operation was essentially a moral movement it could succed only if honest people manage co-operatives efficiently and with integrity.

Gandhi wrote or spoke frequently on various aspects of co-operative movement such as co-operative farming consumer co-operative, adoption and application of co-operative, method of working in cottage industries and other fields. He had made it a point to implement his plans and programmers through co-operative method to the maximu extent possible.

Mahatma Gandhi belived that both the village Panchayats and local state governments have an important role to play for the growth of the co-operative. According to him Gram Panchayats should encourage the unemployed youth to organise cooperative for various sectors.

Besides cottage industries Mahatma Gandhi had also focussed his attention on co-operative Farming. His views on co-operative farming is quoted below as splet by him in the "Harijan" of February 2, 1942.

We shall not derive the full benefit of agriculture until we take to co-operative farming. Does it not stand to reason that it is for betterment for a hundred familes in a village to cultivate their lands collectively and divied the earning there from than to divide the land any how into hundred portions. If for who have small land holdings but do not want to cultivate on the co-operative basis in sprit of knowing this fact these holding, can not give suffering income their it is necessary that on the one hand their (small farmers) misunderstandings about co-operative farming may be removed and on the other hand such programmes schemes be made so as to at tract small farmer towards co-operative farming.

Nehru the first Prime Minister of Independent India was very much in fluenced by the philosophy and ideologies of mahatma Gandhi. Therefore after indepentence when he took charge he laid much emphasis co-operative to translate the thoughts of Gandhiji into practice. The First Five years plan in 1950-51 described the Co-operative movement as an indispensable instrument of planned action in to country.

The first plan statued :

"The principles of mutual aid which is the basis of co-operative organisations and the practice of threft and self-help which sustains it, generate a feeling of self-reliance which is of basic importance in a democratic way of life. By pooling their expenience and knowledge and helping one another, members of co-op societies can not only find the solutions of individual problems but also become better citizens."

The 2nd five year plan set before itself the broad objective of evolve socialistic pallern of societies. For materialing these objectives co-operative was chosen as an important agency and the building of the co-operative sector became one of central aims of national policy. The Third five year plan enusaged a growing co-operative sector particularly in respect of agriculture medium and small industries trade and distribution etc. During the fourth Five year plan "Growth with stafility was expected to be the keynot of the co-operative movement. The fifth five year plan draft stated" co-operative is eminently saited to bring about desired socio-economic challenges in the context of the existing conditions in the country. There is no other instrument as potential powerful and full of social purpose as the co-operative movement. "The Govt of India continued to focus on co-operative movement as an instrument for the growth of rural india in the subseqent plans and programmes.

From the above discussions, it is crystas clear that both state and central Govts have been attaching top most importance on the co-operative movement of the country. This policy of encouraging co-operative has come to place largely due to the influence of Mahatma Gandhi. Gandhiji in his dream of Gramya Swarajya wanted co-operatives to play a pivotal role for the upliftment of the poor rural people. In view of the same, the present co-operative movement of the country owes a lot to Mahatma Gandhi and his philosophy. In short Gandhiji can be held as architect of co-operative movement in India.

B. R. Amendment Act - 2012

Co-operatives essentially are organized on the basis of self help and mutual aid. The co-operative principles that have been designed and re-interpreted from time to time, are the operating principles followed by members for realizing their common goals. The co-operative principles, in fact not only reflect but also reinforce the basic values providing this conceptual clarity that The International Co-operative Alliance (ICA) consciously incorporated the six basic co- operative values; self help, self responsibility, democracy, equity, equality and solidarity, in its Statement on Co-operative Identity (1995). Resorting to external funding and having business dealings with non members by co-operatives is no doubt unavoidable and sometimes even essential in the modern inter connected and inter related world. But such practices should be viewed, as far as possible, as temporary measures and as exceptions. The Principles of Open Membership always comes handy to enroll the present non member users as full-fledged members of the co-operative.

The above mentioned puritan view of a co-operative apart, a discernible legal trend is clearly visible of late which compels the co-operatives to abjure their current wayward practices and return back to their original ways of doing business based on their core values. The provisions of the

97th Constitutional Amendment Act 2011 (CCA 2011) and of the recently adopted Banking Laws Amendment Act 2012 are to be viewed as pointers in this regard. Since enough is already written and said about CCA 2011, and attempt is made in this paper to discuss the recent amendments to the Banking laws pertaining to co-operatives with a view to understand their implications to co-operatives, in particular to those societies accepting deposits from the public (i.e. non members). To place things in perspective, it is worth recalling here about the mandate of Art. 243ZI of the Constitution which require the co-operative laws in the country to be based on certain principles which among others include the principle of member economic participation.

THE BANKING REGULATION (AACS) ACT 1965 POSITION BEFORE 2012 AMENDMENT

Originally enacted as the Banking Companies Act 1949, the law was renamed as The Banking Regulations Act 1949, when certain provisions of the Act were made applicable to Co-operative societies by adding new part V to the existing Act in 1965 by the Banking Laws (Application to Co-operative Societies) Act, 1965 (23 of 1965).

Since the inserted new Section 56 in Part V is self contained and quite distinct, the Amendment Act inserting this new part is popularly known as The Banking Regulation (as applicable to co-operative societies) Act 1965, for short BR (AACS) Act 1965, which came into effect on 1-3-1966. Since the scope of this paper is limited to examining the implications of the recent amendments (of 2012) to co-operatives in Kerala, who are accepting deposits from non members (particularly to PACS) only those Sections that are relevant for the purpose are dealt here.

1.   For purposes of conceptual clarity, it is necessary to have an understanding of some relevant sections of the Act pertaining to applicability to co-operative societies, definition of some relevant terms used there-in, licensing etc.

2.   THE BANKING REGULATION (AACS) ACT.1965
POSITION AFTER 2012 AMENDMENT.

2.(1) Section 3 of the Act explicitly keeps out of its purview a PACS, a PCARDB and any other co-operative society, except in the manner and to the extent specified in Part V thereof.

2.(2)   Banking means the accepting, for the purpose of lending or investment, of deposits of money from the public, repayable on demand or otherwise, and withdrawable by cheque, draft, order or otherwise (S-5). Existence of all the above elements are essential for banking and absence of one or more element result in excluding the business from the definition of banking.

2.(3)   Co-operative Bank means a State Co-operative Bank, a Central Co-operative bank and a primary Co-operative Bank (S.5-cci).

2.(4) Co-operative credit society (CCS) means a co-operative society, the primary object of which is to provide financial accommodation to its members and includes a co-operative land mortgage bank i.e. aPCARDB (S.5-ccii).

2.(5) Primary agricultural credit society (PACS) means a co-operative society- (1) the primary object or principal business of which is to provide financial accommodation to its members for agricultural purposes or for purposes connected with agricultural activities (including the marketing of crops); and (2) the bye-laws of which do not permit admission of any other co-operative society as a member (S.5-cciv).

2.(6) Primary Co-operative Bank (PCB) means a co-operative society other than a primary agricultural credit society - (1) the primary object or principal business of which is the transaction of banking business. (2) the paid-up share capital and reserves of which are not less than one lakh or rupees; and (3) the bye-laws of which do not permit admission of any other co-operative society as a members (S.5-ccv).

2.(7) Primary credit society (PCS) is so defined that it is almost similar to a PCB, except that its paid up share capital and reserves is less than one lakh rupees (S.5-ccvi). Thus, a PCS automatically becomes a PCB once its paid up share capital and reserves touches the threshold of Rs one lakh. Explanation: If any dispute arises as to the primary object or principal business of any co-operative society referred to in clauses (cciv), (ccv) and ccvi), a determination thereof by the Reserve Bank shall be final;

2.(8) Central Co-operative Bank", "co- operative society", "primary rural credit society" and "State Co-operative Bank" shall have the meanings respectively assigned to them in the National Bank for Agricultural and Rural Development Act, 1981 (61 of 1981) (S. 5-ccvii)

2.(9) No co-operative society other than a   C o - operative Bank shall use as part of its name or in connection with its business any of the words "bank", banker", or "banking", and no co-operative society shall carry on the busir...ss of banking in India unless it uses as part of its name at least one of such words (S. 7-1). A Primary Credit Society alone is permitted not only to carry on "banking business" but also carry on such business without the word "bank" etc included as part of its name (S. 7-2-a read with S. 5-ccv).

2.(10) Notwithstanding any law relating to co-operative societies for the time being in force, no Co-operative Bank shall commence or carry on the business of banking in India unless the aggregate (real or exchange) value of its paid- up capital and reserves is not less than one lakh of rupees (S. 11-1). However, two exceptions are made to this general rules that too for only a limited period namely:

(a) any such bank which is carrying on such business at the commencement of the BR (AACS) Act 1965) for a period of three years from such commencement; or

(b) to a PCS which becomes a PCB after such commencement, for a period of two years from the date it so becomes a PCB or for such further period not exceeding one year as the Reserve Bank, having regard to the interests of the depositors of the PCB may think fit in any particular case to allow.

2.(11) No co-operative society shall carry on banking business in India unless it is - (a) a primary credit society, or (b) is a Co-operative Bank and holds a license issued in that behalf by the Reserve Bank, subject to such conditions, if any, as the Reserve Bank may deem fit to impose (S. 22-1). If any other co-operative society, other than the two mentioned above, is carrying on banking business at the commence ment of BR (AACS) Act 1965, it can continue to do so only for a period of one year from the date of commencement of the said Act.

Further, the following co-operative societies are mandatorily required to apply for banking license to Reserve Bank within the period mentioned (S.22-2).

(a) every co-operative society carrying on business as Co-operative Bank at the commencement of the months from such commencement.

(b) every Co-operative Bank which comes into existence (either at the commencement of the BRAACS Act 1965 or at any time there after) as a result of the division of any other co-operative society carrying on business as a Co-operative Bank, or the amalgamation of two or more co-operative societies carrying on banking business before the expiry of three months from its so coming into existence.

(c) every primary credit society which becomes a Primary Co-operative Bank after such commencement shall before the expiry of three months from the date on which it so becomes a Primary Co-operative Bank.

(d) every co-operative society before commencing banking business in India. The proviso to S22-2 enables each of the banks mentioned at (a) to (c) above to continue banking business until it is granted a license or is denied license in writing by a notice by the Reserve Bank in this behalf. It is important to note here that the above mentioned banks should have applied for license with RBI within the said time period for getting this benefit. Equally important is the fact that the law does not mandate RBI to decide either way within any specific time period after receiving the application for license from the bank/s. It is this lacunae in the law that explains the continued existence of unlicensed co-operative banks in the country all these years.

2.(12) No person other than a Co-operative Bank (banking company), the RBI, the SBI or any other banking institution, firm or other person notified by the Central Government in this behalf on the recommendation of RBI shall accept from the public deposits of money withdrawable by cheques (S. 49A). Three exceptions are provided; a PCS, any other co-operative society accepting such deposits at the commencement of the BR (AACS) Act 1965, for a period of one year from the date of such commencement, and any savings bank scheme run by the Government.

3. THE BANKING REGULATION (AACS) ACT 1965 POSITION AFTER 2012 AMENDMENT

3.(1) Following the recommendation of the Committee on Financial Sector Assessment (CFSA), set up by GOI in September 2006 under the Chairmanship of Dr. Rakesh Mohan, not to continue the practice of allowing unlicensed (co-operative) banks beyond March 2012, RBI introduced the policy of licensing Central Co-operative Banks (CCBs) and State Co-operative Banks (SCBs) fulfilling the minimum criteria of having 4% CRAR, The licensing period was later extended up to 30th Sept, 2012. As part of this policy towards consolidation of Co-operative Banks, S. 22 of BR (AACS), who were earlier permitted to conduct banking business are now denied this benefit (cl. (a) of S. 22-1) deleted).

As an interim measure, PCS are now allowed to continue banking business for only a period of one year or for such further period not exceeding three years, as the Reserve Bank may, after recording the reasons in writing for so doing, extend (insertion of 2nd proviso to S. 22-1). Hence, before three years from now all PCS in the country will cease to do banking business.

Further, every PCS which had become a PCB on or before Amendment Act 2012 is required to apply for banking license within three months from the date on which it became a PCB (S.22-2).

3.(2) The above legal changes could impact each of the below mentioned different types of primary credit societies in the manner explained there-in.

(a) Primary agricultural credit societies (PACS), whose

activities strictly conform to the definition of PACS as provided under the BR(AACS) Act 1965(See para 2.2.5.), will be least affected. Such societies could continue to receive deposits from the public (i.e. from non members also), but will have to discontinued the use of the word "Bank" from their name. For purpose of clarity, it is worth mentioning in this context that these societies could not have used the word "bank" as part of their name even earlier, i.e. before the present amendment to the BR Act. Also, these societies cannot allow withdrawal of deposits by public through use of cheques (see para 2.2.12).

(b) PACS in the State, whose object/ business does not conform to the definition of PACS under the BR (AACS) Act 1965 (para 2.2.5), will either fall in the category of "primary co-operative bank" (see para 2.2.6) or "primary credit society". (see para 2.2.7)

See Para 2.2.7 depending upon the amount of paid up-share capital and reserves held by an individual society. In the former case (i.e. PCS graduating into PCBs on or before the commencement of Amendment Act 2012), submission of application for banking license is mandated within a period of three months from the date on which it became a PCB. Such societies who opt and submit application for banking license within the said three months time will continue as banks until RBI takes a decision on their application. Those societies who do not opt to apply for banking license within the said period will cease to be banks. In case of later category (i.e. PCS), they will cease to do banking business within the next 1-3 years, consequent to the present amendment, Thus, except those societies opting for banking license as aforesaid, the other two types will become ineligible to be called banks and shall cease to accept deposits from public, i.e. from non members either with immediate effect or within the next 1 to 3 years, as the case may be. In other words, these societies will function as thrift and credit societies or as CCS (see para 2.2.4).

(c) As regards Urban Credit Society (UCS) what ever is said at (b) above will apply, depending upon the status of individual societies i.e.whether it qualifies to be a PCB (and desires to be one) or not i.e. is only a PCS. PACS There is need to explain as to why this author takes varying views on the question of acceptance of deposits from the public in respect of societies at (a) on the one hand and by societies at (b) & (c) above on the other hand.

On a careful reading of the definitions of PCB and PCS, it would become clear that the law makers have deliberately and consciously excluded PACS from the ambit of these two terms. In other words, it is implied that could take up banking activities (like a PCB/PCS) in addition to providing financial accommodation for agricultural and allied activities etc to its members, the later activity continuing to constitute its substantial business for retaining its status as PACS.

As such, societies who qualify as PACS as at (a) above, can continues to accept deposits from the public, but cannot allow cheque facilities in terms of explanation given at para 2.2.12. As regards societies at (b) & (c) above, they are effectively barred from doing banking business, except those societies who formally apply for banking license within the stipulated period, by the Amendment Act of 2012.

◼

"Democracy is the best form of Goverment. It allows people to have a say in how they are governed and to hold their leaders accountable.

– Jawaharlal Nehru

Co-oprative in Gram Swaraj

Various cooperative institutions and agencies related to development of cooperative movement in the villages also should consider seriously on why the percentage of inactive cooperatives is increasing and how this trend can be reversed.

The entire thinking of Mahatma Gandhi behind the prosperity of villages and villagers was inspired from his high philosophy of life involved with best human qualities and deep feeling regarding extreme poverty of rural people and great desire to remove it.

Gandhiji was too distressed seeing the pitiable condition of millions of rural folk inspite of best contribution being given by them for the prosperity of the cities. Some lines of an article written by Gandhiji about the villages are given here. "I have believed and repeated times without number that India is to be found not in its few cities but in its 7,00,000 villages. But we town-dwellers have believed that the India is to be found in its towns and villages were created to minister our needs. We have hardly ever paused to enquire if those poor folk get sufficient to eat and cloth themselves with and whether they have a roof to shelter themselves from sun and rain".

Gandhiji had this firm opinion that there will be no meaning of the independence of India unless the living standard of rural people is improved. He had seen a dream of Gram Swaraj to bring social and economic changes in the villages. His programme for Gram Swaraj included cooperation also. He was a great supporter of it. He had in an article written that "Cooperative societies are ideally suited organizations not only for developing village industries but also for promoting group effort by the villagers".

Though, Gandhiji was in favour of expansion of cooperation in the villages, he told the need to find the type of society before organizing it in any of the villages. He has written in an article "The social workers should first make a systematic detailed inquiry on the spot as to what occupations could be undertaken in each village. They should then proceed to organize these occupations on a cooperative basis."

Gandhiji's emphasis on expansion of cooperatives was not only for the reason that it is the means of ameliorating the condition of the villages, but it was also for the reason that it has high principles and carry them towards community life.

Here it will be worthwhile to mention that maximum benefits from different schemes being implemented by the state and central governments; use of improved technology; reduction in the expenditure on production; proper arrangement for marketing; generation of regular and gainful employment; protectionfrom exploitation; distribution of profit as per law are only possible through cooperatives of cottage and other.

Besides above, artisans who want to run any of the various cottage and other village industries through cooperative society, need no worry for more capital to industry because state governments provides financial assistance under various schemes to the cooperatives of cottage and other village industries.

From some years self help groups are being encouraged for improving economic condition of villagers also. No doubt, self help groups are useful and they are doing well in direction of collecting the capital, generating employment and increasing income for their members. Policy of encouraging self help groups is good but due to this policy, less attention towards expansion of cooperatives of cottage and other village industries is not reasonable. Because cooperative society in the village is not only the means of generating regular and gainful employment but it is a democratic institution at low level as panchayat which is necessary. For encouraging democratic system at low level, not only panchayats but cooperative societies should also be in the villages and arrangement made to run panchayats and cooperative societies properly by the state governments.

For expansion of cooperatives of cottage and other village industries, gram panchayats of the states can play an important role. Panchayats should encourage the unemployed persons to organize cooperatives of cottage and other village industries. Sarpanchs should contact with the officers of khadi and village industry boards and the officers related to the development of cooperatives of cottage and other village industries and request to them to come in their villages, give training to the unemployed persons for one or two selected cottage industry and tell them about the importance and usefulness of cooperatives of cottage and other village industries. If they agree to run cottage industries through cooperatives, they should be guided about organizing them (cooperative societies).

Role of the officers related to development of

cooperatives of cottage and other village industries should not be only as guide and helper in organization of above cooperatives. But they should also help to the cooperatives to get the financial assistance under various schemes being implemented by the state governments, loans from the banks and raw material which can not be obtained from the market or at reasonable price.

In the states, thousands of cooperatives of cottage and other village industries have been organized, but percentage of active cooperatives is decreasing. This is a matter of great concern.

Various cooperative institutions and agencies related to development of cooperative movement in the villages should also consider seriously that why the percentage of inactive cooperatives is increasing and how this trend can be reversed.

Not to mention if inactive cooperatives of village and other village industries become active. They will be able to generate gainful and regular employment to the large number of their members and to prevent migration of the people from the villages towards cities to a great extent in each of the states.

Gandhiji had also given great emphasis on cooperative farming. Some lines of his article published in the harizan of Feb. 1942 on cooperative farming are given here "We shall not derive the full benefits of agriculture until we take to cooperative farming. Does it not stand to the reason that it is for better for a hundred of families in a village to cultivate their lands collectively and divide the income therefrom than to divide the land anyhow into a hundred portions".

If farmers who have small land holdings but don't want to cultivate on cooperative basis inspite of knowing this fact that these holdings can not give sufficient income, then it becomes necessary that on the one hand their (small farmers') misunderstanding about cooperative farming may be removed and on the other hand, such programme and schemes for joint agriculture cooperative societies may be made so as to attract the small farmers towards cooperative farming.

Gram panchayats, dedicated social workers, voluntary organizations and demonstration of films made on successful joint agriculture cooperative societies before small farmers can contribute to agree these farmers to cultivate on cooperative basis by organizing joint agriculture cooperative societies.

In the last, it will be worthwhile to mention that the cooperatives in the villages also can be useful only when they are run properly, their problems solved and arrangements for regular guidance to them, their inspection and audit timely and properly made.

Agriculture LabourER in India

It is one of the primary objects of the Five year plan to ensure fuller opportunities for work and better living to all the sections of the rural community and, in particular, to assist agricultural labourers and backward classes to come to the level of the rest.

One of the most distinguishing features of the rural economy of India has been the growth in the number of agricultural workers, cultivators and agricultural labourers engaged in crop production. The phenomena of under-employment, under-development and surplus population are simultaneously manifested in the daily lives and living of the agricultural labourers. They usually get low wages, conditions of work put an excessive burden on them, and the employment which they get is extremely irregular.

Agricultural workers constitute the most neglected class in Indian rural structure. Their income is low and employment irregular. Since, they possess no skill or training, they have no alternative employment opportunities either. Socially, a large number of agricultural workers belong to scheduled castes and scheduled tribes. Therefore, they are a suppressed class. They are not organized and they cannot fight for their rights. Because of all these reasons their economic lot has failed to improve even after four decades of planning.

This can also be seen from the Prime Minister's speech made in Lok Sabha on August 4, 1966. **The Prime minister emphasized-**

We must give special consideration to the landless agricultural labour. Although there has been tremendous progress in India since Independence, this is one section, which has really a very hard time and which is deserving very special consideration.

" Seasonal unemployment characteristic feature of Agricultural Industry and under employment of man power is inherent in the system of family farming. According to first A.L.E.C., adult male agricultural labourers were employed on wages for 189 days in agricultural work and for 29 days in non-agricultural work i.e. 218 day in all. They were self-employed for 75 days. Casual male workers found employment for only 200 days, while attached workers were employed for 326 days in a year. Women workers employed for 134 days in a year.

Unlike industrial labour, agricultural labour is difficult to define. The reason is that unless capitalism develops fully in agriculture, a separate class of workers depending wholly on wages does not come up.

Difficulties in defining agricultural labour are compounded by the fact that many small and marginal farmers also work partly on the farms of others to supplement their income. To what extent should they (or their family members) be considered agricultural labourers is not easy to answer. However, it will be useful to refer some of the attempts made by experts in this connection.

1. The First Agricultural Labour Enquiry Committee 1950-55 defined Agricultural Labourer as "Those people who are engaged in raising crops on payment of wages"

2. The Second Agricultural Labour Enquiry Committee1956-57 enlarged distribution to include.

"Those who are engaged in other agricultural occupations like dairy, farming, horticulture, raising of live-stock, bees, poultry etc. In the context of Indian conditions the definition is not adequate, because it is not possible to completely separate those working on wages from others. There are people who do not work on wages throughout the year but only for a part of it.

Therefore, the first A.L.E.C. used the concept of agricultural labour household. If half or more members of household have wage, employment in agriculture then those households should be termed as agricultural labour household. This concept was based upon the occupation of the worker.

The Second Committee submitted that to know whether a household is an agricultural labour household, we must examine its main source of income. If 50% or more of its income is derived as wages for work rendered in agriculture only, then it could be classed to agricultural labour household.

According to the National Commission on Labour "an agricultural labourer is one who is basically unskilled and unorganized and has little for its livelihood, other than personal labour".

Thus, persons whose main source of income is wage, employment fall in this category Mishra and Puri have stated that "All those persons who derive a major part of their income as payment for work performed on the farms of others can be designated as agricultural workers. For a major part of the year they should work of the land of the others on wages."

Classification of Agricultural Labourers :

Agricultural labourers can be divided into four categories -

1. Landless Labourers, who are attached to the land lords;
2. Landless labourers, who are personally independent, but who work exclusively for others.
3. Petty farmers with tiny bits of land who devote most of their time working for others and
4. Farmers who have economic holdings but who have one or more of their sons and dependants working for other prosperous farmers. The first group of labourers have been more or less in the position of serfs or slaves, they are also known as bonded labourers. Agricultural labourers can also be divided in the following manner :

(1) Landless agricultural labouers
(2) Very small cultivators whose main source of earnings due to their small and sub-margining holdings is wage employment. Landless labourers in turn can be classified into two broad categories:
(3) Permanent Labourers attached to cultivating households.
(4) Casual Labourers. The second group can again be divided into three subgroups:
   (i) Cultivators
   (ii) Share croppers
   (iii) Lease holders

Permanent or attached labourers generally work on annual or seasonal basis and they work on some sort of contract. Their wages are determined by custom or tradition. On the other hand temporary or causal labourers are engaged only during peak period for work. Their employment is temporary and they are paid at the market rate. They are not attached to any landlords.

Under second group comes small farmers, who prossess very little land and therefore, has to devote most of their time working on the lands of others as labourers. Share croppers are those who, while sharing the produce of the land for their work, also work as labourers. Tenants are those who not only work on the leased land but also work as labourers.

Characteristics of Agricultural Labourers – Before any attempt is made to evolve a rational policy to improve the living conditions of agricultural labours which happens to belong to the lowest rung of social and economic ladder, it is essential to know the distinguishing features that characterize agricultural labourer in India. The main features, characterizing Indian agricultural labour are as follows:

1. Agricultural Labourers are Scattered – Agricultural labour in India is being widely scattered over 5.6 lakh villages of which half have population of less than 500 each. And therefore, any question of building an effective organization, like that of industrial workers, poses insurmountable difficulties. Thus as the vast number of agricultural labour lies scattered all over India, there has been no successful attempt for long, to build their effective organization even at the state level not to speak of the national level.

2. Agricultural Labourers are Unskilled and Lack of Training – Agricultural labourers, especially in smaller villages away from towns and cities are generally unskilled workers carrying on agricultural operation in the centuries old traditional wages. Most of them, especially those in small isolated villages with around 500 population, may not have even heard of modernization of agriculture. Majority of them are generally conservative, tradition bound, totalistic and resigned to the insufferable lot to which according to them fate has condemned them. There is hardly any motivation for change or improvement.

Since, there is direct supervision by the landlord, there is hardly any escape form hard work and since there is no alternative employment. The agricultural labourer has to do all types of work-farm and domestic at the bidding of the landlord.

3. Unorganized Sector – Agricultural labourers are not organized like industrial labourers. They are illiterate and ignorant. They live in scattered villages. Hence they could not organize in unions. In urban areas workers could generally organize themselves in unions and it is convenient for political parties to take interest in trade union activities. This is almost difficult in case of farm labour. Accordingly, it is difficult for them to bargain with the land owners and secure good wages.

4. Low Social Status – Most agricultural workers belong to the depressed classes, which have been neglected for ages. The low caste and depressed classes have been socially handicapped and they had never the courage to assert themselves. They have been like dump-driven cattle. In some parts of India, agricultural labourers are migratory, moving in search of jobs at the time of harvesting. Government measures to improve their lot by legislation have proved ineffective so far due to powerful hold of the rural elite classes in the rural economy.

5. Demand and Supply of Labour – The number of agricultural labourers being very large and skills they possess being meager, there are generally more than abundant supply of agricultural labourer in relation to demand for them. It is only during the sowing and harvesting seasons that there appears to be nearfull employment in the case of agricultural labourers. But, once the harvesting season is over, majority of agricultural workers will be jobless especially in areas, where there is single cropping pattern.

6. Less Bargaining Power – Due to all the above mentioned factors, the bargaining power and position of agricultural labourers in India is very weak. In fact, quite a large number of them are in the grip of village money lenders, landlords and commission agents, often the same person functioning in all the three capacities. No wonder, the agricultural labour is the most exploited class of people of India.

7. At the Bidding of the Landlord – There is generally direct and day to day contact between agricultural labourers and the landlords on whose farm they are working. Unlike industrial workers, this direct contact between the employer and employees is a distinct feature of agriculture labourer. The above mentioned few important characteristics distinguish agricultural labourers in India from industrial workers. Thus partly because of factors beyond their control and partly because of their inherent bargaining weakness, the farm labourers have been getting very low wages and have therefore to live in a miserable sub-human life.

Agricultural Serfs or Bonded Labourers – At the

bottom of the agricultural cadre in India are those labourers whose conditions are not very different from those of serfs. Agricultural serfdom has been most prevalent in those parts of India where the lower and the depressed classes and most in numerous. The ethnic composition of villages which governs the social stratification is responsible for the survival of the slavish conditions. In Gujrat, Maharashtra, Kerala, Tamil Nadu, Karnataka, Bihar, Orissa, Madhya Pradesh, a large aboriginal population live and the condition of this agricultural labours is very much like that of slaves. These are called in different names in different States.

The following table-3 indicates the number of bonded labourers identified, released and rehabilitated as on 31.12.1995. Statement showing the number of bonded labourers identified and released as on 31.12.1985 as per the reports received from the State Governments.

According to 1981 census, the number of agricultural workers was 55.4 million, which means 22.7% of the total labour force. Similarly as per 1991 census, the total number of agricultural labourers was increased from 92.5 million in 1981 to 110.6 million is 1991. This means the percentage of agricultural labourers over total labour force, increased from 22.7 in 1981 to 26.1 in 1991. This can be seen in the following table.

Population and Agricultural Workers:
Causes for the Growth of Agricultural Labourers:

There are a number of factors responsible for the continuous and enormous increase in the number of agricultural labourers in India. The more important among them are :

1. Increase in population
2. Decline of cottage industries and handicrafts

3. Eviction of small farmers and tenants from land
4. Uneconomic Holdings
5. Increase in indebtedness
6. Spread of the use of money and exchange system
7. Capitalistic Agriculture
8. Displacement of means of subsidiary occupations ang recre
9. Disintegration of peasantry
10. Break-up of joint family system. Measures taken by the Government to improve the Conditions of Agricultural

Labourers :

The Government has shown awareness of the problems of agricultural workers and all plan documents have suggested ways and means to ameliorate the lot of these people. Measures adopted by the Government for ameliorating the economic conditions of Agricultural labourers are

1. Passing of minimum wage Act.
2. Abolition Bonded Labourers
3. Providing land to landless labourers
4. Provision of Housing cities to houseless
5. Special schemes for providing employment :
i)   on Crash Scheme for Rural Employment (CSRE)
ii)   Pilot intensive Rural Employment Project (PIREP)
iii) Food for works programme (FWP)
iv)   National Rural Employment Programme (NREP)
v)   Rural Landless Employment Programme (RLEP)
vi)   Drought Prone Area Programme (It was known as Rural Works Programme)
6. Jawahar Rojgar Yojana (which come in with the merger of NREP and RLEGP)

7. Desert Development Programme
8. National Scheme of Training of Rural ment Youth for Self Employment (TRYSM)
9. Development of Women and Children in Rural Areas (DWCRA)
10. Abolition of Bonded Labourer Act
11. Integrated Rural Development Programme (IRDP) Suggestions for the Improvement of

Agricultural Labourers :

The following suggestions can be made for the improvement of the socio-economic position of the agricultural labourers:
1. Better implementation of legislative measures.
2. Improvement the bargaining position.
3. Resettlement of agricultural workers.
4. Creating alternative sources of employment
5. Protection of women and child labourers
6. Public works programmes should be for longer period in year.
7. Improving the working conditions
8. Regulation of hours of work
9. Improvements in Agricultural sector
10. Credit at cheaper rates of interest on easy terms of payment for undertaking as a low subsidiary occupation.
11. Proper training for improving the skill of farm labourers.
12. Cooperative farming.

"Service to Mankind is Service to God"
                                  – Swami Vivekananda

Co-operatives As Economic Enterprises

*A*ll Co-operative are actually school of democracy where members even in remote villages experience functioning of democratic system by participating in the process of election, annual general body meetings, Board of directors meetings, and getting satisfaction of being a part of decession making process.

Co-operative entity as we know today is more than a hundred years old. We also know that the genesis of cooperatives was in groups of people, generally from the same social groups coming together for benefit of those who were economically not well off and also for mutual benefit of the members of the community. The formation of cooperatives was also prompted by exploitation in society of economically weaker section by more privileged sections and the urge for preserving the self respect and esteem by the exploited class. In short, a cooperative entity was a vehicle essentially to achieve this and economic betterment of members and this is at the core of cooperative philosophy. There was no concept of organising and running a cooperative for the primary purpose of making profits.

Coming to the theme of today's discussions, a question

would first arise whether co-operatives were always excerpts of his speech on International Co-operative Conference organised by IFFCO held at New Delhi, July 5, 2012.

Looked upon as "enterprises" and if so whether they were always "economic enterprises". We all know that cooperatives were definitely not formed to take market competition head on and to maximise profits.

We have to understand very clearly that cooperatives are not just "economic enterprises". They are very much more than that. They are in fact "socioeconomic enterprises" with greater emphasis on "socio" aspect. If we dilute this emphasis, the co-operatives would lose their identity and become followers of pure market led capitalist economic order, just like other corporate entities.

By their very nature cooperatives are not exploitative whereas corporate thrive on exploitation. Success of cooperatives and their earning surplus does not bestow huge rewards on any individual. On the other hand maximising profits is at the core of functioning of all corporate. Cooperatives are expected to be ethical and more transparent. All the cooperatives at primary level with individuals as members still keep their operations simple and effective and have a high degree of member participation.

From what we see the cooperatives are apparently an ideal form of enterprise that provide opportunity to vast majority of population who have the enterprise but do not have enough resources of their gives them an opportunity to participate actively in the own to start other forms of business enterprises. This affairs of cooperatives, and benefit from their participation. Nevertheless, cooperatives do not still match the corporate in visibility and clout.

For whatever reasons that cooperatives are not

occupying the centre stage, the world is, to that extent seeing more turmoil and conflict, both socially and economically. In the developed world that was dominated by large corporate and multinationals holding complete sway, we are witnessing a huge public opinion against them for the mess they have created of the global economy in their greed to maximise profits which is now tailed "obscene profits" and are looked upon with revulsion because the obscene profits were made at the expense of common man.

The campaign called "Occupy Wall Street" in protest against the governments using taxpayers' money to bail out the greedy and avaricious global corporate entities have caught the attention of the entire world. The distrust and disappointment of the common citizen with multinational corporate, particularly the financial institutions have led to serious thinking about the form of enterprises that are different from corporate, and that are closer and less impersonal than the corporate giants. This has led to a renewed interest in the credit cooperatives like cooperative banks and credit unions. The growth rate of cooperative credit sector has been more than double during the last two years than they have been before. People are putting more faith in cooperatives where they are members and where their views are heard and respected.

Our country first adopted socialistic pattern of socio-economic growth with public sector being given the role of engine of growth. As the country had to begin with near zero base, it was but natural for government to come forward to pump in resources for big infrastructure projects and poverty alleviation programmes. After about a decade or so down the line the planning process slowly started losing steam with non-plan and revenue expenditures soaring in relation to developmental expenditure.

Growth rate was sluggish for over two decades during which time other countries developed at a faster pace. After economic liberalisation of the early nineties the growth rate picked up and India moved into the league of fastest growing and most promising economies of the world. However, this also brought in its wake many problems and raised many issues, none more worrying than the growing disparities between different sections of society. Growth of parallel economy or the black money economy, and tax evasion all took the centre stage. The people who were ultimately the worst affected were those at the bottom of the economic pyramid as all the above mentioned factors fuelled price rise, encouraged conspicuous consumption, encouraged industries and enterprises that catered only to the richer class, leaving the development in villages at the mercy of the trickle down effect of free market economy or to the support from govemment schemes.

While all this was happening with the Indian economy, the cooperative sector, contrary to the many negatives attributed to it mostly by vested interest has done a commendable work in the five decades. Had it not been for the framework of cooperative system that has been put in place, the upheavals of last ten years would have had disastrous impact on the vulnerable sections of the rural population. Those parts of the Country where the primary level cooperatives are functioning well, the farmers do not suffer to the extant they do in areas where cooperative movement is not so strong. It becomes duty of the government to provide enabling climate for small cooperatives in villages grow, they are not made to face unequal competition from corporate, and they are patronised by giving preferences. For example a consumer cooperative store stands at disadvantage while competing with a private grocery shop as the former will always draw a bill with tax for the sales whereas the latter will invariably not do so. Can the government not give concessions or support to-cooperatives to face the situation? By doing so, the government is not giving concession, on the contrary, the well being of cooperatives will ensure well being of people of limited means, and to that extant the cooperatives are doing the work that the governments are expected to do.

With all the plus points and good intentions cooperative have not been able to dominate, reasons for which are not far to seek.

One reason that we have touched upon above is the none too supportive climate in the form of laws that impinge on the autonomy of cooperatives and the interference and control of bureaucracy under some pretext.

Another important reason is that the Government considers cooperatives as member run institutions and does not feel obliged to help them although it conveniently forgets the members of these cooperatives are predominantly from weaker section of society who have to be helped by the state. On the other hand Government does not think twice in putting thousands of crores of taxpayers money into public sector banks and organisations like Air India and other PSUs just to help the employees. It is also seen that in some sectors where cooperatives have dominant presence, Government has put many restrictions in their functioning and when the cooperatives became weak and were bought over by private players, get gave relaxations to make their life easier. This has happened in sugar and textile sectors.

I think the media which has heavy urban bias also contributes to the difficulties of cooperatives mostly by ignoring their achievements and highlighting their failures.

Having said this, co-operatives do contribute substantially to the global economy, as can be seen from the following.

The co-operative sector worldwide has about 800 million members in over 100 countries. Overall, it is estimated that cooperatives account for more than 100 million jobs around the world. In terms of percentage of a country's gross domestic product (GDP) attributable to co-operatives, they are quite significant with the proportion.

While these figures provide ample evidence of contribution of co-operatives in global context, the relative figures in India are too well known to all of us to give details here. But still being a cooperator, I cannot resist temptation of repeating some statistics of numerically the largest cooperative movement in the world- comprising of six hundred-thousand cooperatives and 249 million membership, covering 97% of villages and 71% of rural households, 35% of fertilizer distribution, 46% of sugar production, 45% of handloom production, 20% of fair price shops and 19% of institutional credit to farmers most of whom are small and marginal farmers are accounted for by cooperative sector. The overall impact is that cooperative sector accounts for direct employment and self-employment to 16.7 million people.

In the last one hundred years Indian Cooperative Movement has, in its journey, covered a path that has brought millions from helplessness to empowerment. from being exploited to become masters of their destiny and in the process, bringing semblance of dignity in their lives. We now find that cooperatives are slowly donning the role of being purely economic entities. The tide of globalisation is making them swim with it and they are inadvertently moving towards becoming more of purely economic entities, without realising that they have much bigger socio-economic role awaiting them.

Bigger co-operatives tend to imitate larger corporate and multinationals and in their anxiety to improve their financials, they shift focus- to provide services to relatively well-off sections of society. By doing so they could lose their strength and identity in the long run. Today, the need of the hour is to help in arresting the fast growing gap between a small section of the affluent and the better off who are becoming richer at a faster pace than the bottom half of population who somehow have to struggle to be even where they are. Along with liberalisation there needs to be powerful force that keeps a check on growing disparities and this is the new role that cooperative movement should concentrate upon.

The movement should be the custodian of the swabhiman or self-respect of vast majority of less privileged particularly in rural India by ensuring that in the age of information and technology, their self respect is not demeaned by denial of basic needs like pure drinking water and sanitation facilities. We all have to be sensitive to the feelings of millions of our countrymen who have to for lack of any other alternative, drink untreated and contaminated water from village ponds every day, or those who do not have any sanitation facilities both in cities and in rural areas. It is difficult for those who do not experience it to feel as to how these lower the confidence and self-esteem of an individual. Improvement of quality of life and standard of living in the basic sense should be focus and object of an cooperatives in the next five years. It is an herculean job but definitely not an impossible one.

In other words, having seen the immense scope and

potential for co-operatives as economic enterprise, I think they must leverage their position as socioeconomic enterprises and enhance their acceptance with higher involvements in socially important projects that touch lives of the disadvantaged sections of population directly. For example, issues of sanitation, access to pure drinking water and fuel for cooking are the three most basic needs of majority of our population and they spend a considerable time and energy in meeting them. If every cooperative society that is engaged in economic activity takes upon itself to integrate into its operation one of the above areas, with financially viable project, cooperatives will soon be more visible and become dominant form of socio-economic enterprise.

A well-demonstrated system of making access to pure drinking water to those who do not have access to any kind of uncontaminated water can work wonders to the quality of life of millions of households across the country. Any type of cooperative operating in a village/taluka can take up this project. If there is desire to do, it is not difficult to make it viable with the participation of stakeholders and beneficiaries. The purification system will work both with bore well water and with tank or talab water.

The pure drinking water that will be supplied will have international standards purity and will be as pure as bottled water that costs upwards of Rs. 12 per litre. From this purifier kiosks the pure water is available to people through vending machines at a most affordable and nominal price of Rs. 2 per 20 litre can or 10 p. litre. I am advocating adoption of this project by all cooperative societies as their primary social responsibility goal, since we have already put up such 40 kiosks in Gadag area of Karnataka and they are fully functional providing pure drinking water to over four lakh people. In this International Year of Cooperatives we have targeted to set up 150 kiosks in villages with tanks/talabs and we are confident of achieving the target with this not only will the villagers get pure drinking water, the immediate fall out of it is that they will be freed from all the deadly water borne diseases to which they fall pray and spend considerable amount of their meagre resources.

It may be argued by some that these kind of projects have to be undertaken by the government bodies. Knowing fully well the system and pace at which it works, it becomes the duty of the cooperatives to forward to take initiative to work for the benefit of the society. We must remember that by depriving a vast majority of our fellow countrymen of the basic necessities of access to sanitation and pure drinking water, we are forcing them to live a life that is devoid of human dignity. As responsible citizen we must do our bit and not wait for government to help them.

Co-operatives being socio-economic organisations should naturally be the first to take up these projects without any hesitation.

In conclusion I would like to sum up by saying that countries that have vibrant functional democracies and have large population that is struggling to get basic necessities of life, economic entities that involve the masses in their functioning and in which they have a say, like cooperative societies, will be best suited entities. After all cooperatives are actually schools of democracy where members even in remote villages experience functioning of democratic system by participating in the process of elections, general body meetings board meetings and getting satisfaction of being a part of decision- making process.

In this International year of Co-operatives, the Indian

Parliament has given a wonderful gift to the cooperative sector in the form of Constitution (Ninety Seventh) Amendment Act 2012 that clearly proclaims formation of cooperative society as fundamental right of citizen and has enjoined upon state to promote cooperatives in the directive principles. It also makes it constitutionally obligatory upon states to enact cooperative laws with certain provisions that will strengthen the cooperatives in coming years. For this history making reformist legislation we will always be thankful and grateful to the Hon'ble Prime Minister Dr. Manmohan Singhji and Hon'ble Agriculture Minister Shri Sharad Pawarji.

Let us all work towards making the cooperative sector a force to reckon within our economy and take it to the commanding heights that once the founder of modem India and its first Prime Minister spoke about the public sector. Let us all work with single minded purpose to actualise his famous and often quoted-powerful desire to "convulse the entire Country with co-operatives".

"The end aim of all training is to make the man to grow."
– Swami Vivekananda

Co-operative in Villages

PRELUDE :

The greatest movement of the world and the movement with the greatest future before it is the cooperative movement. Cooperatives have been accepted world over, as the only unique agency, capable of improving the socio-economic status of the community, bringing about social transformation. Coop is considered to be a balancing wheel, among the divergent economic systems. It is a combination of the merits of the capitalistic and socialistic economic system.

Definitions of Cooperative :

A cooperative is defined as autonomous association of persons united voluntarily to meet their common economic/ social/ cultural needs and aspirations, through jointly owned, democratically controlled enterprises. (ICA).

A.   What form of co-operative should a village have?

The All India Rural Credit Survey Committee- 1951-52 has looked into the functioning of both the single and multipurpose (fishermen) coops and has concluded that multipurpose coops are too big organizations to be managed at the village coop level So it was suggested to establish large coops, which are intermediate between multi-function and single function coops to substitute the multi-purpose coops. The type of coop suitable for the village level depends on the various factors :

1) Species and quantity of fish available in the area.
2) Communication and transport facilities available. staff.
3) Availability of trained and skilled management
4) Financial status of the members and source of financial assistance
5) Efficiency and education of members to organize the co-operative.
6) Situation of the village with regard to fishing ground, fish market.
7) Areas of fish consumption, consumption patterns, consumers preference.

So it is difficult to recommend what type of coop is suitable for a particular village, because a single purpose coop successful in one area, may not be at all suitable for other area. Similarly a multi-purpose co-operative is also not suitable for all the fishing villages of India. Hence the type of co-operative suggested to be a suitable and viable one for any village, will depend on the local conditions in and around the village and its situation.

At the outset, the form of co-operative society to be organized, single-purpose or multi-purpose co-operative is to be decided, studying the prevailing conditions of business or occupation of the village. So let us see the advantages and disadvantages of different types of co-operatives.

1. Single Purpose co-operatives - Sir Fredrick Nicholson has established the first fishermen co-operative in India in Tamilnadu coast.

Advantages :

1) Principles are easily understood, the main aim of a marketing society is to gain profit for the upliftment of the socio-economic conditions of he fishermen
2) Only limited talent is required, which is easily available in the villages
3) The financial requirements are equally very limited
4) Establishment expenditure is limited for the management, except perhaps a paid accountant

Disadvantages :

a) The requirement of the fishermen members can not be made available from a single purpose co-operative; hence many single purpose co-operatives are required.
b) A middleman is rather capable of looking into all the requirements of the fishermen than a single purpose co-operative.
c) By organization of many single purpose co-operatives, it will be troublesome requiring large nos. of talents, finance and share capital.
d) So these may be integrated vertically or horizontally to cater to the needs of the members and a multi-purpose co-operative can be formed.

2. Multipurpose co-operatives - The idea of Multi-Purpose co-operative has been propagated first in India by Mr. Nanavati of Cooperative Department, Gujarat during 1926.

Advantages :

1) It replaces large no of single purpose co-operatives with singular objectives
2) It can cater to various needs of the participating members.

3) It can help the fishermen like man intermediary for provision of loan, lifting of calding. sorting and packaging, marketing of prodrisk bearing, transportation, storage etc.
4) Business is economical being integrated with various functions of the fishing industry

Disadvantages :
1) It requires multi-talented managers, which is not easily available in rural area, especially from the fishermen community
2) The principle being complex, is not easily defined, so members are not aware of the objectives of the multi-purpose co-operatives
3) It requires large financial implications, dealing with large nos. of co-operative functions, which is not easily available in rural setup.
4) The business transaction being complex and huge, there is possibility of misappropriation and mismanagement of the members in charge
5) It requires large nos. of administrative staff with high establishment cost; trained employees are required, which are rarely available in villages.

3. Marketing Co-operatives :
The producers i.e. fishermen usually gets a minor fraction of the consumers' price for the product they produce i.e. fish, as major portion of the consumers' price, is being eaten away by the intermediary middlemen agencies as marketing margin.

The fisheries resources are not equitably distributed like agriculture, through out the length and breadth of the country. But its concentration is some what localized, situated in specified locations. Accordingly, marketing functions varies in different areas of the same district or state.

Scope of marketing has gone up in recent years, even beyond the production achieved. Planning for obtaining consumers' preference for the fishery products is also included in marketing, much before the production itself. Producers have to plan well in advance, what to produce, how to produce and for whom to produce: since production can not be achieved suddenly at the time of demand.

4. Processing Co-operatives

Processing requires greater expertise and lot of investment, where as in the coop there is a weak financial structure. In agriculture sector there is large nos. of processing coops for production of sugar, oil, fruit juices, pickles, cotton ginning etc. In ideal conditions, a fish processing plant should not concentrate its efforts to produce the fish, already landed by normal endeavour of fishermen but has to plan well in advance to get a steady supply of the desired variety of fish round the year, by supplying suitable crafts and gears to the fishermen. In inland fishery also things should be planned well in advance to produce desired variety of fish, as per the prevailing consumers' aptitude and preference.

Factors responsible for success
1. Plentiful availability of raw materials
2. Nearness of the processing center to the landing center to avoid transport cost
3. Good transportation and communication facilities
4. Assured raw materials as per requirement
5. Water facility, labor availability and equipments

6.   Demand of the finished product and consumers' preference

7.   Consumers' education by extension and advertisement.

5.   Consumers' Co-operatives

Co-operative idea came into existence 1st through the consumers' coops during 1844 by the trade unions in UK to curtail the family expenditure by availing the essential living requisites at producers' price, since the labourers were worse affected and their economic condition has been shattered by the evil effect of industrial revolution.

Need for consumers' co-operative

1.   For proper and effective distribution of the materials
2.   To get good quality materials without any adulteration
3.   To cut short the expenditure of the consumers
4.   To get continuous supply of materials in case of scarcity, avoiding black market
5.   To get materials at a fair price, eliminating the marketing margin taken away by the middlemen intermediaries.

Problems of consumers' co-operatives – The problems confronted in the successful running of consumers' coop, can be discussed under 3 broad heads:

Organizational, trade practices and financial :

1. Organizational problems - The area of operation being small with a very limited nos. of members, the organization is very weak. Management skill and efficiency was not available. Successful running of the consumers' coops depends largely on the locality, where it is organized, skill of the members and other prevailing environments.

2. Trade practice problems - There is hand to mouth financial structure due to limited members of small means and limited area of operation. So the coop runs to the commodities, having maximum discount. The ultimate aim is how the society runs in profit on a marginal level but in none of the situation there should be loss. The coop should deal with goods, which are having heavy demand; otherwise purchase may result in money idling, without further chance of circulation leading to loss.

3. Financial problems - The source of finance being limited, there is a very less share/ working capital. Where share capital is more, being contributed by the members and working capital being supplied by the government, the society becomes capable of running profitably, otherwise the success of the coop is very much doubtful.

Constitution Guarantee to Co-operative

The Constitution (97th Amendment) Act, 2011 Cooperative Societies and its functionaries in respect is provided certain Constitutional guarantees to the organization functioning and other matters. Formation of Cooperative Society has been made as a fundamental of their rights and responsibilities relating to the thirteen articles from article 243-Z H to 243-ZT, has the Constitution. A new point as "Part-IX-B containing night of the citizen of India by amending the article 19 of and obligation of the Cooperative and functionaries there been inserted in the constitution which prescribe the rights of Some of the important rights and obligation enshrined in the constitution as amended are given in brief below-

1. Formation of Cooperative society has been made as a fundamental right of the citizen of India.
2. It guarantees for voluntary formation, democratic member control, member economic participation and autonomous functionary of Cooperative Society.
3. State has been saddled with the responsibility functionaries, democratic control and professional to promote voluntary formation, autonomous management of Cooperative Society.

4. It restricts the maximum member of Directors and reservation of one seat for SC or ST and their seats in the board of a society to 21(twenty-one) directors for women as their the said 21 directors of societies consisting of individual members and having members from such category of persons.

5. The term of office of elected directors and office bearers shall be five years from the date of election and the term of office bearer shall be coterminous with the term of the Board.

6. Election of the Board shall be conducted before expiry of the term of the Board so that the members take over office from the outgoing Board.

7. Casual vacancy shall be filled up by nomination of the Board, only if the term of office of the Board is less than half of the original term and such co-opted member shall be from the same class of members in respect of which casual vacancy has arisen.

8. Besides the 21 members, the legislature shall by law would form co-option of person act exceeding two on the Board having experience in the field relating to the objects and activities undertaken by the Cooperative society. Such co-opted members shall not have the right to vote in any election of the society or to be elected to any office in that capacity.

9. Conduct of election control, superintendence's preparation of electoral roll etc shall vest on the authority or body as may be provided in the state law by the legislature.

10. The Board of Cooperative society where there is no govt share holding or loan of financial assistance or any guarantee by the Govt. shall not be supersede or suspend or suspended in respect of other Cooperative

society the Board can be suspended or the Board can be superseded on the grounds which are prescribed in article 243-XL in part-IX B of the institution in part IX-B of the constitution as amended for a maximum period of six months. In the case if societies doing banking,business it may be one year.

11. The accounts of every society shall be audited within six months from the date of the close of the financial year to which the accounts relate by an auditor or auditing forms appointed by the General body of the Society from the panel approved by the state Govt. The audit reports of an apex society shall be laid before the state legislature.

12. The Annual General Body meeting of the society shall be convened within six months of the close of the financial year as provided in the state law.

13. Every member shall have the right to the books of accounts of the society kept in regular transaction of business of such member.

14. Every society shall file return in respect of the matter prescribed in article 243-ZA of the constitution as amended within six months of the close of the financial year to the designated authority.

15. Porvision may be made in the state law to ensure member participation and utilization of maximum level of service by the members and the cooperative education and training.

16. The state Act may provide provision for offences which shall include members mentioned in article 243-ZQ of the constitution as amended. The constitution (97th Amendment) Act-2011 come into force with effect from 15th February, 2012.

Article 243-ZT of the constitution as amended

provides that the provision of the State cooperative Act in force immediately before coming into force of the constitution (97th Amendment) Act 2011 which are inconsistence with the provision of the 97th Amendment Act,2011 aforesaid shall continue to be in force until amended or until the expiration of one year from the date of its commencement which ever is less. In other words, the sate Cooperative Act needs amendment of the provision which are inconsistence with the provision as brought out in the constitution (97th Amendment) Act, 2011, by 14th February,2013 or else such in couristente provisions of the state law shall become in operative with effect from 14th February, 2013.

Rural Employment Guarantee Scheme

However after a long lapse of nearly five decades of the formation of an independent India, the weak rural sector, now can have a sign of relief, with a ray of hope of a guarantee of income of Rs. 500 at the minimum, per month. Of-course, at present it is not for the entire country, rather it is for 200 Districts in the 1st year, with an aim of covering the entire nation, 1000 districts, within the coming 5 years and that credit is to be awarded to be Congress-laid UPA Govt., at the centre.

In the past, hundreds of Schemes for rural development have been worked out, but also all are in vain, only because of the utter failure of the machinery deployed to operate such projects. Almost all such schemes have not given the expected result, due to lack of expertise, efficiency and honesty of the organization kept in-charge of it's implementation. For illustration, we can look to the KBK area. Uncountable amount of funds have been pumped in to this region, but the result is still prominently visible to any open eye.

Even today it earns the credit of the Hungriest Region of Asia. It seems it would have been far better, had we distributed the entire funds invested in this region in the past years, in the shape of hard cash directly to the poor tribal beneficiaries of the region, instead of handing over them to the most corrupt Govt. machinery, including the ever hungry politicians, who usurped them in broad day light for their self-interest.

It seems our policy framer rulers have not learnt any thing from the past experience.We are going to repeat the same mistake of keeping the implementation of this project also in the hands of the Panchyati Raj, that has already earned bad name and fame for it's efficiency in adoption of corrupt practices and expertise in mis-using public funds rampantly. Latest example is recent detection of misappropriation of Rs. 9 cores in Maharastra State in operation of such a State operated scheme this is only one example of hundreds and thousands occurring almost every day around the country.

Our 1st Prime Minister Nehrujee, along with father of the Nation Gandijee, dreamt of Ram Rajya, a Developed Modern India, where not a single citizen would ever go to bed in an empty belly, for effective implementation of which, he conceived of 4 institutions for the development of the Indian Rural Sector.

These are - **Gram Panchayat** - For political and an overall development with local people participation.

Village School - For education & Socio- Cultural Development.

Primary Health Center - For solving rural health hazards.

Village Cooperative - For Economic Development. and with this end in view for the over all economic development of the rural sector, credit was linked with marketing and supply of essential commodities of the rural poor folk.

But after Nehrujee, the entire out-look has been changed and the media for the rural development has been completely changed, throwing the Co-operatives to the Bay of Bengal, and bringing the Gram-Panchayat to replace it.. just like an Engineer being kept in charge of a Hospital, ending in an un-usual health hazard.

Gram- Panchayat is the lowest strata of the Administrative Machinery run by political parties leaders with a partisan bias. It's aim is admittedly development of the rural sector but not to directly handle the operational part of any economic development project. We know Governor is the administrative head of the State. Every thing is done in the name of the Governor but the actual work is done by the respective Departments.

Similarly, when economic development is the function of the village Coop. society, why it is not allowed to do it's function under the guidance of the Gram Panchayat. It seems from our past experience, we have not learnt any thing or even if we have learnt our mistake knowingly we have closed our eyes in our vested interest.

At the out-set, the Co-operatives are the only organized institution of the rural folk, mostly of the targeted poor community. The scheme envisages organization of groups of at least 7 males and 3 females for it's implementation, but here we have already an existing well established organization of 700 males and 300 females or still more in number and if not we can make it in no time, in which a Panchayat would take decades after decades to achieve. Is it not better to go for an already existing and well established Institution, than to go for an institution to start afresh?

To the credit of the Cooperatives, it's the only organization, in the rural sector, having a vast & wide financial resource starting from the Block level Branch of the District level Central Co-operative Bank, ending with the RBI viza-viz, the NABARD at the national level. In order to meet any urgent financial need for short or longer period, it can arrange within a short span of time, which is never possible in a Governmental machinery, run under heavy red tape along with an un-ending deficit/overdraft.

Further the Co-operatives have the hundred years, vast experience in implementation of the scheme, which they executed successfully in the past, whereas the Panchayati-Raj, in their past few years of undertaking rural development work have admittedly failed to deliver the goods.

The Co-operatives have a well greased machinery, with technical know-how men and materials to operate the Scheme, where-as, the Panchayats are to start it afresh.

The Book-Keeping & Accounting system of the Co-operatives, with it's Profit 7 Loss accounts, with the accountability of the person, in-charge, is more perfect than the Accounting system with Income & Expenditure system of the Panchayati Raj.

In a Co-operative Society Peoples participation is more perfect than that of it in the Panchyati Raj. Members of a Co-operative Society are more vigilant of their rights & duties and they have better command over their management. Last but not the least is the distinction as between an organization of a century and half a century.

The advantages of the Co-operatives. Over the Panchayat is it's non-Political bias. In principle Co-operatives are Independent of any political, religion & creed., whereas Panchayats, basically stood on alignment to certain political faith, likely to favor their followers at the cost of their rival folk. sigmi to Above all when Gram Panchayats do the job there is no other organization at the village level to point out their loop-holes, if any, but when a Co-operative under-takes it, the Gram-Panchayat is there to conduct an independent & effective supervision of its working.

Thus it may be seen that for implementation of this massive project, the Co-operatives are better placed as compared with that of the Panchayati-Raj sector. It has the organization, resources, experience, expertise & the vital fac-tor, the managerial as well as technical know how with man power even to add to all these factors, it has the greatest advantage of the widest range of Marketing net-work of the rural products through its Regional, State Apex & even the NAFED & NCCF at the national level. They are effectively handling such schemes through the Labor Contract Cooperatives. With the revitalization of the Labor Co-operatives they can better handle, take care & regulate the scheme and can no sooner deliver the much expected result.

In the above contents, the program conducting authority, the State Govt. should consider the entire issue in proper context of the programme & try to convince the Govt. of India & see that the programme may be executed through the cooperatives. We know, it is not an easy task, since the vested interest working at the back-ground of the implementation of the scheme through the panchayati Raj is so strong a rock that it can not be blasted by a much power-less, peoples welfare dynamite.

It is high time that the Cooperators, whether in the Govt, semi-Govt, even out-side the Govt. forgetting their socio-political or regional differences, should join their hands to bring this highly ambitious rural development project under the fold of the Coops. Even if we fail to convince the National level leadership to bring in the entire scheme to the fold of the Coops, we may move to get the project implemented in certain selected pockets having a base of comparatively stronger coops, under capable leadership. During the current year the Govt is undertaking 200 districts under the scheme & Orissa quota, would not be less than 14 districts. On experimental basis, let the Coops be allotted with 7 Districts & on completion of the 1 year, let us evaluate & compare the result achieved by both. The organizations and the successful organization there after should handle the project.

In this connection it may be added that, last year, after the UPA Govt. coming in to power at the Centre and their inclusion of this Employment Guarantee Scheme in their CMP. I prepared a Model Scheme, for Orissa, especially for the Kendrapara District, a programme for 5 years, and handed over to Mr. Bhagabat Prasad Mohanty, Ex-Minister, Senior Congress Party leader and a known Cooperator to place it before the Central Govt. for consideration to implement the Scheme through the Co-operatives. It seems he handed over the Scheme to Mr.Chidambarm, Finance Minister as well as to I some other Central Cabinet Ministers for consideration but it seems it was either not taken in the consideration or if it was taken in the consideration, it was turned down.

However it is high time that the Cooperators should give a serious thought to the matter and the State Coop. Union should take the lead-ership by constituting a Committee, under the Chairmanship of Humble Minister Cooperation, and membership of Cooperation Secretary, Registrar & other Official and Non-official, Cooperators and convince the Central Govt. and try to get the Project for the Coops. At - least for few Districts, even if possible on experimental basis at the initial stage.

Let the attempt to get the Employment Guarantee Scheme to the Coop. Sector be our motto for the coming year & if we succeed that would be a great achievement for the Coop. movement at the close of it's Centenary & be a great gift for our posterity. 'V' for the Victory of the Co-operatives.

"People were starbed not for want of food, but for want of Co-operative effort".
— Mahatma Gandhi

Panchayat Raj Adminstration in India

Introduction :

Panchayat Raj is a system of governance in which Gram Panchayats are the basic units of administration. It has 3 levels: Village, Block and District. The term 'Panchayat Raj' is relatively new, having originated during the British administration. Raj literally means 'governance or government'. Mahatma Gandhi advocated Panchayat Raj, a decentralised form of Goverment where each village is responsible for its own affairs, as the foundation of India's political system. The term for such a vision was Gram Swaraj (Village Self governance).

This system was adopted by State Governments during the 1950s and 60s, as law were passed to establish Panchayats in various states. It also found backing in the Indian Constitution, with the 73rd amendment in 1992 to accomodate the idea. The Amendment Act of 1992 contains provision for devolution of powers and responsibilities to the panchayats both for the preparation of economic development plans and social justice, as well as for implementation in relation to 29 subjects listed in the eleventh schedule of the Constitution. The Panchayats receive funds from three

Sources :

(1) Local body grants as recommended by the Central Finance Commission.

(2) Funds for implementation of centrally sponsored schemes.

(3) Funds released by the state Governments on the recommendatoins of the State Finance Commissions.

In the history of Panchayati Raj in India, on 24th April 1993, the Constitutional (73rd Amendment) Act 1992 came in to force to provide constitutional status to the Panchayat Raj Institution. This Act was extended to Panchayats in the tribal areas of eight states, namely Andhra Pradesh, Gujarat, Himachal Pradesh, Maharastra, Madhya Pradesh, Odisha and Rajasthan starting on 24th December 1996. Currently the Panchayati Raj system exists in all states except Nagaland, Meghalaya and Mizoram, and in all Union Territories except Delhi.

The Act aims to provide a 3-tier system of Panchayat Raj for all states having a populatoin of over 2 million, to hold Panchayat elections regularly every 5 years, to provide seats reservations for schedule caste, scheduled tribes and women to appoint a State Finance Commission to make recommendatoins as regards to the financial powers of the Panchayats and to constitute a District Planning Committee to prepare a development plan draft for the district.

The 3-tier system of Panchayati Raj consists:
(1) Village level Panchayats
(2) Block level Panchayats.
(3) District level Panchayats.

1) Village level Panchayats -
Powers and responsibilities are delegated to

Panchayats at the appropriate level. Preparation of the economic development plan and social justice plan, implementation of schemes for economic development and social justice in relation to 29 subjects in given in the Eleventh schedule of the Constitution. This schedule covers important topics such as Panchayats powers, rural development, poverty alleviation, markets, roads and drinking water, etc. To levy, collect and appropriate taxes, duties, tolls and fees.

2) Block level Panchayats

A block level panchayat (Panchayat Samiti) is a local government body at the tehsil level in India. This body works for the villages of the tehsil that together are called a Developent Block. The Panchat Samiti is the link between the Gram Panchayat Samiti link between the Gram Panchayat and the District administration.

3) District level Panchayats

There a number of variations of this institution in different states. It is known as Mandal Praja Parishad in Andhra Pradesh, Taluka Panchayat in Gujarat, Mandal Panchayat in Karnataka, Panchayat Samiti in Maharastra etc. In general, the block Panchayat is a form of the Panchayat Raj but at a higher level.

Constitution :

The Constitution is composed of ex-official members (all sarapanchs of the Panchayat Samiti area, the MPs and MLAs of the area and the SDO of the subdivisions), co-operative members (representative of SC/ST and women), associate members (a farmer of the area, a representative of the cooperative societies and one of the marketing services), and some elected members. The samiti is elected for 5 years and is headed by the Chairman and the Deputy Chairman.

Departments :
(1)   The common departments in the samiti are as follows:
(2)   General administration.
(3)   Finance.
(4)   Public work
(5)   Agriculture
(6)   Health
(7)   Education
(8)   Social welfare
(9)   Information technology and others.
(10) Drinking Water

There is an officer for every department. A Government appointed Block Development Officer (BDO) is the Executive Officer to the Samiti and the Chief of its administration.

Functions of Village Level Panchayat :
1)   **Implementation of schemes** for the development of agriculture.
2)   **Establishment of Primary Health Centres** and Primary Schools.
3)   **Supply of drinking water,** drainage and construction/repair of roads.
4)   **Development of cottage and small-scale industries,** and opening of cooperative societies.
5)   **Establishment of youth organisations.**

Sources of Income of Village Level Panchayat :
The main source of income of the Panchayat Samiti

is grants-in-aid and loans from the State Government. District Level Panchayat The governing system of district level panchayat Raj is also popularly known as "Zilla Parishad". Chief of administration is an officer from IAS Cadre.

Functions of Block Level Panchayat :

1. Provide essential services and the facilities to rural population.
2. Supply improved seeds to farmers. Inform them of new farming technologies.
3) Set up and run schools and libraries in the rural areas.
4) Primary Health centres and hospitals in villages. Start vaccination drives against epidemics.
5) Executive plans for the development of the scheduled castes and tribes. Run ashram schools for adivashi children, set up free hostels for them.
6) Encourage entrepreneurs to start small scale industries and implement rural employment schemes.
7) Construct bridges, roads and other public facilities and their maintenance.
8) Provide employment.

Sources of Income of Block Level Panchayat :

1) Taxes on water, pilgrimage, markets etc.
2) Fixed grants from the State Government in proportion with the land revenue and money for works and schemes assigned to the Parishad.

Conclusion :

However to give a boost on women empowerment the Union Cabinet of the Goverment of India, on 27th August 2009, approved 50% of reservation for women in PRIS (Panchayati Raj Institutions). The Indian States which have already implementated 50% reservation for women in PRIS are Madhya Pradesh, Bihar, Uttarakhad and Himachal Pradesh. As of 25 November 2011, the states of Andhra Pradesh, Chhatisgarh, Jharkhand, Kerala, Maharastra, Odisha, Rajasthan and Tripura also reserves 50% of their posts for women. Now the women are no more stagnant and isolated as they used to be in the past. They are now emerging as a big force in every walk of life.

Agricultural Marketing

1.1: INTRODUCTION

Market reforms and marketing system improvement has now become an integral part of policy and strategy for agricultural development. For this, an efficient and organized marketing system is necessary to enable producers to realize a better price for their produce and to reduce their exploitation by middlemen, commission agents and traders. The role of the domestic agricultural market is vital for overall agricultural growth of the state.

However domestic agricultural markets remain undercapitalized, rudimentary, relatively thin and scattered. Our rural habitations are often poorly integrated into commercial markets. About 84 per cent of our agricultural producers are small & marginal farmers. Their marginalization in the marketing system is evident on account of complex tenure systems, low market access, lack of information, extension services, transport, credit and most importantly, lack of institutions to facilitate sustainable engagement with market. Moving beyond food grain self sufficiency, it is required to augment the capacity of small producers for reliable production and profitable marketing of products to meet consumer's satisfaction and preference.

The complex interplay of food security and income

generation warrant government intervention in agricultural marketing. Besides, private sector participation is required for development of infrastructure and introduction of innovative marketing practices. The present system of agricultural marketing has lot of bearing with the market infrastructure associated with the regulatory mechanisms prevailing in the State. Market Regulation in the State came into force under the Odisha Agricultural Produce Markets (OAPM) Act-1956.Objective of the Act is to provide better regulation of buying and selling of agricultural produce to ensure fair price to the farmers, establishment of markets for the purpose and making available up-to-date market intelligence to the Producers. Odisha State Agricultural Marketing (OSAM) Board was constituted during the year 1985 as per amended provisions of Section-18(A) of OAPM Act, 1956.

The Board has the objective of having superintendence and control over the Regulated Market Committees (RMCS) to increase their efficiency and to facilitate creation and development of marketing infrastructure.

1.2.Market infrastructure; There are 163 Wholesale Assembling Markets and 1150 Rural Periodic Markets in the state. There are 65 RMCS covering 55 Revenue Sub-divisions of the State, out of which,61 have Elected Committees. There are 427 Market Yards in the State which include 53 Principal Market Yards and 374 Sub Market Yards. Besides, there are 326 Seasonal Market Yards, mainly for paddy procurement. There are 43 Krushak Bazars of which 32 are functional. Out of the total blocks of the State, 111 blocks don't have any regulated market. The periodic Hats and assembling centres have not got minimum phyto-sanitary standard and cemented floor to maintain the quality of the produce. Even dry fish marketing/arrival/ processing centres don't have such facilities.

1.3.Godown infrastructure; All the RMCS of the state are having 549 no.s of Godowns with a Capacity of 1,30,588 MT. Odisha State Warehousing Corporation (OSWC) is having warehouses of capacity of 3,95,050 MT(own) & operating godowns of 13,557MT on rent basis. OSWC has also planned to construct 1 Lakh MT capacity of Godown in the coming year. Central Warehouse Corporation is having 12 nos of Godowns with a capacity of 1,62,312MT of its own and about another 2 lac MT capacity on rent. Marketing Federation (MARKFED) of the state is having 40 godowns with capacity of 98,000 MT.Besides, FCI is having godown capacity of substantial tonnage. 292 Godowns with capacity of 5.60 lakh MT has been created in the state under the Rural Godown Scheme of Govt. of India. Inspite of all these, the storage infrastructure for grains is not adequate and there is a need for enhancing the storage infrastructure for grains by 11 lakh MT.

1.4.Cold Storages; There are 101no.s of cold storages in the state with a capacity of 2.91 Lakh MT The corresponding numbers of Privately-owned, Cooperative-owned and Government owned Cold Storages in the State are 81,16 and 5 with capacity of 2.48 lakh MT, 38,100 MT and 4200 MT respectively. Out of the total, 39 cold storages with a capacity of 139630 MTs are exclusively meant for potato storage only. Still an additional requirement of another 2 lakh MT is estimated for the purpose. Besides these, the availability of cold storages   products are 35, 22 and 4 respectively. Barring few meant for multipurpose use, meat & fish and horticultural cold storages meant for potato meat & fish,rest of such structures are yet to become fullyfuctional. cortification products like honey, oils and spices and Laboratory which tests the samples for AGMARK

1.5.Grading and Standardization: State Grading Grading Laboratory is used for creation of awareness programmes among the farmers on FAQ (Fair Avarage Quality) standards in RMCS. Mobile All the Wholesale Assembling Markets and Rural Periodic Markets are yet to avail grading and standardization facilities.

1.6.Market Information; 91 Computers have been Information Network (MRIN) Scheme of Govt. of India provided to 91 markets under the Market Research and for collection and dissemination of market information Kiosks have been supplied to 28 RMCS from out of the to the farmers through AGMARKNET Portal. 28 IT funds provided by GOI under MRIN Scheme. In addition to price/ market information, farmers can also access other related information. RMCS should conduct programmes to create awareness among the farmers on quality/grades of the produce, prices of commodities, market opportunities, production as well as post harvest management in collaboration with different line departments. However farmer producers in the vicinity of majority of markets are still deprived of getting up- to-date market information.

1.7.Peculiar Conditions of Existing Markets in Odisha : Primary or Periodic Markets (haat / bazaars) are most neglected - basic amenities not available.

Condition of cattle markets most appalling.

Farmers have to travel long distances as the density of regulated markets is very low.

Weak governance of APMCS-management not professional.

Licensing systems creates entry barrier to new trader/ buyers.

Multi-Point Levy of Market Fee (Varies from 0.5 to 2%) and Multiple Licensing System.

Restrictions on movement of goods-intra-state and also inter-state

1.8. High Marketing Margin in the supply chain; So far as the supply chains of fruits and vegetables are concerned, the total margin in the chain comes round to 60 to 75 per cent, out of which the margin from farmers to wholesaler comes around 30-35 per cent wastage 15-25 per cent and transportation 10 per cent. The producers' share, however, varies from crop to crop. On an average the producer get 25 to 40 per cent out of the rupee paid by the consumer. In case of perishable commodities like vegetables, the price in the market ranges widely depending upon the time of harvest and flow to the market. For an example, brinjal sales at a price ranging from 2.50-17.00/kg in one season while tomato sales at a price ranging from 1.50-22.00/kg within the same season.

2.   COMMODITY-WISE SUPPORT MECHANISMS & CLUSTER APPROACH OF AGRI-MARKETING :

2.1. Market Support Mechanisms for Agri-Commodities Paddy – The existing marketing institutions need be revitalized so as to address marketing issues. Procurement of paddy is suggested to take place through Primary Agricultural Credit Cooperative Societies (PACS), Pani Panchayats and Women Self Help Groups to facilitate procurement within 5 km radius of farm yard. There are seasonal paddy procurement centers located at 625 RMCS. Recently 2017 PACS have been identified for paddy procurement. Paddy procurement through PACS was conducted last year from 3,9 lakhs farmers RMC has provided necessary infrastructure for the PACS. The PACS should be covered under "agmarknet" scheme of the Government of India to disseminate market information and act as single window for credit, output marketing and market led extension.

2.2. Cluster Approach of Agri-Marketing – All commodity specific cooperatives need reorganization like that of OMFED with more participation of growers. Promotion of partnership based cooperatives particularly for horticultural produce (like Maha-Mango, Maha-Banana, Maha-Grapes of Maharastra) is needed to tap export market and also domestic market. Based on production potentialities, cluster approach of marketing should be promoted in an integrated manner in following localities of the State.

3.   MARKET REFORMS –

In keeping with the provisions of the Model Act circulated by the Government of India, the OAPM Act was amended in June, 2006 to allow "Establishment of Private Markets and Contract Farming" by any person or company or a Cooperative Society.

3.1.Private Markets & Contract Farming – Not much progress has been done towards establishment of Private Markets in the State. However several efforts have been in progress towards functioning of contract farming in commodities like cotton, sugarcane, niger, sesame, ground nut and horticultural crops like onion, water melon & litchi etc since the amendment of OAPM Act in Odisha. The State Government have to follow policy initiatives with a cautious approach while granting contract licenses to a company for any specific agricultural commodities.

3.2. The National Spot Exchange Ltd. has been granted licence for establishment of private e-marketing facility to facilitate trading of commodities such as maize, cotton, oilseeds, pulses. But still the Spot Exchanges have yet to popularize e-marketing facilities in a large scale,

3.3. The Forward Market Commission (FMC) has decided to set up 18 Price Ticker Boards in identified RMC Yards through NCDEX. But no much progress has been done.

3.4. Terminal Markets – It has been decided by Government of Odisha to set up of Terminal Markets at least at four important trade centres of our state viz. Sambalpur, Cuttack, Berhampur and Rourkela. These markets will operate like Hub and Spoke Model of Market Infrastructure with proper forward & backward linkages with a special provision of 70 per cent of throughput from Horticultural Produce (Fruits, Vegetables, Flowers, Spices etc) and rest 30 per cent from grains, pulses and other perishables (dairy, me egg etc.) Although work had been initiated in the construction of Sambalpur Terminal Markets yet much progress has not been made till today in this direction

Conclusion –

Of late, the development of agriculture and its marketing is getting due attention for accelerating the growth process of a poor State like Odisha. In view of the forthcoming 12 Five Year Plan the Agricultural Marketing System of the State should be restructured to ensure higher net profit to farmers on sustainable basis. In this process, the objective should be to ensure them a better share of the consumers' price, to improve efficiency in the marketing chain and reduce transaction costs through strengthening & modernization of marketing and credit infrastructure as well as by adoption of a farmer friendly regulatory mechanism.

"Co-operative farming or dairying is undoubtedly a good goal promoting national interest. Such interest can be multiplied."

– Mahatma Gandhi

H. R. Development and Co-operative

A group of co-operators (persons) united voluntarily to meet their common economic, social and cultural needs and aspirations through a jointly owned and democratically controlled Co-operative is an autonomous association enterprises.

The aim of cooperation is to care for the felt needs and socio-economic interests of the poorest and empower them for their development and self sustain. The concept of cooperation is regarded as a special mode of doing business.

The co-operative system is based on the values of Self Help, Self responsibility, equity and solidarity. Co-operative members of their respective organization based on ethical values of honesty, openness, social responsibility and caring for others.

Human Resource Development :

HRD is a process by which the employees helped in a continuous and planned way to or sharpen capabilities to perform various functions associated with present or future role.

Organizations are systems. Success depends on its people. It should be clear that the human capital and intellect should drive business growth. Cooperative Organizations have to treat human resources an investment and a crucial asset for long term competitive advantage.

The Word HRD was first applied in 1968 in the George Washington University of America and in 1969 it was need in Miami at the American Society for training and Development Conference (ASTDC). By middle of 1970 it was more acceptances but was being used by many as merely a more attractive term than "Training & Development." Term HRD was introduced for the time in the State Bank of Indian in 1972. It is believed that the concept of HRD is a philosophical value concept developed by Dr. Udai Pareek and Dr. T.V. Rao at the IIM, Ahmadabad by the late seventies.

It is sure that the Coop. Movement in India plays a pivotal role in the mainstream of Indian Economy, particularly in the field of rural credit, distribution of agriculture inputs, storage, fertilizer etc. It is said that the cooperatives are the only model for upliftment of disadvantageous and weaker section of our economy and more relevant today for the inclusive growth. Therefore, the 12 plan document heads special mention about the cooperative.

The Co-operative Movement has entered into the twenty first century Land completed one hundred eight years. Human Resource Development has been intitialy present in cooperative philosophy since the times of Rockdale pioneers. The cooperative identity statement enunciates the HRD in the principle of cooperative.

The fifth cardinal principle is co-op education, Training and intermations and the seventh principle is concern for community. HRD is headed by any cooperative society that wants to be dynamic and growth oriented to succeed in a fast changing environment HRD converts ordinary cooperatives into extra ordinary Members, Board of directers and employee are three pillars of a cooperative. The development of human resources like employees, members and board of directors has become a key factor, in today's competitive world. The important of HRD lies in developing and empowering the human resources need for HRD in Co-operatives In the context of present day competitive business the quality of human capital of an organization determines the degree of success which it can achieve. As there is keen competition for human resources, then human capital can be created within the organization.

It is to mention here that cooperatives in the entire country are facing the biggest financial difficulties towards implementing HRD programmed Land activities. In order to work on professional lines with enlightened and active membership and inspiring leadership, it is highly percived prereanise is for the sector to strengthen.

HUMAN RESOURCE DEVELOPMENT

India has the biggest in structure and HRD institute in the cooperative sector in Asia but the existing infrastures and fund availability from govt and cooperative sources is inadequate. The HRD institutions funded by govt. of India are doing excellent job but lack of adequate funding pattern adversely affects its training and education activities. The institution funded by state govt. like state Co-operative Union are not in a position to deliver the training and improve the efficient due to lack of adequate financial support from the state Govt.

The institutions are owned, controlled and funded by the cooperatives such as state cooperative Banks, KHRIBCO, IFFCO and NABARD etc. don't have much difficulties in development the infracture and organization need based training and education activities for their target group.

Due to vast change in the business transaction. and human resource strength of the co-operatives, the need for proper human resource development system in cooperative is highly perceived as following.

For efficient and effective utilization of all human resources associated with the very wide structure of cooperatives.

Improving system, service, avalilty of goods, productivity and over all image of cooperative.

To face the challenges which arise after the initiation of new economic policy.

Formulate suitable strategies to encounter the challenges.

Preventive of dormancy sickness and poor performance in co-operatives.

To bring better co-ordination among different tiers and sector of the co-operative movement.

There are success stories in developed states of coop. movement.

These success stories should be shared at regular internally documentation of success stories for replication in meetings, conference and workshops.

The united Nations has declared 2012 to be the International year of Cooperatives and advised a year of Cooperative. The NCUI is organising seminars conference, meetings throught the country. The East countries in the world to celebrate the International Zone Conference i.e is 4th in series is organising at the temple city of Bhubaneswar. The apex level cooperative of our country, the NCUI under takes the responsibilities of co-operative education, tranning and information activities. The financial provision for discharging the above activities in this competative era is not satisfactory.

As well as the same situation of the state co-operative unions in state level. These institutions are not business organisations. They only depend upon govt. grant-in-aid and cooperative education fund in the state acts. But after amandmend of the provision of cooperative education fund in the state acts, the cooperative organisations are not mandatory to pay the such fund to state cooperative unions. So, the entire HRD activities of the cooperative movement is in a cross road. This issue may taken into consideration seriously as HRD is the first and formost requirement of a vibrant and florishing cooperative movement in our country.

Future of Co-operative Bank in India

Our country had the first Bank i.e. Oudh Commercial Bank in the year 1881 followed by Punjab National Bank in the year 1894. Banks, basically, are institutions to safely keep the surplus money of the people till they withdraw their deposits. A major portion of such resources are, however, deployed as loan and investment and out of the return against such transactions, the depositors are paid interest. Lending, therefore, is not only the second priority activity of a Bank, but also is required to be made very carefully with adequate security covers to ensure return of such loan and investment back to the Bank to meet the depositor's withdrawals.

Occurrence of severe droughts, floods, epidemics and other natural calamities during the 19th century and the prevailing exploitative and irrational land revenue and taxation system almost compelled the farmers most of whom were very poor and disadvantaged to abandon agricultural production operations. In absence of willingness of the aforesaid limited Commercial Banks which had limited area of operation, the farmers became credit starved and had to go to the money lenders who demanded exorbitant rate of interest and mortgage of land and moveable properties which made the rich richer and the poor poorer leading to serious nature of social instability.

This situation at the end of Ninteenth Century compelled the British-India Government to think of alternatives to take care of the credit needs of the poor and to introduce cooperative system to pull meagre funds from the poor people who join as members to form a "common wealth" out of which temporary lending of grain or cash to the needy members could be possible. The Government of India, therefore, enacted the Cooperative Credit Societies Act, 1904 which was subsequently elaborated into a more comprehensive Cooperative Societies Act in the year 1912 facilitating organisation and registration of non-banking cooperatives also. Although many Commercial Banks came up as an impact of Swadeshi Movement in the year 1906 onwards, most of such Banks faced crisis during and after the First World War and as many as 588 Commercial banks suffered failure during the Forties perhaps as an impact of the Second World War.

The RBI which was established on April 01, 1935 was nationalised on January 01, 1949 and the banking Companies Act passed in February, 1949 was subsequently amended and renamed as Banking Regulation Act, 1949 providing powers to the RBI to regulate the Banking system in the country. Subsequently the Imperial Bank of India was nationalised in the year 1955 and was reconstituted as the State Bank of India which, later was massociated with seven more Banks constituting State Bank of India group of Banks.

In absence of financial support from the Govt. of India and under influence of Swadeshi movement thousands of Co-operative Banks were organised in almost all the parts of the country during the first two decades of the twentieth century which were amalgamated into district level banks having strong financial base by the time similar transformations were taking place in the commercial banking sector.

Although Cooperation became a provincial subject after 1919, the Govt. of India continued taking interest to respect the cooperative banking system in view of their ramification in to the nook and corner of the country and accessibility of the poorest farmers through their local primary societies. Due to reluctance of the commercial banks to provide risky, micro-credit to the weaker sections of the rural areas, whatever insignificant service could be rendered by the Co-operative banks appeared conspicuous and that is why the Maclagan Committee appointed by the Government in the year 1915 observed that "there should be one Co-operative for every village and every village should be covered by a Co-operative. The Rural Commission of Agriculture in India in their report submitted in the year 1928 also recommended that the State should protect and patronise the Co-operatives for utilising the cooperative credit structure as a resource provider to the rural population. To quote the Rural Commission's report "If Co-operation fails there will fail the best hope of rural India".

As a result of such recommendations the RBI Act, 1934 was amended providing for establishment of Agriculture Credit Department (ACD) to take care of refinance support to the Co-operative banks. The Co-operative Banks, however, had a stunted growth during and after the Second World War which saw sickness and liquidation of many commercial banks.

Recognising abundant presence of the Co-operative credit structures in the villages and the accessibility of the rural people to the Co-operative Banks, the All India Rural Credit Survey Committee headed by Prof. Gorewal, recommended for the State partnership with the Co-operative Banks, not only in providing equity-contribution, soft loan and grants, but also in terms of governance and management support. Prof. Gorewal reduced his observation into a sentence, as "Co-operatives in India have failed but they must succeed" No doubt, a lot of financial and logistic support were provided by Central and State Govt. to strengthen the Co-operative Banks through the Five Year and Annual Plans.

But the Co-operative banks got recognition only. Further the 1965, when the Banking Regulations, Act. was amended, considering the State a scheme, Central Co-operative Banks and some past, Urban Co-operative Banks complying to few stipulations of the said Act, as "Banks" igncork the Land Mortgage Banks and the Prima Credit Societies confining their deposit collections and agricultural credit disbursements to their members only. In effect, the vast network of Co-operative credit structures at village, Gram Panchayat and block level were prohibited to tap public deposits except from their members, which limited their resource mobilisation capabilities, and made them more and more dependant on Govt. and higher financing agencies like District and State Co-operative Banks, NABARD etc. at the cost of adequate profit margin and which adversely affected the process of viability of the Primary Co-operatives.

The credit disbursal system became highly regulatory and time consuming for which the farmers could not get loan at the time of their need and that distanced the farmers, from having a sense of belonging to the Co-operative societies. There were, perhaps, reservations in the mind of policy makers may be under the influence of Commercial Banking professionals to give a free hand to the Co-operative Banking structures to operate in the rural areas for financing for agricultural and allied purposes, after infusing professional management in Co-operatives and keeping them free from political intervention. Rather, Co-operative Banks were discouraged to go for non-farm sector financing and for personal loans till NABARD advised to go for such lendings during early nineties.

The Govt. of India nationalised fourteen major commercial banks during April, 1969 and six more during April, 1980 to converge the class banking system to the mass banking system to make their-branches accessible to the relatively poor and disadvantaged people of the rural areas.

Subsequently the Regional Rural Banks were organised, utilising the huge financial resources and professional approach of the commercial banks, contemplating that the branches of the RRBs would play the role of windows of the commercial banks in the rural areas. At the instance of RBI, a number of Primary Co-operative Societies were ceded and adopted by the commercial banks during late seventies on experimental basis as a parallel system to the RRB structures.

National Bank for Agriculture and Rural Development (NABARD) was constituted in the year 1982 for providing not only credit for promotion of agriculture and allied sector but also small scale industries, Cottage and village industries, handicrafts and allied economic activities in rural area. Since, in spite of all these arrangements resource of the commercial banks could not adequately flow into the rural areas, *service area approach was enforced during late eighties attaching different villages to specific branch of the commercial banks and RRBs to compel the Banks to open up their activities in the said villages attached with such branches.

As it appears, since the resources of the commercial banks were mostly the depositors' money and since the commercial bankers had no confidence to get back their money which they were to pump as rural credit as direct finance or through the cooperative system infested by vested interests, the aforementioned arrangements did not have the desired result. That is why the Govt. and the RBI set up many Committees during the eighties including Ardhanariswaran Committee, Choudhury Brahma Prakash Committee, Khusro Committee etc. all of which give specific recommendations to make the Co-operative member driven free from political intervention and to function professionally so as to earn the confidence of the depositors, equity investors and lending Model Act were framed by the agencies.

Govt. of India and circulated to different State Governments to improve the existing Primary Agriculture Credit Societies. But, as it appears, most of the States, although amended their existing in actual practice, many Co-operative Act, Govts. failed to show the right spirit to ensure democratic system of management and fix responsibilities on those who caused mismanagement and losses to the societies. Fortunately, many Governments pioneered by Andhra Pradesh and followed by Bihar, Chhatishgarh, Jamu & Kahsmir, Jharkhand, Karnatak, Madhya Pradesh, Orissa and Uttaranchal, have legislated a parallel Co-operative Act providing sufficient autonomy to such new generation Co-operatives which would be member driven and will be fully free from financial and administrative control of the Govt. hoping that people with strong leadership personalities would come up and bring out the real Co-operative movement that will compete with the commercial banking structures in resource mobilisation and rural credit dispensation.

After the financial reforms in the banking sector as per the recommendation of the Committee on Financial Systems with Sri Narasingham as Chairman which was set up on 14 August, 1991 the commercial banks and RRBs which fall under the Union list in the Constitution of India, were provided with huge financial support for cleansing of their balance sheet. The Co-operative banking system were denied of such support on the ground that the recapitulation is made by the owner and since the State Govts. are the owner (equity holder) of the Co-operative Banks, the State Govts. should provide similar financial support to the Co-operative Banks.

However, except few State Governments like Andhra Pradesh, Punjab, Uttaranchal and West Bengal etc. most of the State Govts. did not come up for substantial financial support for cleansing of the balance sheet of the Co-operative Banks. As a result, as many as 144 Central Co-operative Banks out of 367 DCCBs have eroded their net worth and are not complying to Section-11 of the Banking Regulation Act and not eligible to receive financial support from NABARD and strictly speaking, they are not eligible to perform banking business.

However, the Govt. of India have come to understand in the mean time that it is not possible to attain the targetted 8% growth rate of G.D.P. unless the Agriculture and allied sector are improved and that there is no alternative to the Co-operative credit system to fulfil such objectives and that it would be easier to revitalise the cooperative credit structures than to enable the Commercial Banking sector to serve the rural credit seekers generously. Accordingly, Jagdish Capoor Committee followed by Patil and Vyas Committees strongly recommended for cooperative sector reforms at the beginning of the current century and even budget provisioning was made by the Govt. of India to provide financial support to Co-operative Banks and societies, subject to taking up of certain corrective measures by the State Governments and sharing of the required financial package. It was, however, observed that the strategies suggested by such Committees for revitalising and funding the cooperative banks were neither realistic nor implementable.

The Govt. of India, therefore, have constituted another task force in the year 2004 with Prof. A.Vaidyanathan as the Chairman to suggest for an implementable action plan for revitaling and restructuring the Co-operative Credit structures both in long term and short term sectors and exercise is going on about the financial package and strategic measures to be taken within a petraft, Further the years in the country.

The Capoor Committee and Ve scheme, Committee have almost reiterated the the past, tion of the Committees set up earlier that few Co-operative credit structures have to prk revitalised to meet the credit needs of the rural people. The recent developments like legislation of parallel Co-operative Acts to strengthen the Co-operative leadership and infuse professional management system free from control and financial support of Govt., the declaration of National Coop.Policy in the year 2002 i.e. 98 years after the Co-operative system was introduced in the country by the Government, the amendment of NCDC and NABARD Act to allow direct financing to the Co-operatives without Govt. guarantee and recent decision of the Govt. to double the flow of agricultural credit as it existed as on 31.03.04 within the next three years and the present expression of the Govt. of India to ensure adequate flow of credit to weaker sections of the community including small, marginal and tenant farmers and the present proposal of the Govt. of India to amend the constitution for enforcing democratic management of Co-operatives, timely elections, involvement of RBI in the management system of Co-operatives etc. generate a strong hope that the time has come when the Co-operative Banking credit structures would stand reformed to function as an efficient financing system in the country.

Once leadership is developed and Co-operative activities take shape of a movement, and professional management is infused Co-operative societies would start making profits and distribute dividend to the equity holders and resource will not be a problem as that would also lead to adequate deposit mobilisation by the Co-operative Banks, once- they deserve the confidence of the people.

"We will not measure the success of the movement by the number of Co-operative societies fromed, but by the moral condition of the cooperators."

– Mahatma Gandhi

Proper Management is the Key to Success

Time management is the most key factor for the highly successful people. Each and every person has 24 hours a day, but how one manages that time completely depends upon person to person. There are some people who do a lot of work and then also manage to have sufficient time to enjoy; on the other hand, there are some people who always complain about not having sufficient time. This is not the matter of the shortage of time; it is all about the management of time.

Therefore, the success of any person does not only depend upon the hard work; but it depends upon how efficiently and effectively one manages the time. If we look at the data - relating to the business world - published by O.K. consulting - 54% of executives work more than ten hours a day, 71% of workers usually take their work home. 75% of workers 64% suffer from insomnia due to time constraints at work, 61% have already cancelled or postponed their vacation several times due to pressure of relief their job in their dreams, work, and 74% of executives feel, they do not have time for their family.

This is today's scenario of the business world. Time

management is, therefore, an important key to lead a successful and as well as less stressful life.

Successful people in the world attribute their success to effective time management activities which they do in their routine life. So, if we distribute our time according to the work priorities, then it helps us to reduce the wastage of time and energy and also to do the right thing at the right time which will result in increasing the productivity and efficiency, which is the crucial part of the journey of success for any person.

In order to lead a successful life, we should keep some points in our mind like our goal, priorities etc. The golden rule of time management is completing high priority tasks first. One must prepare daily, weekly and monthly schedules of activities so that one can start the new day with clearly scheduled activities.

"India leads in villages and villages perishes, India perish too."
— Mahatma Gandhi

Strengthening Credit Institutions

There is a need to support short-term cooperative credit structure to enable it play an important role in inclusive growth of our country.

Credit delivery system has been envisaged as an effective channel for creating an environment for inclusive growth of the society. The institutional credit system for agriculture comprises of short term (ST) and long term (LT) cooperative credit institutions, commercial banks(CBs) and Regional Rural Banks (RRBs), under the supervision and regulation of Reserve Bank of India (RBI) and National Bank for Agriculture and Rural Development (NABARD). The Institutional credit delivery system or urban areas comprises of CBs, Urban Cooperative Banks (UCBs), and Urban Cooperative Credit Societies (UCCS).

The rural Co-operative credit and banking system consists of two wings - ST and LT. The short term cooperative credit structure (STCCS) deals with short and medium term credit and also credit disbursement for agricultural purposes and it is federal in character. It is mostly based on a three-tier pattern with the state cooperative banks (SCBs) at the apex level, district central cooperative banks (DCCBS) at the intermediary level and primary agricultural credit societies (PACS) at the village level. At national level, the National Federation of State Cooperative Banks Ltd

(NAFSCOB) was established on May 19, 1964 with a view to facilitating the operations of state and central Co-operative banks in general and development of cooperative credit in particular.

Inclusive growth may be defined as the opportunities and helps in reducing poverty, It means having access to essential services in health and education by the poor. It includes providing equality of opportunity and empowering people through education and skill development. It also encompasses a growth process that is environment friendly, aims for good governance and helps in creation of a gender sensitive society. Special efforts to increase employment opportunities are essential as it is a necessary condition for bringing about an improvement in the standard of living of the people. The concept of inclusive growth was introduced under the 11th Five Year Plan.

Inclusive growth ensures that the benefits of a growing economy extend to all segments of society Unleashing people's economic potential starts with connecting them to the vital networks that power the modern economy. Inclusive growth is the integration of virtual networks (financial services, market and supply chains & digital platforms), physical networks (electricity, transportation, water) and social networks (local community, family and friends & Investors & mentors). Access to and integration into these neteworks increases their productivity, which can set in motion a various cycle of sustained poverty reduction and inclusive growth. Thus, the cycle of inclusive growth include business innovation and investment, rising income and job opportunities expanding and more prosperous middle class and more robust domestic demand.

A key component of inclusive growth is financial

inclusion which connects people to secure ways for receiving, storing and managing money. While financial inclusion is a point of entry to lift people and markets out of poverty, inclusive growth is the key to move them towards shared prosperity.

Financial services are important for inclusive growth. STCCS are playing a very major role in inclusive growth by providing financial services to the under privileged mass in rural India. Viz, farmers, rural artisans, landless labourers and women etc. Financial services extended by STCC contribute in capital formation in the economy. Formation of capital is a very important prerequisite for inclusive and sustainable economic growth.

Therefore, access to financial services and identical opportunities enable underprivileged people to participate better in the economy, thereby helping them to actively contribute to the development and help in poverty eradication. The role played by STCCS in this regard is very important. The cooperative movement has a long history in India. Cooperative societies were set up in India towards the close of the nineteenth century drawing inspiration from the success ofbexperiments related to the cooperative movement in Britain and the cooperative credit movement in Germany.

The co-operative movement consists of autonomous association of persons united voluntarily to meet their common economic, social and cultural needs through a jointly owned and democratically controlled enterprise: Mutual help, democratic decision making, voluntary and open membership, economic participation, autonomy etc.vare the basic principles on which the co-operative structure is designed. Thus the principle of mutual aid which is the basis on cooperative organization and the practice of thrift and self-help which sustain it, generate a feeling of self-reliance and empowerment.

With appropriate fund support Co-operative banks, with the following achievements and advantages can be the most appropriate and effective agencies to ensure inclusive growth.

Number of KCCs issued by cooperative banks(short term)-3.34 crores(As on 31.03.2018).

The percentage of KCCs issued by cooperative banks to total KCCS is 73.31% (excluding commercial banks). Amount disbursed under KCC-Rs.1,24,484 crores.

The share of cooperative banks in total loans disbursed under KCCs is 52.34% (excluding commercial banks)

Number of PACS at grassroots level-95,595 (as on 31.03.2017)

Number of members of PACS-13.12 crores Percentage of borrowing members to total members-39.63% Amount of loans issued - Rs. 200678 crores.

Number of SHGs linked with cooperative banks-13,02,981.

Percentage share of Co-operative banks in total SHGS linked with banks-14.90% Amount of savings of SHGS-Rs.2120 crores.

Percentage share of Co-operative banks in total savings of SHGS-10.82%.

Number of women SHGS-11,40,776

Percentage share of Women SHGS in total SHGS linked with cooperative Banks-87.55%

Amount of savings of women SHGS-Rs.1855.81 crore 87.51 per cent of total savings of SHGs belong to women SHGS.

The Labour CO-OPERATIVE SOCIETY

The Labour Cooperative Movement actually emerged after the independence for providing protection to economically weaker section of the Society from private contractors. In India there are nearly 46,179 Labour Contract Cooperatives out of which 12.5% are tribal labour cooperatives. These cooperatives have nearly 416.700 members. But unfortunately most of the societies are loss making ones. The working capital of labour cooperatives comes to Rs.297 crores along with business turn over of Rs. 665 crores.

Labour Cooperatives are also extended to forest areas. The Government of India has started taking interest in improving the conditions of labour cooperative for which National Advisory Council on Labour Cooperatives has been constituted under the chairmanship of Union Minister of Agriculture. The States like Delhi, Panjab, Haryana, Maharastra, Andhra Pradesh and Himachal Pradesh has accepted the recommendations of the Advisory Council.

The Labour Cooperatives faces a number of problems. The major problems are insufficient work contracts, lack of financial resources to execute work contracts. There is also need for promotion of skill among unorganized labour force and weaker section. In the second National Labour Cooperative Congress held on 15" March, 2000 emphasis I was given to withstand Janata Personal Accidental Insurance Scheme to Labour Cooperatives. In the Ninth Plan a grant of Rs.10.50 Crore had been earmarked for labour cooperatives. However, stress was given to make the labour cooperatives self- reliant. In view of the competition with private contractors, there is the need for labour cooperatives to assimilate the various components of Information Technology to reduce the cost of building operation and to increase per worker productivity. Vocational training should also be extended through specialized courses.

Labour Cooperatives by and large represent land rural poor, agricultural labourers, artisans and the weakest of the weaker section of the country. The difficulty encountered by Labour Cooperatives are generally-labour force at the bottom level are mostly scattered, illiterate and unskilled, lack of initiation to organize labour cooperatives. lack of proper leadership and migratory character of Indian Labour force etc.

The labour cooperatives in India are formed in three-tier basis, Primary Labour Cooperatives at the village level, Central Labour Cooperatives at district level and State Labour Cooperative Federation at the state level. To represent the labour cooperatives at the national level in the year 1981, a National Federation of Labour Cooperative was set up. All these bodies were constituted only to arrest exploitation, providing better quality of life to the members by safeguarding their interest.

As regards Orissa is concerned, we are having 92 numbers of labour contract and Forest Labour Cooperatives. But unfortunately, 56 have become dormant. Membership of these societies stands at 11,239. The paid up share capital of these societies comes to the tune of Rs. 29,20 lacs. If we make an assessment of the financial condition of the societies it is revealed that, the number of societies which are making profit are quite negligible which clearly shows that the performance of the clabour cooperatives of he State is not up to the mark.

It is suggested that if steps will be taken in the line of recommendations made by National Advisory Council on Labour Cooperative then the Labour Cooperative Movement can be strengthened. Measures like:

1. All unskilled works may be exclusively reserved for labour cooperative.

2. Skilled work up to Rs. 30.00 lakhs may be earmarked for labour cooperatives.

3. Preference in case of work, rate and price may be given to labour contract cooperatives and they may be exempted from payment of earnest money and security deposit.

4. Arrangement to financial assistance thorugh cooperative banks to these societies.

5. Promotion of labour/artisan cooperatives of rural women workers.

6. Preparations of action plan, conduct of HRD programmes are the need of the hour.

Labour Cooperative Movement has remained as the neglected area in the cooperative sector. However, if we take initiative from now even, then the labour cooperative movement may stand as a milestone in the cooperative arena and we can bring a ray of hope for the weaker section of the society who deserves a better quality of life in the future. In our state the activities of labour Cooperatives is far from satisfactory.

The major problem being non allotment of work

order or in the otherwords though a circular was issued long back by the Works Department of Govt. of Orissa to give preference to labour Cooperatives still then the work alloting authorities are not assigning the job to the Labour Cooperatives. This has crippled the Labour Cooperatives. Presently our Labour force generally migrate to Mumbai, Gujrat, North Eastern States in search of a job. There, they are being exploited and do not even get the minimum wage. They do work in an unhealthy condition as a result of which they suffer from a number of ailments.

Even the young boys and girls are not spared. Secondly, poor knowledge about labour market also compel them to accept the job offer whatever they get. And there after they are exploited by the employer. Even today we find Goti and Dadan labourers. For the success of labour Cooperatives movement in the State effective leadership, will power and patronage by the state Government are required. In a developing state like ours which is fast moving towards industrialisation, the Labour Cooperatives can play a vital role in nation building.

A Duty of a Public Servant

During any tenure as Public servant in coop. Deptt. of the State for about three and half decades from 1966 to 2001, one of the OCS Officer successful in solving some difficult and problematic situations outside the fame work of law in uncommon way which he wants to narrate as memorable incidents for the information of the readers through this article. During 1973 to 1976 I was working as ARCS, Aska, Rampant paper transaction of loan had taken place by the Secretary of one near by S.C.S. of Aska town namely Magalpur S.C.S. with the connivance of the supervisory and staff of Aska Central Coop. Bank & office bearers of the society: Came to light when the fact came to knowledge allround legal steps like supersession of the committee of management of the society was resorted to besides filing of dispute cases against large number of defaulted loanee members of the society after supersession of the committee of Management. The Secretary of the SCS who was involved in such unlawful activity of paper transaction of loan had absconded and it was reliably leant that he had taken shelter at Surat (Gujrat) with his relatives who were working there. The loanee members got panic and were terribly afraid about the consequence of realization of loan through legal process of disputes and E.P. cases.

They came to the office of ARCS Aska in large

numbers every day for solution of the problem. The Officer could not help the situation when dispute cases were pending in the court of the ARCS, Aska. It was not possible to solve the problem out of the court pending disposal of the cases. It was also clear and evident that documentary evidences like loan ledgers and loan disbursement/ statement etc. would defi-nitely go against the interest of the loanee members and truth can not be established in the dispute cases when the signatures & LTI of loanee members are genuine in all relevant documents relating to disbursement of loan and ultimately the lonee members will have to suffer to pay the dicrotal amount with cost of litigation although they had on received the entire loan as per the relevant documentary evidences as stated by one and all loanee members. In such a situation it was difficult to solve the situation to establish the truth.

In absence of Secretary of the society record of the society was seized by breaking open the locked admiral in presence of Magistrate as per provision embodied in the statute and another staff of the Aska Central Coop. Bank by posted as Secretary of the society. For disposal of disputes, the presence of the Ex-Secretary of the society was also necessary at the time of hearing of the cases who bad been impleaded as one of the defendant along with the concerned loanee member. It was made clear to the members of the society that they should ensure attendance the Ex-Secretary by putting pressure on the near relatives of the Ex-Secretary who belonged to same Managalpur village. Accordingly they succeeded in ensuring attendance of Ex-Secretary by bringing him from Surat through his near relatives as they were their co-villagers. Pending disposal of dispute cases, physical verification of loan was ordered and he also attend the physical verification of loan in the office room of the society located in Mangalpur village which was attended all the lonee members, Ex-Secretary & concened officials, of the Aska Central Coop. Bank & Deptt.

Before taking up physical verification of loan due procedure of asking the concerned loanee member and Ex-Secretary to admit the loan liability and loan-disbarment with reference to relevant loan statements & loan ledgers. It struck to me that to find out real truth as the time of physical verification some fear complexion linked to religion & god / goddess should be infused and it was ascertained that all villagers of Mangalpur and near by villagers are devotees of near by Jhadeswari goddess worshipped in a temple situated in hilltop adicanent to Mangalpur village.

So it was decided to swear in the name of Goddess Jhadeswari touching the used flowers of the Goddess to speak the truth about the actual amount acknowledged as loan by the members and disbursed by the Ex-Secretary case by case. Accordingly the physical verification of loan commonced and it was seen that actual truth had been established in admitting the loan liability and loan disbursement both by loanee members and Ex-Secretary without any exception and signatures / LTI of both were taken in support of their admittance in physical loan verification statement which was taken as documentary evidence in proper and quick disposal of dispute cases.

The undisbursed loan amount misappropriated by the Ex-Secretary as per the physical loan verification statement was deposited in full in the names of loanee members concerned by the near relatives of the Ex-Secretary immediately by pressure put on them by the co villagers (loanee-members). This incident still alive in my memory even after lapse of about 30 years as memorable work piece in my entire service career.

Another memorable incident had taken place in the year 1999 six day after his joining as General Manager & M.D. of OSCARD Bank. At about 7P.M. when was working in my office chamber about more than 50 employees of the Bank lead by President and other office bearers of the employees union entered in my office chamber without asking for my permission and threatened me to pay all their pending dues. He instead of arguing with them said them politely that he being new to the office is not acquainted with their problems within very short span of about one week since assuming office and shall look into their problem tomorrow as he knew that the employees union in the past have pressurized the Ex. M.Ds and have resorted to agitational Programmes for fulfillment of their demand. But on the next day he did not go to the Bank and applied for leave to the President of the Bank (Commissioner-Cum-Secretary to Govt., Cooperation Deptt.) who was away on tour to Karnatak as observer appointed by Election Commission of India.

The office bearers of the employees union came to house without finding him in office to persuade him to go to the Bank. But he did not accede to their request protesting against their behaviour shown to me as a new M.D. of the Bank. Next day they again came to his with senior officers of the Bank to beg apology and persuade him to attend the Bank but he told them that he will reconsider the matter of continuing on leave after discussion with the president on his return to headquarters from Karnatak two days after on Monday as it was Friday. But they tried their level best to convince him to attend the Bank telling that they shall never repeat the incident anymore in future. Lastly he told them that he will attend the Bank next day but they should keep on waiting with a garland near the portico of the Bank at about 10 A.M. to which they agreed with rejoice Accordingly he reached Bark at the appointed hour and they came rushing to garland him near the portico of the Bank.

But he stepped them telling that the garland is not meant for him but for "Purusottam" who has come to the Bank with him and the garland should be offered to him in his office chamber. Then all of them came along with him to his office chamber. Standing near his office table he took out the holy glass bound images of Loard Jagannath, Balabhadra & Subhadra alongwith a packet of mahaprasad (Nirmalya) from his bag and placed the same on his office table he asked them if any one staff of the Bank was Christian or Muslim and they replied negatively. Then he asked them if they are all agreeable to his proposal of solemnly swearing before the idols after garlanding and touching the Mohaprasad that they shall no more resort to any agitational programme including of hearing M.D. in future and give their best in developing the Bank which was in very bad shape being imbibed with the spirit of "work is workshop".

They agreed to his proposal and then asked them to call each and every staff of the Bank to his office chamber and swear accordingly. They all did one by one which continued after about half an hour. Then he asked them to paint with the help or one staff (painter) at all conspicuous places of the Bank starting from main entry of the bank to all entrance points of all rooms with the slogan "work is workshop" which he was done nest day. He also suggested them to coopt. him as advisor of their employees Union to guide them properly in constructive way like a senior professor being nominated as advisor of college union by the Principal. They readily agreed to his suggestion and came up with a resolution passed by the executive committee of the their union adopted in an emergent meeting coopting him as chief adviser with all Managers as advisors endorsing copy to the President of the Bank. From that day on wards job culture and work atmosphere pervaded in the Bank as he marked explicitly with in office and field. Recovery performance took momentum even during post-super cyclone period.

He also tried his level best to look into the personal claims of staff like his own claim to the best possible manner within parameter of rules and stringent financial position of the Bank gradually looking into genuineness of the-claim and hard cases as on priority basis which satisfied the employees removing their long pending heart-burning grievances and ill feeling against the management. He explained politely and humbly to the President of the Bank that stringent legal and disciplinary action against the erring employees would have aggravated the situation creating atmosphere of fear for the management to work properly and efficiently which would not have brought favourable and conducive work atmosphere in the Bank with suspicious feeling between the employees and the management The President well appreciated the approach and thanked him. The employees of the Bank still remember the incident and always appreciate his advice when they meet each other.

In the said Bank another new approach to meet the big and wilful defaulting members of the primary CARD Banks by their field staff in a group with a banner had bought an impact in the climate of recovery due to the very fact that single approach by one supervisor had concealed the real repaying attitude of the loanee members for some secret understanding between the two due to non-repaying attitude of the loanee member and selfish interest of the supervisor which was not possible in group approach. Besides the fame and position of the affluent defaulting loanee member in the eyes of his co-villagers was degraded due to publicity in the village through group approach with banner. The willful defaulting member of the primary Banks who had capacity to pay but were not paying with a view to avoid the tarnishing of the their name and fame in the village paid sizeable amount by arranging fund including to disperse the group with banner standing in front of his house attracting attention of his villagers.

This approach when proposed to the President of the Bank was readily approved and was also acceptable to all field functionaries who were depressed for very poor recovery performance of the primary Banks leading to deprive them form their bread and butter in near future due to closure of the Bank which was always appreciated by them. - Lastly he will cite another incident as to how development of business was made in Cuttack wholesale consumers Coop Societies. Ltd. (Namuna super market) which is now under liquidation) during the year 1972-73 when he was posted as administrator on his return from Pune after doing Diploma in Co-operative. Business Management (DCBM) with specialization in consumers business which was 11 months in service course from VMNICM There I applied one business development policy called "loss leader policy" which he had known during his training by application of that theoretical policy in to practice he selected four essential consumer articles used by all types of consumers daily namely (1) Salt (2) Match box (3) shaving blade and (4) Sun light soap to sell in the super market at cost price without adding any element of profit margin in costing to attract customers from vicinity to come to the supermarket to purchase those items as no other business man could sell them at that cost price and it was definitely cheaper and no where available at that price undoubtedly. The said items were demanded heavily by customers standing inquer.

The stock was exhausted at very short intervals for which arrangement was made to replenish the stock by keeping heavy stock in godown and to place orders for supply immediate before stock out in the godown so that customers were not returned for stock out. This created and impression in the minds of the customers that the Co-operative. Store is selling goods cheaply and other businessmen of the locality who were selling those items at higher price received complain from their customers for which they came rushing to him to enquire as to how those items were sold by the store at that price by sustaining loss and asked him to check up the costing sheet in which some mistake in costing must have been committed. He told them that he will look into the same but did not disclose them his trade secret.

After application of this policy the sale of other good also in creased multifold as compared to sale of previous months as the customers who came to purchase those four items also purchased other items comparing that other items are also little cheaper as compared to other shops since the margin of profit taken in other items was less as charged by other shops which was at all known to the customers as they seldom visited the supermarket previously and were accustomed to purchase from other shops regularly and were not in a position to compare the price which was also partly due to lack of advertisement by the supermarket. Any how when monthly sale turn-over statistics for about six months after introduction of "loss leader policy" was analyzed, it was seen that the sales thee increased gradually from month to month by more than ten times, he found that the loss sustained in selling the identified four items as cost price was made up by increase in sale at other items multifold and also the loss sustained was nothing if cost of advertisement was taken into consideration which could not have forced the customers to visit the store by way of advertisement only unless they are convinced. Selling of four items cheaply as compared to market price could not have put impact on the public through advertisement as compared to news spreading from person to person automatically among people and also due to gathering of large crowd in the store always as seen by persons passing by the store out of curosity to know about the gathering of large number of customers mostly from middle and lower middle class. Audit objection raised for selling the four items at cost price was complied with over all sales turnover of the store increased abnormally in other items to make up the gap which was justified and self- convincing to waive out the audit objection.

"My outlook at present is not the outlook of spreading the Co-oerative movement, gradually, progressively as it has done, my outlook is to convulse India with Co-operative movement or rather with Co-operation".

– Jawaharlal Nehru

Management of Milk Producers' Co-operative Society

The Indian Constitution describes cooperative societies as organizations "based on the principles of voluntary formation, democratic member control, member-economic participation and autonomous functioning" vide provisions under Article 43-B and 243-ZI. Section 4 of the Odisha Coop. Societies Act, 1962 provides that, unless the organization have its object, the promotion of economic interest of the members and comply the cooperative principles provided under Sec. 2 (d-2) read with Schedule-ll of the Act, it can not be registered.

The said co-operative principles, accepted world-wide, differentiate a cooperative from other group-based economic ventures like companies, partnership farms, corporations etc.

India is not only the largest democracy, but also, with more than six lakhs cooperatives involving about twenty four crore members, has the largest network of cooperatives, in the world. But, Indians were allowed to practise democratic governance through cooperative management with enactment of Cooperative Credit Societies Act, 1904, much before political democratic rights were bestowed upon them in the year 1935 and finally in the year 1947, onwards. "Rule of Law" being the essence of democracy, one has to be acquainted with the provisions of law, practice and procedures in that regard, whether he is interested for political governance through Panchayatiraj Institutions, Urban Local Bodies, Legislative Assembly or Parliament, or is interested for applied economic-activities through cooperative leadership.

The General Body of members is the final authority of a cooperative Society, as per Section 27 of the Odisha Coop. Societies Act, 1962. The General Body meeting must be held at least once in a year to transact business described u/s 29 of the said Act, which includes most important functions like review of performance of previous year, approval of Annual Action Plan and budget for the current year, co sideration of Inspectic and Audit Reports, distribution of surplus Pofit), matters relating to Election and amendment of Bye-laws etc. So the General Body is the ultimate governing authority in a cooperative, subject to the Provisions of Co-op. laws, rules and byelaws of the society. The members of the General Body, elect the Managing Committee including office bearers like President, Vice- President, as per provisions of Act (Sec. 28, 28-A, 28-B), Rule and Byelaws.

The said Committee manage the affairs and business, as detailed under Sec. 28 of the Act, by help of paid employees headed by Chief Executive Officer and others. So, the real function of a cooperative is run by the employees, with the C.E.O. appointed by the Managing Committee (u/s 28 (3-b)) as leader.

Pandit Jawaharlal Nehru, the first Prime Minister, and the architect of modern India had said "All the enthusiasm in the world will not be enough unless we have trained personal to run the cooperative societies". The cooperative principles as provided u/s. 2 (d-2) and schedule II of the O.C.S. Act, require provisions for education of the members, office-bearers, officers and employees of a cooperative, as well as for general public, on the principles and techniques of cooperation, both economic and democratic. Since attainment of business target would ensure proper return to members by way of dividend and services, Management Development Programme (MDP), which aim at enhancing the organizational as well as individual performance capacity, by adopting best practices, is the best H.R.D. exercise.

The concepts covered under the acronyms "POSDCORB" (P=Planning, 0 = Organization, S = Staffing, D = Direction, CO = Coordination, R = Reporting, B = Budgeting) and "SWOT" (S= Strength, W = Weakness, 0 = Opportunities, T = Threats) which generally apply to any organization, also applies, more or less to the Cooperatives, including the M.P.C.S.

"Co-operation" being a subject under List II (state list), in i schedule, under Article 246 of the Indian Constitution, The Cooperative Societies Act, and Rules framed thereunder, are the regulatory laws to bind the Governance and management of the Cooperatives. After the 9i" Amendment of the Constitution was enacted, the O.C.S. Act 1962 have been suitably amended and the Odisha Self-Help Cooperatives Act, 2001 have been deleted, to make the state cooperative laws compliant to the Constitution. But, although the said Amended provision of the Constitution provides for matters relating to election of Managing Committee, its tenure, cooption, reservation for weaker sections etc. the Coop. Societies (Election to Committee) Rules, 1992 has not been amended by the Govt. of Odisha as yet.

In case of Milk Producers' Coop. Societies at primary, Central and Apex level, the rules relating to composition, tenure, election procedures etc. are not guided by any separate set of laws / rules framed by State Govt. and the existing relevant provisions of byelaws and guidelines/executive-directions regulating constitution of Managing Committee audit, inspection etc. have been made by modifying the relevant provisions of OCS Act, in exercise of powers conferred on State Govt., u/s. 123 of the Act.

The State Govt. therefore, perhaps have to take a policy decision, whether the M.P.C.S. would be allowed to continue their existing governance and management pattern, or to provide a new set of provisions of law/rule to bring their management system in conformity with the amended provisions of the Constitution of India.

Balance Sheet in Co-operatives

Truely speaking the balance sheet of any business organization is the mirror which reflects the actual state of financial health as on a particular date & cooperative Societies being business enterprises by and large are not exception to this Balance sheet should be transparent, trust worthy & reliable piece of document for the share holders, investors, depositors & other stake holding associates & as such it should not be routine or ritral to comply with the statutory provisions only.

Interpretation of Balance sheet & working out various ratio yardsticks as well as net worth services very useful & meaningful purpose for which it should furnish the true, actual & correct position of properties & Assets alongwith capital liability. Both in letter & spirit without hiding or suppressing any material aspect to make the balance sheet rosy & attractive so onorous responsibility lies on the Auditors to ensure. It is seen that the Balance sheets are prepared keeping in view the vested interests of the Management & as such many hidden essential matters are not disclosed & the auditors are necessary bilature parties with the management to prepare the balancesheet as per the sweet will of the management for the reasons best known to the auditors for their selfish vested interests.

The auditors are Primary responsible for not

disclosing very impartment & valuable information in the balance sheet & deliberating either under pressure, fear or otherwise for their selfish & malafide motives. As such instead of being in dependent & neutral play their role as yes as dectated by man of the management them & dance as per the tune set by the Management. This attitude of auditors not only ruin the organizations but also betrays the share holders, investors, depositiors & other stake holders resulting in landing them in to serious financial loss due to non realization by their invested capital in the organization.

In order to check & curb such type of under hand malapractices of auditors by daring to the tune set by the management there should be checks & balances on the auditors by a third party so as to detect the omissions of frauds & errors of the auditors in suppression of most valuable pieces of intimation like misappropriation of funds & embursement by employees throughfraudulent documents non-receiving of dues from debtors non-realization of assets of the organization information and sharing misleading about realization nonperforming assets and so on.

The following practical suggestions unholy may be considered desirable to infuse a sence of fear to prompt the auditors to refain from relationship with the management & employees so as to curb their unbealthy practices as deterrent measures.

1. Test Audit : To avoid perfectory audit some percentage of test audit of audited organizations may be conducted by fixing on random sampling basis every year in societies with high turner & profit making organizations in remote in accessible & flaged areas to test by the efficiency and veracity & testimony of the auditors.

2. Surprise visits : The programme made by the auditor should be verified at the field and his job performance must be checked by surprise visits to ensure actual auditing by auditors at head quarters of the society & not at his residence with records brought to unauthorized place of auditing.

3. Re- Audit : Where it is noticed that the audit is perfunctory, reaudit should be conducted.

4. Insisting for special confident report and audit objection menus.

5. Disciplinary proceeding

6. In Initiating of surcharge proceedings :

Audit serves no purpose if audit recoveries are not realized from the person or persons who are made responsible and accountable specifically to make good the loss sustained by the society for their illegal, fraudulent, malafide actions involved misappropriations & irregularity basing to diminishing the asset of the organization is any manner whatever supported with material & documentary evidences detected in course of audit pin - printing their extent of liability very clearly and specifically beyond all reasonable doubt. This is very important aspect of work audit organization as no steps are taken by the audited organizations to year in audit reports without any action there on as such in many cases.

The surcharge proceedings initiated if not disposed of within reasonable time losses it worth & remaining in pen & paper only for eye washing. Time bound programmes with targets should be fixed for both for initiation of surcharge proceedings and disposal which should be reviewed on monthly basis. This serves as exemplary, lesson & deterrent for others to refrain from such types of retarious activities both for employees and management. This step shall be expeditions based on audit reports which are admissible in evidence & shall reduce the volume of disputes cases which are mostly only filed for realization of overdue loan dues of members, loanees from the societies based on loan transaction records.

It would not be art of place to mention that the auditors should not only be very honest, dutiful & diligent not only to detect the errors but also give concrete suggestions & advices to improve the business opportunities by playing the role of friend, philosopher & guide to the organization & make valuable suggestion for improving accounts keeping with built in system of internal checks & balance insisting on four eyed principle of checking each and every transaction by two persons and not by one person alone, rotation of all vernable seats at prescribed periodical intervals for innumerable detection of fraud, errors, embezzlement & misappropriations as they are not truly grey hards as after remarked to highlight their possetive role for finding out faults only and nothing else Auditiors should hear as much as necessary but spark as less as necessary to discharge their onerous.

It is true that audit of any type of post responsibility of playing their role as honest neutral and impartial observer. Mortem examination of accounts after commission of & irregularities, fraud, misappropriation embezzlement. But it cannot detected earlier in course of transactions unless accounts are written. so audit should not confused within fault system of interval checks and balance which takes care of preventing any type of defects in accounts keeping immediately to rectify the irregularities in course of transactions by the cross checking & vigilant eye of the superior passing authority unless he deliberately connives with his subordinate who prepares & originates the transactions.

So it is necessary and very essential to ensure that no single person is entrusted with the work to supervise and pass the transactions prepared by them. Each transaction should be seen at least by four eyes and not by two eyes only. Shortage of staff should not be any excuse for this. It is therefore necessary to build up a system of interval checks and balance which cannot be avoided even though internal audit or concurrent audit system is in vogue which cannot detect the errors committed before close of transaction of the day as both the system of internal audit and concurrent audit are postmortern in nature which audits the accounts not on same any of transaction but on the next day.

So no type of audit whether internal, concurrent, interim, final can in any case replace the strongly built in internal check & balance system and internal auditor should be made accountable to felt very important transaction fixing a minimum financing limit before any transaction are finalized and pay rests effected for any expenditures or loan and arrears giving him fully automatically to object the transition of any type with reasons and the ultimate anything to agree or disagree with internal auditor, should lie with the chief executive who should state his reseason to agree or disagree with internal auditor. This is required also in case of loans & advances sanctioned by his sub-committee Executive Committee / or committee of management / Board of directors as mere sanction by competent authority is not enough unless all the terms & conditions fixed by the competent sanctioning authority are complied meticulously in letter and spirit by the disbursing anything before disbursement. It shall suffice to pay that "prevention is better than cure" as said in case of disease.

Similarly the same is well applicable to prevent the frauds. So the golden words "Trust is good but control is better" should be always remember in mind by all business transcation including all cooperative organizations and auditors.

"All the enthusiasm in the world will be not enough unless we have trend personnel to run our Co-operative Socities."
– Pandit Jawaharlal Nehru

97th Constitution Amendment

Cooperation is the very basis of social existence. In common parlance it refers to mutual working together for the pursuit of a common goal. Human beings satisfy many of their needs and fulfill interests through joint efforts. The idea of the cooperative movement took birth with the realization of people that they can find solutions for many of their problems through cooperation. Since interdependence is widespread in all walks of life, cooperation is all the more needed. Society advances through cooperation. Progress can better be achieved through united actions.

In India, the co-operative movement was initially started with dispensation of rural credit. After independence, "co-operation" was accepted as an instrument of planned economic development, particularly to bring about all-round socioeconomic transformation of the weaker sections of the community. At present cooperative movement has touched all fields of economic activities.

The constitution of India devides the legislative powers between the union and the states in three lists-the union List, the State List, the Concurrent List (Art 246 Subject-matter of laws made by Parliament and by the Legislatures of States). The states have exclusive power to make Laws on subjects mentioned in the state list. In our constitution cooperative societies are included in the state list. Under state List Entry 32(Seventh Schedule to the Constitution of India) it is open to the state to legislate on any or all aspects of co-operative societies including their management etc. The Entry is as under: 32. Incorporation, regulation and winding up of corporation, other than those specified in List I, and universities; unincorporated trading, literacy, scientific, religious and other societies and associations; cooperative societies.

Year 2012 has been declared by the United Nations as the International Year of Cooperatives. It has been declared to highlight the valuable contributions of cooperatives in economic and social prospects. On the occasion of the International year of cooperatives let's take a few moments off to reflect on the cooperative laws in Odisha.

1. It was in the year 1904 the first Legislation on cooperative was born. The Act was termed The Co-operative Credit Societies Act, 1904. (Act 10 of 1904)

2. The above mentioned Act was repealed by The Cooperative Societies Act, 1912. (Act 2 of 1912)

3. Then came the following Acts after co-operative became a provincial subject consequent upon the Govt of India Act, 1919.

The Bihar & Orissa Co-operative Socieies Act, 1935 (BO Act No 6 of 1935).

The Madras Co-operative Societies Act, 1932 (Madras Act 6 of 1932)

The Orissa Co-operative Land Mortgage Bank Act. 1938 (Orissa Act 3 of 1938).

The above mentioned three Acts were replaced in the state by the The Orissa Co-operative Societies Act, 1951(Orissa Act 11 of 1952).

The Orissa Co-operative Societies Act 1962 (Orissa Act 2 of 1963) which is now in force repealed the Orissa Co-operative Societies Act, 1951.

The Orissa Self Help Co-operatives Act, 2001 (Orissa Act 4 of 2002) followed The Orissa Co-operative Societies Act 1962. The Act is in force.

Both the 1962 Act and the 2001 Act are in force in Odisha. The Co-operatives formed under the 2001 Act enjoy full autonomy in their Management and functioning. Late Utkal Gourav Madhusudan Das the founder of the state of Odisha is also the pioneer of the Co-operative movement. He had introduced the concept and organized Co-operative institutions much before the enactment of The Co-operative Credit Societies Act, 1904.

Following are the Acts made by the Government of India from time to time for the formation of cooperative societies whose area of operation touches more than one state.The Multi unit Co-operative Societies Act, 1942 (Act No 6 of 1942)

1. The Multi-State Co-operative Societies Act, 1984 (Act No 51 of 1984) The Multi unit Cooperative Societies Act, 1942 was repealed.

2. The multistate Co-operative Societies Act, 2002 (No 39 of 2002). By the enactment of this Act The multistate Cooperative Societies Act, 1984 was repealed.

Year 2011 was a golden year for the Co-operative movement in India. 97th amendment to the Indian constitution, has made the right to form cooperative societies a fundamental right under Article 19(1)(c).

Article 19(1)(prior to the Amendmend) ran as –
Article 19. Protection of certain rights regarding freedom of speech etc.-

(1) All citizens shall have the right to form associations or unions.

Article 19(1) (c) guarantees the right to form association or unions. Under clause (4) of Article 19. However the state may by Law impose reasonable restrictions on this right in the interest of public order or morality or the sovereignty and integrity of India. The right guaranteed is not merely to form the right to form association but also to continue with the association as such. Now Article 19 (1) (c) will be read as "to form associations or unions or cooperative societies".

The amendment also inserts a new directive principle into Part IV of the constitution, Article 43B, which reads. "The State shall endeavour to promote voluntary formation, autonomous functioning. democratic control and professional management of cooperative societies" and after Part IXA of the Constitution, Part IX B (Part IX B the co-operative societies).

Part IXB contains the following

(i)   Incorporation, regulation and winding up of Co-operative societies based on the principles of voluntary formation, democratic member control. member economic participation and autonomous functioning;

(ii) specifying the maximum number of directors of a Co-operative society to be not exceeding twentyone members;

(iii) a fixed term of five years from the date of election in respect of the elected members of the board and its office bearers; and an authority or body for the conduct of elections to a Co-operative society:

(iv) a maximum time limit of six months during which board of directors of a Co-operative society could be kept under supersession or suspension;

(v)   independent professional audit;

(vi)   right of information to the members of the Co-operative societies;

(vii)   empowering the State Goverments to obtain periodic reports of activities and accounts of Co-operative societies;

(viii) reservation of one seat for the Scheduled Castes or the Scheduled Tribes and two seats for women on the board of every Co-operative society, which have individuals as members from such categories;

(ix)   penalties in respect of offences relating to Co-operative societies.

The Amendment aims at encouraging economic activities of Co-operatives, ensuring autonomous and democratic functioning of Co-operatives, and accountability of the m gement to the members.

The amendment to the Costitution came into force w.e.f. 15th February 2012 it has also been provided in the amendment that not with standing anything in Part IXB, any provision or any law relating to Co-operative societies in force in a state immediately before the commencement of the constitution (Ninety seventh Amendmend) Act, 2011 which is inconsistent with the provisions of this part shall continue to be in force until amended or repealed by a competent Legislature or other competent authority or until the expiration of one year from commencement of the amendment whichever is less. In other words the state Acts are to be consistent with the 97th Amendment within a maximum period of one year from 15th February 2012. In our state Odisha, the Act and Rules on Cooperative Societies are suitably amended from time to time in order to meet to the changing needs of the masses.

Co-operatives have played a pivotal role in national development and empowering the community. It has given a boost to India's agriculture and allied sectors. The 97th Amendment to the Constitution of India thus reiterates that cooperation is the main spring of our collective life. It gives strength in union, it builds, it nurtures, it brings prosperity.

Second Green Revolution

India became independent on 15.08.1947. Credit starved poverty stricken farmers were exploited under 200 years British colonial rule. Only 8% agricultural families had received institutional credit out of which 3.1% belong to Co-operative credit 0.9% to commercial Banks and 4% to Government Taccavi loan. The rest 92% had been exploited by Money lenders, Feudal kings, Jamidars, Landlords etc. They received credit from them with high compounded rate of interest, out of which 66% from Usurious money lenders. 90% people were below poverty line and 98% land were unirrigated.

Famine was frequent. There was lack of communication. The population of partition India was 350 million during 1950-51 and food production was only 50 million ton. India was deficit in food production to feed its entire people for which Government of India was compelled to import wheat from America under Marshal Yojana of USA Major Share of our foreign exchange were utilized for importing rice and wheat.

Government of India formulated five year plans and introduced mixed economy to eradicate poverty and to make the country self sufficient in food grain production. Though cooperative failed during last 50 years of its operation due to poverty stricken and illiterate people I still then the planners make cooperative as 3rd economic sector for rapid socio economic progress to eliminate poverty, to raise living standard of common people, to make the country self sufficient in food production by adopting Japaneese method of intensive cultivation inirrigated lands which was called first green revolution since second five year plan in 1957 onward.

The credit is major input for achieving these objectives. So according to recommendation of rural survey committee in 1954 Cooperative became multi-purpose in providing farm credit for purchasing surplus land of landlords by tenant farmers under land reform, loan for land improvement, irrigation, mechanized farming instead of traditional ploughing, loan to purchase hybrid and high yielding seed, fertilizer and insecticide.

These schemes helped for more crop yield, Government of India set up agricultural price Commission in 1954 to declare support price of each crop before their sowing taking into consideration of investment in agricultural operation and harvesting. RBI introduced seasonal crop policy to advance crop loan on crop wise basis instead of on prior pre-independence policy of land security. PACs are advancing crop loan both in cash and kind like fertilizer etc. for agricultural operation by preparing scale of finance annually for each crop and are collecting loan after 2 to 3 months of harvesting of each crop by giving opportunity to farmers for marketing their crop to repay crop loan by scheduled date in order to avoid defaulters for availing fresh finance in raising new crop.

Food Corporation of India was set up in 1954 to purchase surplus crops of farmers at support price. PACS, regional, Mandi, State and National Marketing, Cooperative Societies. Tribal Development Cooperative Corporation,

Forest Cooperative Societies are also purchasing crops and other forest produce at support price especially by linking credit with marketing to avoid distress sale and for good recovery. R.B.I. had also extended facilities to distress farmers for loosing crop in natural calamities to convert, to rephase, to reschedule for repayment of crop loan in 3 to 5 installments and there by for availing fresh crop loan to raise new crop and in extreme adverse condition to write up crop loan.

PACS and Co-operative Banks are compensated for such written up loan by both state and Central Governments during 5th plan. These measures are helping farmers for food production and security of farmers in their crop failure. Commercial Banks were not in field of crop finance till 1969. PACS and Cooperative Banks had monopoly of crop loan.

Short term credit Cooperative Societies, Cooperative banks had played vital role in financing subsidized farm loan during 5th plan period in 1971 for small, marginal, farm labourers, Harijans, Tribals, drought stricken farmers under small farmers, marginal and farm labourers, Tribal and drought prone agencies to raise the living standard and repaying capacity of these weaker section.

The State and Central Govts. Compensated PACS and Co-operative banks in bearing the subsidy loan portion to the extent of 14, 1/3, ½, as in case of small, marginal and Harijan and tribal farmers respectively. These agencies had also provided risk fund to PACS and Cooperative Banks for financing these weaker section. Cooperative is still playing major role in advancing farm loan. State and Primary Cooperative Banks for Agriculture and rural Development are advancing long term investment loan for land improvement, irrigation, housing and ancillary farming loan for dairy, poultry,fishery and village artisan loan to eradicate poverty and to raise living standard of people. The Cooperative took Onerous responsibilities of operating 11 out of 20 economic points as announced by Late Prime Minister Indirajee 1975-76 to liquidate rural indebtness and poverty, IRDP poverty alleviation scheme was introduced in 1980 to eliminate poverty of poorest people of our society wherein cooperative had undertaken responsibility of executing these schemes.

For all these measures our country became self sufficient in food production during 1992 and was able to export food products inspite of increased population from 35 crores in 1951 to 90 crores in 1991. The people below poverty line narrowed down gradually to 22% in 2003-04 from that of 90% during 1950-51. Co-operative farm loan was raised to Rs. 37252 crore in 2005-06 from that of mere Rs. 22.90 crores in 1950-51. Food production raised to 210 million ton in 2005-06 from 50 million Ton in 1950-51.

Still then our country is far behind than China regarding food production and alleviation of poverty. China has got population 1050 million during 2000. Cultivated land 30.5 Million hector, rice production per hector 6.2 Ton, total rice production was 190 million Ton against India had got population of 1020 million, cultivated land 44.6 million hector, rice production per hector was only 3 Ton. The total rice production was 134 million ton. That means India has got more cultivated land less rice production than China. 22% of total population or 2.36 crores people in China were below poverty line during 2003-04 against 225 of total population or 23 crore in India were below poverty line.

Rice production per hector land was double of India. Similarly wheat production per hector inFrance and U.S.A. was much more than India. Crop production of some countries of world during 2000 are enclosed herewith for reference. In this context Government of India under Hon'ble Prime Minister Mr. Mana Mohan Singh took bold policy decision on 18;06.2004 to double the farm credit within 3 years from level of 86981 crore rupees as on 31.03.2004 which is main input for agriculture production through second green revolution to compete with China, Japan and other south eastern Asian countries some Uropean developed countries and U.S.A. in order to reduce further % of people below poverty line.

Cooperative Credit structures are fraught with low resource base. Dependence on higher financial institutions, poor business diversification, poor recovery, huge accumulated loss, managerial inefficiency especially due to State Govt. interference, politicalisation and high management cost etc. For which credit cooperative is to be strengthened for helping doubling farm credit as the share of cooperative in farm finance is reduced from 62% in 1991-92 to 50% in 2002-03, 26% in 2004-05 & 25% in 2005-06. The measures may be taken to strengthen ST and LT credit cooperative structure

a) Membership drive is taken for enrolment of new members and fresh credit flow to them as a result 29 lakhs people became new member in PACS of India during 2004-05. Orissa State Cooperative Bank had taken door to door approach by special campaign "Cooperative at your door step" during 1st to 15th August 2003 for which 111632 new members admitted, Rs. 30.18 crores an advanced to them, 29515 Kisan Credit Card issued for instant finance. 24.38 crores were collected and there by 31452 indebted members became non-defaulters. 1681 members opened deposit account of Rs. 8.31 crores.

This campaign may be followed by other states to revitalize cooperative credit structure for 100% enrollment of members atlest admission of all agriculture families as members of P.A.C.S from level of 1354 lakhs members as on 31.03.2004.

i) Debt restructuring may be taken for reschedulment of loan for distress indebted members for easy repayment by installments

ii) One time settlement scheme may further extended for lessening loan burden of indebted farmers

(b) revised scales of finance to meet realistic need of farmers for agriculture operation and technological up gradation in agriculture, agro-processing and agribiotech

(c) monthly state level meting with all concerned be held to review action plan collection etc.

(d) recommendation of vaidyanathan Committee may be implemented for immediate contribution of Rs. 18435 crore, under capital adequacy scheme to cleanse the balance sheet, to wipe out accumulated loss of PACS, DCC Bank, S.C. Banks OSCARD and of PCARD Banks.

e) Loan Recovery: The recovery to demand as on 31.03.05 at the level of SCB was 83.47%, at the level of DCCB was 71.28%, at member level was 63%, 43.70% at SCARDS and 50.6% at PCARD level. NPA was at the level of SCB 16.25%, at level of DCCB 19.87%, at level of SCARD31.27%, at level of PACARD 31.9% that is beyond normal of 12.5%.

High NPA is creating concern for Co-operative ST and LT structures, for which imbalance is mounting. 90% recovery will consolidate weak ST and LT structures. Low recovery percentage is due to govt. policy of interference in loan recovery for which number of willfull defaulters are mounting. An- other genuine factors for non-recovery are crop loss of crop borrowers in natural calamites and distress sale of crop for less than support price. Farm borrowers are getting compensation in natural calamites against crop loss since 1985 and all farmers for all crops since 1998. But all insured borrowers are not getting crop loss compensation inspite of they are paying compulsory premium against Creal, oilseed, Pulse and Sugarcane crops for area approach like Block at a Unit. There should be attempt to compensate crop loss of each crop borrowers by individual approach.

At least crop loss in natural calamites should be assessed on basis of village or chaka circle as unit. So that they will repay the loan out of crop loss compensation and will not be defaulter to receive fresh loan. Govt. of India has also introduced crop price fluctuate insurance for certain crops against price fall since 2003 to compensate short fall of price against support price. Interest rebate scheme by OSCB since 26.04.2000 for honest crop borrowers and loan collection incentive to Secretary and other employees of PACS by Orissa State Co-operative banks are encouraging good collection of 69% at member level during 2003-04 against 58% in 2000-01. the said policy may be followed by other states. One time settlement scheme should be further extended to recover old chronic loan. Govt. of India should provide fund within one year to cooperative banks as recommended by

Baidyanathan Committee under capital adequacy scheme for cleansing their balance sheet in order to get uninterrupted refinance and revitalization of S.T. and L.T. Credit cooperative structures. Govt. of India and state govts. Should hence forward be refrained from loan waiver scheme not to encourage willfull defaulters and to create recovery climate for achieving at least 90% collection, which will I solve all problem for revitalizing Cooperative Credit Structures in order to issue fresh farm credit for success of second green revolution.

f)   Interest rate: Govt. of India has reduced the deposit interest rate from 10 to 7% and there by crop loan lending rate of 11% has been reduced to 9% since 2003 incase of C.B. & R.R.B. Govt. of India has further reduced interest rate from 9% to 7% since 1.4.2006, for I which Govt. of India is subsidising 2% interest rebate to evade loss of these banks. But Govt. of India has not yet agreed to compensate interest loss of Cooperative Banks.

There shall not be any discrimination against farmers irrespective of their borrowing crop loan from Commercial or Cooperative Banks. However Orissa Govt. has come forward on 23.09.06 to bear interest loss of Rs. 33 crores of Orissa Cooperative Banks & PACS for Khariff & Rabi Crop loan with effect from 01.04.2006. So that Cooperative Banks & PACS will lend crop loan at 7% interest rate at par wit CB & RRB. Other State Govts should follow the said interest rebate scheme of Orissa Govt.

But this may create hurdle in operation of PACS and co-banks as it was happened in past in case of Keral state Government's subsidized interest scheme on S.T. Loan due to want of timely budgetary provision. Rather NABARD should refinance ST loan of Cooperative Bank at nominal rate of 12% in stead of 2% % like many foreign banks.

So that farmers will receive ST loan at 7% from PACS which will stimulate farmers for crop production with less Agriculture Operation cost and there by to accelerate second green revolution. India is the largest producer of Milk of 91 million Ton during 2004-05, 45.2 million eggs, 44.5 million Kg. wool, Rs. 2.12 million Ton meat was produced during 2004-05. Milk Cooperative Societies and Unions are organized to advance loan for Milch cow, buffalo and to purchase Milk at support price. India is third largest producer of fish of Rs. 6.3 million ton in 2005-06. Fishermen Cooperative Societies are organized to catch, collect and marketing of fish with cold storage facilities. Poultry cooperative Societies are organized for purchasing poultry birds and selling their meat. Socio economic, progress: 60% people are still dependant on Agriculture, Agriculture is greatest employment sector.

The Co-operative is the second largest employment sector. Many people engaged in agro production and on livestock Agro, industries like IFFCO, Khribhco etc. Agro processing, agro marketing, agritransport and distribution of consumer articles like rice, sugar especially through PACS, agro service centre for mechanization of farming. As a result poverty has declined from 90% in pre-independence era to 54.8% in 1973-74, 29.9% in 1987-88, 26.1% in 1999-2000 and 22% during 2003-04. Second green revolution since 2004 will certainly further reduce poverty stricken Indian people.

The Co-operative is one of the major media for executing the various poverty alleviation programmes of both central and state Governments especially since 5th five year plans like small farmers, marginal farmers, 'farm labourers, drought prone and tribal development agencies in 1971, 20 point economic progrmme in 1975, IRDP in 1980 etc. Indian Agriculture is for subsistence and has not yet declared industry as in case of America and other European Countries. But agriculture is now for commercial production for success of doubling farm production from level of 2000-05 during 11th five year plan under second green revolution.

g)   210.4 million Ton food grain was produced during 2005-06. 26.7 million Ton oil seed, 273.7 million Ton sugarcane and 16 million Ton cotton was produced. India is largest producer of Tea of 667 million ton in the World and Coffee 2.81 lakh ton during 2005-06. Fruits 57.6 million Ton and vegetable 991.4 Ton was produced during 2005-06. Rubber 7.8 lakh ton produced during 2005-06. The Cooperative has extended to al- most all segment of socio-economic programmes, The Cooperative had already generated 13.86 million direct and self em- ployed persons till end of 9th five year plan period.

Agriculture inputs will led for success of second green revolution to increase food grain production in rain fed dry land especially in more production of wheat, sugar, pulses, corn, oil seeds, fruit, vegetable.

i)   Seed 54700 Quintal breeder and 7.4 lakh quintal foundation seed was produced and 127.4 lakh quintal of certified seed distributed during 2004-05.

ii)   Fertilizer, IFFCO, Khribhco and other fertilizer Cooperatives are major producer of fertilizer out of total 15Million Ton. Consumption of fertilizer was 18.39 million Ton. Consumption was 96.60 per hector during 2004-05. PACS, RMCS, Mandi, State Cooperative Marketing Federation were distributing IFFCO fertilizer.

iii) Irrigation- Cooperative are advancing loan for minor, lift, dug, Tube, fountain and drip irrigation to increase irrigation potential in country. 68% or 95.13 million hector land has been irrigated so far by all means of major, medium, minor irrigation project including through Cooperative. There are many lift and other irrigation Cooperative Societies to increase irrigation potential of our country.

iv) Cooperative had advanced credit Rs. 37252 crores during 2005-06 to finance for all agriculture inputs.

v) 590.55 lakh farmers were covered with crop insurance under Rastriya Crop insurance scheme from 1999 Rabi season to 2005 Kharif. Still then crop insurance scheme and crop cutting procedure should be simplified to compensate crop loss in natural calamites of all insured farmers as security measure to farmers inducing them for doubling farm production and success of second green revolution.

vi) Agricultural Marketing Various marketing organization like F.C.I., Corporation for Jute, Cotton 7521 regulated markets and specialized Marketing Boards for rubber, coffee, tea, coconut, tobacco, spices, horticulture products are operating to purchase commodities at support price. Net work of Co-operative, like PACS, RMCS, State Cooperative marketing Federation, NAFED are also purchasing Paddy, wheat, Onion, groundnut etc. Cooperative marketing Societies are advancing pledge loan to farmers for which they are selling farm produce at profitable price. Credit link with marketing is for assured collection of loan.

The Cooperative and other agencies had procured 41.2 M. Ton rice and wheat during 2005-06 at support price to avoid distress sale, PACS and RMCS in Raipur District of Chhatishgarh and Baragarh, Sambalpur, Bolangir Districts of Oriss are purchasing paddy at support price linking with crop loan collection. Still then price fluctuation scheme should fully operative to compensate farmers in selling their all crops short of support price.

vii) Kissan Credit Card (KCC) scheme has been introduced for instant crop finance since August 1998 for instant S.T. Loan in seasonal Agricultural operation. Out of 590.93 lakh KCC since inception to 31.03.06. The Cooperative Banks have issue d304.12 lakh Commercial Bank 218.03 and R.R.B. 68.78. that means Co-operative played major role in issuing 51% KCC out of total.

viii) Electric Cooperative Societies are energizing lift irrigation points for irrigating high land. All these measure will help for second green revolution, doubling of farm production during 11th five year plan and elimination of poverty through many such socio economic schemes.

Certainly the Cooperative will be key for second green revolution and Socio-economic progress as Cooperative played major role for success of 1st. green revolution and Socio-Economic progress as Cooperative played major role for success of 1st green revolution and self-sufficiency in food production of our country.

Rural Development
Through Co-operative

India is essentially a village oriented country because it consists of around 6 lakhs villages where in about 80% of her population resides and derive their livelihood from agriculture and allied sector. The economic property of the country therefore depends on the integrated and all round development of the rural economy.

Until the socio-economic conditions of small farmers, agricultural labours, scheduled castes and scheduled tribe people are ameliorated, village economy cannot be considered to be developed. Development of rural India means not only the aggregate development of rural areas but also the development of socio-economic and cultural status of the people living in the rural areas.

The objectives of development include sustained increase in per capita output, income, expansion of productive employment and greater quity in distribution of the benefits of growth. The objectives of rural development are therefore multidimensional as well as multi-directional. It aims at increased employment, higher productivity, higher income, as well as minimum acceptable level of food, clothing, shelter, education, health etc. and to build up a round value system which helps in keeping with the high cultural heritage of the country.

Its pertinent to mention here that cooperative movement has been paying a pivotal role for the development of the rural economy of our country. Cooperative movement in our country was introduced in 1904 with an objective to eradicate rural poverty, accelerate the pace of agricultural production and to ameliorate the soci-economic conditions of the rural people. Ever the father of the nation, Mahatma Gandhi was an order believer of cooperatives system. According to Pandit Jawaharlal Nehru, "there are three essential pillars of an Indian village, viz a cooperative, panchayat & school". The All India Rural Survey in the year 1954, reiterated in the similar voice when it had rightly observed that in cooperative lies the best hope for rural India.

The cooperatives for last 100 years have helped in the shaping, regulation and development of rural economy of our country. The specific development brought about by cooperatives till date can be narrated section-wise in the following lines. The cooperative credit is the most important source of institutional credit in rural area in meeting the increasing agricultural credit requirement of small and marginal farmer, landless labourers, workers etc. village level primary Agricultural credit cooperative Societies (PACS) have been organized in rural areas to cater the short term credit and input needs of it 120 million members. They have been successful in providing timely credit at reasonable rate of interest as well as fertilizers, agricultural implements, improved seeds, pesticide, insecticides etc. They have implemented the instant and hassle free dispensation of agricultural credit through Kissan Credit Cards.

They have been successful in protecting the farmers from the exploiting clutches of the village money lenders as they usually charge an exorbitant interest rates. Moreover these all farmers service cooperative societies which are framed to reap the benefit of large scale or joint farming on scientific lines. Besides there are large size multipurpose cooperatives (LAMPS) organized in tribal areas to promote the economic interest of tribal members. The concerted effort of these credit cooperatives, have not only increased the agricultural production of our country but also improved the economic conditions of rural people.

Besides the short term crop. loan, the co-operatives also provided investment credit to farmer members through primary cooperative and rural development banks, operating in sub-division and Taluke level. They provide long term loans to farmers for acquisition and development of assets with a view to enhance production, productivity in agriculture by adopting advance technology which ultimately help the farmer members to generate more income. Schematic finance of NABARD for plantation, horticulture, sericulture, piciculture, farm mechanization, small road transportation, small business, small scale industries under both farm and non farm sector come under this category which are financial by CARD banks, DCCB and PACS.

As we all know, agriculture is the most risk prone enterprise in India, on account of natural calamities like flood, drought, cyclone, hail storm, fire etc. To cover the risks of crop loss and crop failure, the PACS and DCCB are playing a very important role in implementation of crop insurance schemes of the government. The earlier comprehensive crop insurance scheme and the present National Agricultural Insurance schemes have been successfully implemented through cooperatives by which more than 1.5 crores of farmer members have been benefited in our country. The crop insurance scheme not only give protection to the farmers but also protects the interests of the financial institutions by giving repayment guarantor for their loan.

To prevent the menace of distress sale of paddy and to help farmers get remunerative price for their agricultural product, the marketing cooperatives, the regulated market committees and the grain banks have come to the rescue of the farmer members. National Federation of Agricultural Marketing Cooperative (NAFED) is the nodal agency to provide support to marketing cooperatives in the domestic market as well as in the field of exports. IFFCO & KRIBHCO, the fertilizer giants have significantly contributed to augment the farming community agricultural productivity by producing quality fertilizer and promoting their judicious use amongst the farming community agricultural productivity by producing quality fertilizer and promoting their judicious use amongst the farming community.

Dairy is one area where cooperatives have excelled. Dairy cooperatives have been instrumental in providing subsidiary occupation to small and marginal farmers, landless labourers, women, folk and other poorer sections of the society. Thanks to formidable presence of milk producers cooperatives at village level, milk producers Union at district level and milk Marketing federation at state level for which India has emerged as the largest producers of milk in the entire world.

Cooperatives have also carred out a riche in the field of textiles, handicrafts, handlooms, cottage industries and small scale industries in village area. The weavers cooperative societies facilitates the weaver members in producing and in marketing of textiles & handloom products and has there by raised their economic condition.

Sugar cooperatives have been formed to procure sugarcanes from the members and pay remunerative prices. The sugarcane growers of Maharastra & Gujrat have already established their credentials in uplifting their social, economic & political status.

Fishery cooperatives are providing finance for fishing, nets, boats, etc and pays remunerative prices to amelionate the economic condition of fisherman community. Similarly poultry growers cooperatives and goter societies have been promoted to benefit the members.

Tribal cooperatives are engaged in collection & marketing of miner forest products & surplus agricultural products collected on cultivated by tribal. Similarly the tree growers cooperatives have been promoted for creation of common forest property that are diverse, economically which cater to all the range of survival needs.

In fine, the above cooperative societies have acted as a catalytic agent for raising the level of productivity, providing income source, extending improvement in technology and expanding employment in rural areas.

Women in Management

The growing level of literacy among the entrepreneurial fair sex and women development pro-grammes have motivated the prospective and fairly educated women to venture in the field of science, engineering, technology and industrial entrepreneurship simultaneously with other traditional jobs and professions like farm cultivation, livestock, forestry, fishing, plantation, mining, manufacturing, servicing, repairing, advertisement, trade and commerce, transport, storage, communication, cinema and other services. In short, there is no field in this world untouched by the women.

So the access of women in the field of administration, science, management, technology and industrial entrepreneurship, especially in tiny and small scale sector is rapidly increasing year by year. They are getting proiority assistance from the government of India under the scheme for aid given to self-employed women and an equally high priority is being accorded to them under the national award scheme for rewarding best producers. These may look as the stories of the past, because they have now entered in all types of industries in all the sectors.

After independence the country has witnessed the growth of industrialization, education and democratic system. With result the tradition bound Indian society has under gone a sea change. One striking evidence of this is that women have started seeking not only in gainful employment in many fields in increasing numbers but also in entrepreneurial field is haunted by a number of difficulties and problems faced by women entrepreneurs. They are as follows: Stiff competition from male entrepreneurs. Managerial constraints. Financial constraints. Technical difficulties. Inferiority complex among the lower and middle class women community. Family affairs, child and husband cares. Unplanned and haphazard growth of women entrepreneurship in the country.

Lack of specialized entrepreneurial training programmes best suited to the temperament of women entrepre-neurs. Low ability to bear economic risk, social risk, technical and environmental risk. Discrimination in the selection for developmental training. Low level or favourable family background in the field of family cooperation, education, occupation and entrepreneurial base. Lack of infrastructural facilities both in urban and rural areas. Late commencement entrepreneurship in the country. Thus the problems of women are many and varied. Several studies in women entrepreneurship have focused on some specific problems and a total approach to all such problems and possible solution could help the planners to give impetus for women entrepreneurship.

In our country the central and state governments and private agencies are trying hard to develop women entrepreneurship. Several schemes and incentives are exclusively available for women. The result has been the emergence of women entrepreneurs on the economic scenario in recent years.

Suggestions:

The following recommendations are made to facelift the participation of women in business and other enterprises. Women comprise about 50 percent of the total population of India. So developing business acumen among women is equally important for its allround development of the country. In majority of cases, the women have to depend on the male-members of their family for their existence. Besides after finishing their household work, most of them sit idle inside the house. This is equally applicable even in the case of educated and affluent women. In such a situation if efforts are made to develop their entrepreneurial skills it will not only solve the problem of women in making them economically independent but it will also help in adding to the national income.

A package of assistance covering product selection, market information and marketing outlets, training in management is required to accelerate formation of indigeneous organisations Such a programme for promotion of women entrepreneur-ship's self employment depends on the solid foundations that are laid through preparation of realistic and bold action programmes and in providing necessary organisational frame work and to set their financial assistance.

Though the entrepreneurial movement among community have been started recently, the promotional agencies are firmly determined to turn the smouldering fire into flames. Thus, in the active support of the promotional agencies and the good family occupational background rapidly increasing and it is expected to develop in every nook and corner of the country in the years to come. women entrepreneurial is Dr.P.Vijayalakshmi, in her doctorial study entitled "problems interalia sugesstions.

entrepreneurs" has offered the following The training programme should include sensitivity training developing communication skill, interpersonal skill and time management Training in organisational behaviour may also be imparted.

Government must provide financial assistance with 50% subsidy for purchases of a small sized personal computer to all women entrepreneurs followed by a six weeks training to them in its operation. This will very much help them to store, retrieve and know where they stand. This will surely give a psychological boost of having a friend in need and guide.

Women have to play the dilemma of dual role as a family member and an entrepreneur. They have low risk taking, coupled with low intemallocus of control. They are also highly prone to stress. So big corporate houses in ? India and abroad other than stress management methods also adopt Mediation and Transcendental Meditation. Indian women entrepreneurs can also be inducted to this area so that they would get internal peace and discover their immense potentialites.

Commercial banks may have separate women entrepreneurship assistance department which could help in preparing perfecting the project report and also adopt successful ventures for full scale financing and expansion.

An exclusive industrial state for women entrepreneurs may be established by the government at important metropolitan cities and in their outskirts on a vast area and constructed plots with assured power, water and other infrastructure facilities, must be provided at concessional rate. In such a sprawling area other than school, creeches, market place and park, a strong police contingent set and a women police booth for watch and ward develop women entrepreneurs to a great extent.

Globe over, the increasing participation of women in the workforce has been one of the instable characteristics of the recent past. Much is being said, done planned not only to sustain this trend but to enhance it further. Politicians, economists, psychologists and socio-logists have all supported this movement on different accounts and rationals. No doubt the increased participation is not only quantitative but implies women's entry into non-conventional areas of work. That is why this century has seen women making a dent in the business world in a major way.

It is appropriate to quote a recent happy news of Fortune magazine magnets of the world. This list includes three Indian women stalwarts who are none other Kooneer Chanda Kochar, Deputy Executive Director, ICICI, Nainalal Kitwai, Top Executive officer, HSBC and Iran Majumdar, chairman of Pyokhan., This happened due to employment of women and active women entrepreneurial development. But the empowerment of women is still a far cry to about 50 percent of their population living in rural areas and in remote corners of our vast country.

Co-operative in Post "Kalia"

The Direction of Agricultural Extension-

Extension is the carrier of knowledge and technology from lab to land and also the mechanism for feeding back the experience to lab for refining as per users need. Extension and capacity building of personnel is a continuous process by adopting the method of refreshing and retooling the machinery. Field Extension is Mostly performed by the Development Departments of Government of Agriculture and Farmers Empowerment Department (include Agriculture, Horticulture and Soil Conservation), Fisheries and Animal Resources Development, Department of Handlooms Textiles and Handicraft Department (Sericulture) and Cooperation Department.

The Institutions like State Agricultural Universities, ICAR Institutions play a major role in bridging the knowledge gap of Departmental Personnel. In case of Cooperation Department the Odisha State Cooperative Union (OSCU) is the apex Institution and at National level the Vaikuntha Meheta National Institute of Cooperative Management (VAMINCOM) is the knowledge provider. In case co Cooperative Credit NABARD has now emerged as the major knowledge provider and it is imparting training through its

Nationational level Institutions like Bankers Institute of Rural Development (BIRD).

Regional level institutions and at the State level the Agriculture Staff Training Institute under Odisha State Co-operative Bank has taken the lead role. Gradually credit aspect is being distanced from the OSCU and on the other side the Extension Institution Institutes in Cooperative Banking sector have probably taken the responsibility of credit related issues.it is now found NABARD has entered into other aspects and rather it can be said it has taken Credit + approach. Most important aspect is collectivization of Small Holders who constitute not less than 87 % of total workforce in Agriculture Sector.It has come with many new products to fill the gap.the approach for organizing Joint Liability Groups (JLGS) to address the issue of inability of major farm force to access credit in the absence of bankable title over the land they ttill. The Agricultural Extension wing led by IMAGE (which has come up in place of Grama Sevaka Talim Kendras) also distanced from credit aspect (so also collective marketing) and abolished the post of Instructor manned by an Assistant Registrar of Cooperative Societies who happens to be a Resource Person for Credit, Collectivization and Marketing. So far it is known the scope of work of OSCU also covers Marketing, Fisheries, Khadi and Village Industries, Textiles etc. In Odisha the Cooperation Department owns the Marketing Directorate and Odisha State Agricultural Marketing Board (OSAMB) who facilitates marketing by creating infrastructures like storage, Market Yard and in the latest an e-marketing platform (eNAM). Besides the cooperatives are are visible in marketing Cooperatives those participate in trading., Cold Storages etc.

The Paradigm shift :

Presently the paradigm has been shifted from Production Oriented Extension to "Market Led Extension". The planners have realized that "Profits are in the market and not in the farm" The very purpose is to make Agriculture profitable and attract younger generation to accept Agriculture as a vocation. Stress is also given to look into consumers' choice and Food Safety. The flow chart of the agriculture as an enterprise has been explained as follows. (Soil/Capital/Credit/ Investment)

1. What variety to Produce)
2. Analysis of land holding for suitability of crops
3. Market Situation Ahead

Decision on how much to produce / what practice to follows :

1. Adoption of INM, IPM, GAP, Harvesting
2. Post-Harvest Technology, Application of ICT
3. Value Addition, PSS*, Food Safety
4. Storage/Transport
5. When to sell
6. Where to sell, e-marketing
7. At what price to Sell
8. Market Yard/NAM
9. Rupees
10. Savings, Repayment of loan, Capital formation
11. *PSS-(Phyto Sanitary Standard)

Innovative Steps by the Government-

Odisha has a well considered Agriculture Policy (Latest being in 2013) which has touched almost all aspects. During last decade a number of farmer friendly steps have been taken which are eye opener for other States. Of all procurement of paddy and payment through bank accounts is most important one. In this initiative Odishi was ahead of many States as payment to farmer was then made through Agents.A separate "Agriculture Budget" is being presented in the State from 2013-14. thereby The budgetary outlay of agriculture & allied sectors was only Rs.5627.87 crores in 2012-13.This has gone up to to Rs.13181.89 crore in 2016-17.Allocation of Rs.14, 930 crore has been made for Agricultural sector through separate Budgetary Provision for the year 2017-18.The State is accessing funds from various Central Sector Schemes. The RKVY, MIDH are the major sources for funding projects. The outlay for the Agriculture Budget is about 14% of the total Budget and Estimates of the State for the year 2017 18.The same trend is also continuing. In cooperative sector ditization of cooperative credit is in the progress.In Agricultural Marketing Sector Reform measures have been taken on priority basis.Producers usually approach private traders for money in advance to give them their output after harvest obviously in a term disadvantageous to him.Keeping this problem in eye the Government of Odisha have floated the Scheme "Krushak Assistance for Livilihood and Income Augmentation. (KALIA) started infusing funds to the farmers accounts with hope that they will use this as working capital.

Remembering Royal Commission on Agriculture :

Remembering Royal Commission on Agriculture had viewed in the year 1938 that "if Cooperation fails there will Fail the Best Hope of Rural India.'It is a proven fact that all development in Agriculture and Allied Sector have come due to cooperative action. Always it may not be a registered Cooperative Society but may be collective action. Credit or any funds provided from any source need be utilized for productive activities so as to generate income.

New Role of Cooperative Extension-

It is time for Cooperative Extension sector to adhere to the system of "Market Led Extension" under the leadership of Odisha State Cooperative Union. The OSCU should reqoent its Training Centers as advanced Centre for Cooperative Training. It should promote Commodity Based Cooperatives like such Cooperatives in Maharastra.The New Agriculture Policy 2013 has viewed for promotion of Rural Producer Organizations. It is pertinent that During last few years the Agriculture Sector has shown good progress in production of Food Grains, The total production of Food Grains, Oil seed, Fiber and other crops has gone upto 12106(in 000 MT) during the year 2014-15 against 7991 (in 000 MT) in 2011-12. In case of Horticultural crops 34675 Quality planting materials have been supplied during 2014-15 against 27406 in 2010-11. And spectacular change has taken place in production of Fruits, Vegetables, Spices and flower.The OSCU may takeup organization of Cooperatives or adopt existing Cooperative Societies to establish farmers linkage with these Yards.eNAM can only be successful if such collective organizations are created and nourished.The OSCU may adopt some PACS also.

Profit Orientation-

The Government of India have enacted a Special Provisions in Indian Companies Act during the year 2013 by way of amendment to incorporate Producer Companies which are almost based on the 7 Principles of Cooperation. But the important section is regarding assurance for limited payment on the share contributed. But in case of cooperatives there is no assurance regarding payment of dividend. Hence the Extension Machinery should take all care to ensure earning of distributable profit to pay dividend.

The OSAMB to Come Forward-

Once again I repeat that "Profits are in the market and not in the farm". Hence Odisha State Agricultural Marketing Board may consider to come up for organization of Commodity based Cooperative Societies focussing Market Yards in coordination with Extension Officers of the Department and OSCU. The farmers may be sensitized to make productive use of "Capital" created at farmers level by way of infusion of funds under KALIA. This will generate income at the level of farmer.This will also enable eNAM platform to function successfully. The OSCU may also guide formation of Cooperatives under KVIB programme to create employment for surplus agricultural labour. The OSAMB may patronize the Kalyani, Samabaya Samachar and commodity based issues may be published. The OSCU may take up research market surveys. A tentative production clusters in Odisha is mentioned in the table below where Cooperative Societies can be promoted or existing PACS may also have Sub-Groups for the purpose.

"Whatever steps we take in regard to Co-operation have to be in the democratic contest, i.e. it has to get the good will of the people"

– M.K. Gandhi

The Indian Co-operative Society's Law

The progress of amending State cooperative laws based on Model Act has been rather slow. So far, Orissa, Madhya Pradesh, Karnataka and Kerala have amended their cooperative law with reference to Model Act. In the meantime, important development in the sphere of cooperative legislative reforms has been enactment of parallel cooperative laws on the lines of Model Act with the sole purpose to provide complete freedom and autonomy to those cooperatives that do not take Government assistance and at the same time to retain the already existing cooperative laws. Eight States, Andhra Pradesh, Bihar, Jammu & Kashmir, Madhya Pradesh, Karnataka, Rajasthan, Orissa and Uttrakhand, have enacted parallel law.

In the year 2002, the Government of India brought out a comprehensive amendment of Multi Cooperative Societies Act with the twin objective of enabling cooperatives to promote economic and social betterment of their members and to ensure their democratic functioning as people's institutions to provide them functional autonomy and freedom of enterprise. Important changes in the 2002 law are as follows:-

(i)   Simplification of registration procedure by providing for deemed registration;

(ii)   Provision for deemed amendment of bye-laws;

(iii)   Provision for promotion of subsidiary organizations;

(iv)   Codification of duties and functions of federal cooperatives;

(v)   Conferment of affirmative duty upon cooperative for organizing cooperative education programmes for its members, directors and employees;

(vi)   Restriction on the Ministers to hold any position of office-bearers in cooperatives;

(vii)   Responsibility to hold election placed on the cooperative society itself;

(viii) Nomination of Central or State Government on the Board of Co-operative restricted to a minimum of one where the share of capital of the Government is less than 26 percent and to a maximum of 3 where the same is 51 per cent or more;

(ix)   Powers and functions of the Board and Chief Executive elaborated and clearly demarcated;

(x)   Investment of funds of cooperative in other cooperatives is allowed;

(xi)   The cooperative society vested with the power to appoint auditors to ensure timely conduct of audit.

(xii)   Provision for settlement of disputes by arbitrators introduced.

(xiii) The Government vested with the power to supersede the elected Board of Management only of the co-operatives having 50% or more share contribution by the Government. Basically Cooperatives societies are economic organisation to serve the economic interest of interest of common members with upliftment of their economic condition.

Miracles in Co-operative

The then Prime Minister Pandit Jawaharlal Neheru in a message said "I do not claim much knowledge of the co-operative movement in India but I definitely know that the movement has failed to evoke the necessary response. It may have produced some good results here and there but taken as whole its impact on the masses has been insignificant. What is the reason? The reason is that absolutely wrong and worthless methods were adopted in running this movement in India.

Let us study the methods adopted by other countries and follow the lead of those who have made cooperation a road to prosperity".

This was the view of the Premier after 50 years of Co-operative movement in India and Chamanlal a widely travelled having varied activites took the task of high-lighting the method and growth of the movement abroad in this book "Miracles of co-operation" published in the year 1957. He had travelled the world extensively and spent so many years meeting people of different lands. He was a person of varied activities. Sri Manoj Das, the international repute author in his book 'Smrutira Pradipa' has stated Chamanlal as the most respectable journalist of the era and the first person to introduce reward for working journalists.

He is the author of so many famous books which include the precious 'Hindu America.'

Regarding the success of the movement in Scandinavian countries the author remarks "It is true nothing man-made is perfect, but it is equally true that God only made the men and men alone by hard work and cooperation have created countries like Switzerland and Denmark, Norway, Sweden and Finland".

About agricultural cooperation in Denmark Chamanlal states - Ask a Danish farmer how many Co-operative associations he belongs to and he will stop his work, push his hat back and probably reply. "Well there's the diary and bacon factory". He will then wipe his brow and reflect for a moment before mentioning several move. There are, for instance, the cattle export society, the egg-export association, the feeding - stuffs society, the fertiliser society.

The three main groups of farm organisations in Denmark the Co-operatives, the farmer's union and small holders unions are all non-political. The farmer's Co-operatives are mainly concerned with economic activities. One group of Co- operatives is concerning with production and marketing. Another group consists of supply societies for feeding stuffs, fertilisers and other farm requisities.

Regarding the movement in Japan the Lal notes: The whole of Japan can be described as a family of eighty million Co-operators. The Co-operative system which was imported there form Germany found a fertile ground for its growth since the Japanese national character has co-operation as one of its strong pillars.

Realy ideal Co-operation practised in Japan. Japan's Co-operative system boasts a village where the Co-operative society controls the size of village population and the entire village income is pooled together and spent for common good.

Likely Switzerland is the best democracy not merely due to the presence of patriotic leaders in the Federal Parliament but mainly because of the rule of Co-operative in most villages which with their own initiative have made Switzerland a paradise of Co-operation. The prosperity of rural Switzerland is the result of land labour of ten thousand Co-operative societies which rule every department of rural life.

Germans the pioneer Co-operators, in connection with the social and economic success of the Co-operatives, mentionx must finally be made of their moral and educational value.

The first five year plan (1953-57) of China made tremendous change in its economic geography and the number of agricultural producers' Co-operatives crossed the million digit and the highest number of peasant living country solve the food crisis through Co-operative ladder.

The book shows the wonderful success of the movement abroad.

Regarding the failure of the movement in India the answer of Chamanlal is in three words only i.e. "WE LACK CHARACTER". These three words of Chamanlal 50 years back is also applicable to us even after celebrating 100 years of the Co-operative movement in the country.

"Never give up ! Failure and rejection are only the first step for succeeding."

– Jin Valvalo

Crisis on Co-operatives

Co-operatives in Orissa was established initialy in non-credit sector in the year 1898 by Utkal Gourva Madhusudan Das at Silver city Cuttack named as Cuttack Cooperative Store. This was followed by domain of rural credit to deal with the problems of exploitation of the Unprivileged farming community by money lenders. Latter or it spread and developped into peoples (Organisation) movement and have brought the weaker section into their organisational structure.

In pre-Independent era promotion and development of cooperatives were very slow but after Indendence the advent of planned economic development ushered in a new era for the cooperatives. It possess as a distinct sector of the national economy. Mohatma Gandhi, father of the nation rightly said, the development of down troden people lies with the successful implimentation of cooperative and Panchayat Raj. A successful strong & vibrant Cooperative movement requires:

1. Enlightend and informed membership. Though coverage of membership have increased up to mark. but active participation is very nominal.

2. Participation of borrowing members in election for the post of Directors in the committee of management

is very much required to vacate the domiance of vested Interest groups.

3. Regular conduct of General Body meeting which can banned autocratic management and will create apathy among the members towards management.
4. Infrastructure development for diversification of business with new out looks.
5. Immediate fixation of responsibility on the person (s) responsible for causing the cooperative non viable.
6. Proper training to the employees and Cooperators at their door step.
7. To change the mindset of exploytive bureaucratic interference.
8. Above all introduction of Information Technology in the Cooperative sector to provide better services and to make the facilities to its members about the latest plan and priveliges available for them.

But the Co-operatves of the day have been paralyised and it becomes puppet in the lands of vested interest groups. Other constrains for not achieving the success of co-operative movement inour state are Infrastructure development, lack of awareness among the (people) members, erosion of democratic content in management, tight bureaucratic preceivation, needless political interference, implementation and revision of policies like withdrawal of priviliges, disinvestment, debt relied etc.

Mounting of over dues, high level of Non performing asset, Imbalances of demand, collection, balance position amongest members vrs Primary Co-operatives and apex Co-operatives in each year, high cost of management above all lack of recycling of funds together with an inability to mobilise internal resources have made a large number of cooperatives sick and defunct.

It is a matter of great regret that non-credit sector of cooperatives like marketing sector, consumer sector and housing sector including long term credit sector like Co-operative agriculture Development bank previously known as land development Bank are now being failure, leaving only short term credit structure in to operation.

In the wake of structural changes and economic reforms the Co-operative sector have faced unprecedented changes and challanges. Co-operative credit sector have strived hard to sustain. We must have to convere challanges to oppertunities by adopting of innovative schemes and reforms. It is inoperative for the Co-operatives to keep pace with the changes and srestain challanges. Though Co-operatives is in crisis, but failed. There is no such alternative to Co-operative organisation whose foot prints are available in every knock and corner of the word.

"All the Buddhas of all the ages having telling you a very simple fact. Be-don't try to become. Within these two words, be and becoming your hole life is contained. Being is enlightenment. Becoming is ignorance".

– OSHO

Woman a Perennial Source

The role of woman in India today has been formed by traditions. The nature and role of women in the society is presented by great heterogeneity, divergence and multiple paradoxical appearing phenomena as India itself. In order to remedy these conflicts, women have to play an active role in the society.

While travelling through India, we will notice that we cannot erude ourselves from a spiritual omnipresence. The principle of 'being' forms this country far too much and play a crucial role at every level of human existence. In order to understand her role in modern times, one must look to the past. It is important to recall that the feminity is seen as a creative manifestation of the cosmic principle.

The devotion towards the superior and also toward the family and the willingness to sacrifice, forms the existence of women in India at all societal levels in all periods. Unfortunately today woman is discriminated at all levels. Surprisingly, Indian society considers women as an embodiment of love and kindness. She is also considered as creator and destroyer (as powerful). The same society which is patriarchal and subjects her to oppression and humiliation in political, social and economical aspects of life.

There is a need for women in modern India to be

aware of their strength and their potential. They have to oppose any thing that is meant for their suppression. In order to do this they must be educated and made eonomically independent. They have to assent themselves and must change the social frame work in order to stand up for the goal and values, which are important for them.

The turning point in India can only be achieved through active participation of women in national movements in which education must precede. Education and freedom, as well as its acceptance by the male side would arrange a new self confidence, a newly defined image. She can then no longer let herself be subordinated, but operates on equal weight with men in the society.

Man and woman are still trying to find their place in a society which balances between spiritual tradition and market based modernity. Woman is and will remain a source of strength and love. She always remains the embodiment of the values of Dharma.

"Learning is not attained by chance, It must be sought for with order and attained to with deligence."

– Abigail Adams

Co-operatives: Alignment to Agility

INTRODUCTION

In a rapidly changing environment, the professional competencies of the organisation needs a relook. Co-operatives being a dynamic organisation, must be alert to possibilities where others see problems, they see potentials. As observed by Mckinsey; "Co-operatives do well on alignment and motivation but need to improve their agility." In this context, the first striking factor is to train or retrain by upskilling the existing employees for an innovative mindset. It is well said that like people, don't get a second chance to make a good first impression. For such an eventuality, Benchmark against the competition is a key tool to keep your business fit to the contemporary market situations. In other words, co-operatives should be market–friendly to commensurate with the immotional expectation of its members and users as well. In consonance with the OKR (Objectives and Key Results), Management always has operative goals in terms of enhancement of delivery system for targeted business in the right time, in a right way and with the right price to the market segment. The multi-generational workforce must be ready with a focus on standards and customer satisfaction.

AGILITY : The Concept

The concept of agility has existed since the 1950s in the system theory of Organisations. The so called AGIL scheme was developed by Sociologist Talcott Persons on four functions that each system must fulfill in order to maintain its existence i.e.

1) Adaptation (Adjustment) : Ability to respond to changing external conditions.

2) Goal Attainment (Target Tracking) : Ability to define and pursue goals.

3) Integration (incorporation) : Ability to link the various elements of a system and ensure cohesion (inclusion)

4) Latency (Perpetuation) : Ability to maintain basic structures and Value Pattern.

The general connotation of agility is capability. People, teams, and entire organisation can have agility or agile – meaning that they can pro actively sense and respond to the change around them. For individual employees or managers agility involves anticipating what might happen, managing the unexpected, adapting to new situations. Agile organisations are good at fostering conditions that promote experimentation to determine what may work in an ambiguous situation. It often involves new products or services in front of real users earlier than later. Agility is the freedom and capability to 'act otherwise'. As defined by Martin, Andreas & Christrane; "Agility as the ongoing development and maintenance of decision-making capability under changing circumstances." Eventually, agility prepares for managing under uncertainty and overcoming the new normal. As reinforced by Mckinsey, 'Agile decision making requires effective performance management systems that surfaces issues quickly and enable corrective action'.

*Former Principal, IGICM (NCCT), Lucknow

DIFFERENT DIMENSION

The various dimensions of agility in an Organisation encompasses mostly the following features.

Technology : These are the various tools, techniques and methods that organisations can use to become more agile.

Organisational Design : This speaks about the workspace and the organisation that enables cross-functional creative and effective work.

Employees : Agility enables employees to work across functions using techniques, coaching, advance training and developmental paths. The hallmark of agile business is improved teamwork and staff effectiveness.

Leadership : It's about trust, empowering employees and giving decision-making power to the people with the best assessment of the situation.

Culture : It is a humane, trusting and respectable culture of conflict about the best solutions for everyone. Be everything you love.

Preparedness for Cooperatives : Key Points

- Agility in pursuing adjacent opportunities.
- Agility in developing and sourcing talent
- Becoming efficient and commercial to give customers the right product at the right price at the right time.
- Explore new sources of revenue, particularly in emerging markets.
- Emotional proximity to the customer's expectations
- Find out new ways to engage members and interact with them
- Remain close to your members, and never forget their needs
- Making Organisations more sustainable
- Be united on Strategic Goals

- Aim to use flexibility to deliver best-in-class service to their members at a competitive price.

A Point of Caution :

"Co-operatives shouldn't think that customers are going to come flocking to our door just because they have a different model of governance, because that won't happen." (Mckinsey on Cooperation).

Point to Ponder :
- Can Co-operatives renew and maintain their membership base in the light of shifting trends in ownership ?
- How can Co-operatives capture the growth opportunity in emerging markets ?
- Which advanced capabilities could Co-operatives turn into a strategic advantage ?
- How can Co-operatives anticipate shifts in consumer tastes ?
- How can Co-operatives better prepare members for regulatory change ?

ACTION PLAN :
- Clearly state your purpose and proposed deliverables.
- Include a SWOT (Strength, Weakness, Opportunities and Threats) analysis that will help you identify the appropriate opportunity for business.
- Leverage your public relations to get feedback
- Increase employee engagement by multitasking
- Innovating as a business culture
- Apply OKR (Objectivea snd key results) to measure outcomes in terms of "Corresponding Behaviour".

- Never stop learning from the rhythm of business training through Digital platform
- Accept the change and evlove with it together.

Learning Lessons : Be Resilient

Agility is an organisatin's ability to sense and respond to change quickly and confidently. Innovation is the creation, development and implementation of a new product, process or service with the aim of improving efficiency, effectiveness or competitive advantage. Agility and Innovations are inseparable twins with the goal of delivering differentiating and customer obssessed business outcome. Looking to the challenges of business due to post pandemic, Co-operative organisations should use this as an opportunity and going forward by considering the actions to increase agility and become more resilient in the future. It is well said by Anita Roddick:

"Speed, Agility and Responsiveness are the keys to future success".

"Kaizen", Japanese - Work Culture

"Our people are our most important asset" goes the saying. How many times have we heard or seen these words? They appear in most annual reports, they are heard at meetings around the globe and they are never far from the lips of the leaders of the world's most influential organizations. Any organization needs adequate finance, appropriate technology, achievable plans and it is work force. No plan, however sophisticated, can be achieved unless the staff understand and are committed to it. No amount of investment can deliver success unless the staff are the best people to do what you want them to do. No amount of bright shiny leading-edge technology operates effectively without a positive interface with human beings.

Thus any successful organization needs to respond and embrance change successfully and speedily in order to achieves its goals, it is vital to consider how to encurage the whole work force to learn to live and work comfortably in the fast changing world we now inhabit. To motivate staff, they were placed into teams with a good deal of autonomy about how they worked. They were apprised as a team, coached to improve performance and provided with skills training on an ongoing basis. With this vital human backdrop to concept that the Japanese Call "KAIZEN".

WHAT IS KAIZEN ?

Kaizen as it is practiced in Japan is a very simple concept which is formed from the two characters. KAI meaning change and ZEN meaning good. Thus, "Kaizen" literally means "Improvement".

"KAI" "ZEN"

Change + good =

Improvement

Kaizen become part of Japanese management theory in mid- 1980s and management consultants in the west quickly took up the term using it to embrance a wide range of management practices which were regarded as primarily Japanese and which tended to make Japanese companies strong in the areas of continual improvement rather than innovation.

Kaizen advocates a process-oriented approach. While the western philosophy is based on the result orinted thinking, the Kaizen philosophy emphasizes attention to processes rather than results. They concentrate the efforts of everyone in the organization on continually improving imperfection at every stage of the process. In the long term, the final results is more reliable of better quality, more advanced, more attractive to customers and cheaper. It means that if we take care of the process the result will come as a by-product and we need not be unduly concerned about the results.

TEAM BUILDING / GROUP WORK

Kaizen is mostly based on group work or working together with a spirit of cooperation and mutual complementation or in other words it is termed as working with synergic relationship. Organizations are sometimes unsure whether they have teams or simply groups of people working together. It is certainly true to say that any group of people who do not know they are a team cannot be one. To become a team the group of individuals need to have a strong common purpose and to work towards that purpose together rather than individually. They need also to believe that they will be achieve more by cooperating than working individually. Team work with synergic relationship can be described as that one and one can be more than two and it can be even eleven. On the other hand in terms of energy relationship one and one can at best be too or even zero depending upon wheather both are positive or one of them is negative.

The classic defination (from Bernard Babington Smith, training in small group) is "A group in which the individuals have a common aim and in which the jobs and skills of each member fit in with those of others as to take a very mechanical and static analogy in a Jigsaw Puzzle prices fit together without destoration and together produce an overall pattern".

This defination spells out that team members can complement each other and that a team can produce more than the some of individual components. A team constituting a group of people are bestowed with different capabilities, per se, some may be good as a ideators, some may be good as a critiques, some may be good as a evaluators and so on. An effecting team having differnent capabilities and if we group their strengths together we will achieve the result in a most efficient to way and is then ready to take on more challenging tasks if so required. In otherwords it can be said that ordinary people can achieve extra ordinary results. Thus the key factors for success of an organisation is how the management is perceived about team working. Team work and team building needs careful consideration for achieving better performance.

CORE VALUES OF KAIZEN PROGRAMME

Kizen programme is a step-by-step approach in direct contrast to the great leaps forward in innovation. Its core values are :

- Each individual should value and respect every other individual, not Just people in their own department, their own specialization, or their own level.
- Every individual should be able to openly admit any mistakes he/she made or any feelings that exit in his/ her Job and try to do a better Job the next time. Progress is impossible without the ability to admit mistakes.
- Kaizen culture goes without speaking that developing team spirit in organizations team leader plays an important role, A good team leader is the one who has all the qualities of a good team builder.

Kaizen team leaders recognize the primary of their human relationship skills over craft or technical skills. Their responsibilities as coach, counsellor, educator trainer motivator and team manager differentiate them from traditional supervisiors, who can be more responsive to and driven by quantitative outputs than the quality processes/ relationships and the working environment.

Further, a leader who is self-confident, confident in his or her team and capable of managing the team consensually should be able to delegate much command and control to the team itself, thus encouraging a self directed or a leaderless, team. This will enable the leader to develop their role as a boundary manager, managing by exception, and to plan the assignment of short and longterm roles to goals with regard to individuals competencies and needs. Japanese team leaders often say that the team leader's role is significantly different from that of the old-style supervisor because there is a much greater emphasis on developing and motivating the team, rather than performing specific work duties. Existing supervisors are not necessarily the best to become team leaders. Organizations which want to change their culture need to do much more than rename their supervisors as team leaders.

CONCLUSION

Kaizen tells us that only by being constantly aware and making hundreds of thousands of small improvements it is possible to achieve the desired result, Kaizen principles can be summarized through an old poem, which spells that it is generally the smallest things that cause the biggest disasters. It is merely always the straw that breaks the Camels' back rather than a heavy load.

"For the want of a nail, the shoes was lost
For the want of shoes, the horse was lost
For the want of a horse, the general was lost
For the want of a general, the army was lost
For the want of an army, the battle was lost
For the want of a battle, the war was lost
For the want of a war, the country was lost
And all for the sake of a nail".

This old poem reveals the truth that small is beautiful and according to Einstein. "If you are not failing, you are not trying". Thus Kaizen approach for creative organization is one which.

- is not afraid to act.
- responds flexibly and quickly.
- Accepts failures as part of the process.
- Challenges accepted "Wisdom".
- Is committed to learning.
- Communicates with markets and people.

- Develops and involves people.
- Celebrate success.

In the reform process, present day market oriented economy, Indian co-operatives have to face many a challenges. In the light of ever changing competitive business world   co-operative sector needs to group itself and make a vibrant one. This is full of challenges and calls for a developing work culture and environment within the organizations. It is an admitted fact that Indians are intelligent enough as individuals as compared to the people across the globe. However, it is discouraging that when they come together they fail to act with the spirit of natural cooperation and synergic relation. while thinking about the organization tomorrow, now it is high time to keep pace with the changing needs.

In fine, the Kaizen work culture as described above, would be considered seriously for bringing about a healthy work culture for the cause of success and development of the co-operatives in the wake of the new millennium.

"Business love nothing more than stability"
— **John Leo Weber**

Benefit of Co-operative Credit

Predominantly, India is an agricultural nation with huge reserves of cultivable land. At the time of independence, the country was suffering from severe food storage. Obviously, the first property of the Government was to increase the agricutural production by improving the farm production. The Government and the planners at that time had visualized the imprtance of Co-operatives was recognized as an instruments of socio economics development of rural India. According to Nobel Prize winner Amartya Sen "The progress of a Society and the economy of a country can never be judged by the wealth and leaving standard of the rich. In order to evaluate the economic prosperity of the country, we must take into account the standard of the leaving of the poorest of the poor.

Keeping it view Co-operative have remained the prime institutional agencies with vast network all over the country. Since the introduction of Co-operative movement in 1904 in India. Earuer money lenders were to dominate source of providing credit to farmers. The Co-operative credit institutions continued to play crucial in advancing of credit for agricultural and rural development in the last changing economic scenario and in the contest of liberalization and globalization.

In the present study an attempt is made to find out the benefit of co-operative credit in the central Co-operative Bank of Jaipur, the third Central Co-operative Bank (Koraput) of Odisha establish in 1914. The study is based on primary data collected from 300 borrowers covering 24 villages in Jaipore block of Jaipore. The simple borrowers obtained from the Central Co-operative Bank, Jaipore. In the research study data have been collected in printed question were from the borrowers. In the first phase out of total list 153 small and marginal farmers, 78 medium and large farmers, 39 businessman and traders and 30 transport operators were included.

BENEFIT ON INCOME

Generally poor people in rural area want to increase their income by means of different productive activities. So credit is essential to them. The most important objective of economy planning is to increase the percapita income of rural people. So there is an urgent need for directly benefitting the rural people with the target obtained rural financing programmes. The present section is intended to assert of borrower householders. The benefit of income due to credit are present in table No. I

The annual income increased by Rs. 5575/- in post loan period of small and marginal farmers due to the impact of credit. So there was 45% increase in annual income of small and marginal farmers which is very significant. The medium and large farmers also benefited from Co-operative credit. Their annual income increased by Rs. 9400 in post loan period compared to pre loan period.

There has been 45% increased in annual income of medium and large farmers. If all farmers are taken together the average annual income has increased by Rs. 7400 which is 45% more than the previous period. Businessman and traders have also benefited from Co-operative credit organization. The reanalysis revels that there is tremendous impact of Co-operative credit when pre loan and post loan annual income of farmers compared.

Co-oerative is one of the essential tools to be used in combating rural poverty aims to increase the productivity, income and food security at the rural poor by Co-operative credit. The credit Co-operatives are the most suitable forms at organization for the rural area. In a country of small and tiny farms Co-operatives are the most cost effective delivery system with a termendous outreach, until over a hundred ten years.

Liberalisation of Indian Economy

Economic reforms were initiated from the year 1991 and this helped India to achieve the high economic growth of 6.3 percent in the year 1994-95 and the growth during the year 1991-92 was only 0.8 percent. The inflation rate decline to less than 5 percent.

Foreign Investment in India will play a big role for economic transformation in India an efficient and honest administration is also another factor which would help for the economic transformation. Further there need not be any expansion in the size of bureaucracy.

The saving rate of India is 22 percent and this has to be increased so as to have enough funds for investment. To upgrade our technology foreign investment is a must in the process of liberalisation. Our industry can be integrated with the global economy. All the managerial resources can be transferred in one package.

Direct foreign investment need not be allowed when there is development in domestic capabilities and when they were not utilised to the maximum extent. Foreign investment in the field of consumer goods like motor car units, ice-cream parlours, soft drinks etc, cause will decline in country's resources since dividends and interest are to be paid. Instead we have to increase the rates of saving and investments. But this is not in line with today's concept of "Swadeshi".

There was much emphasis in economic self-reliance in Gandhiji's concept of "Swadeshi" and this is not consistant with today's concept of globalisatin and liberalisatin. The concept of "Swadeshi" instead that foreign goods should not be allowed inside the Indian markets. Under the present economic scenario, this strategy is not required.

The concept of "Swadeshi" is feasible in certain fields like consumer goods, indigenous goods, goods of SSI sector, cottage industries etc. Foreign investments can be made in few areas like infrastructure, telecommunications, roads, petro-chemicals power and other Hi-tech industries.

After liberalisation we have been facing an increase in scams and scandals. More than hundreds of crores of rupees are lost every time due to scams and scandals. The reasons for this might be the lack of a proper system of checkings in the economy and also there is erosion of country's money. This paves way to every wrong doer to escape without any punishment.

Therefore the system has to be refined by introducing built in check and balances. In coming years our country cannot lose money further due to scams and scandals.

Most industries and imports have been delicensed and due to economic liberalisation political morality has improved. Much emphasis should be given to the concepts of autonomy, accountability and transparency.

Private companies or public sectors have to inform the consumer about the cost, quality and other aspects of its products when the consumer insists. Thee is lack of accountability or commercial spirit especially in public sector. Therefore work culture has to be oriented towards accountability and transparency.

The Government has the aim to render more social service to the poor. When the Government increases expenditure on social services, the living condition of the poor would improve. The focus may be on the efficiency in rendering the services. For this, strategy of the Government has to be refined.

Accountability of the strategy/methodology to the beneficiaries has to be included in the system. A good and clean Government is very essential for the success of economic reforms.

People should be motivated to understand the importance of hardwork and patriotism. People should be taught about the skill to work for better living in the context of globalisation. They are to be oriented for sincerity and dedication to exam their livelihood. The government should also take efforts to utilise the people's talent suitably for the development of our country.

Report of Kapoor Committee

The Government of India had appointed a Committee under the Chairmanship of Jagdis Kappor, Dy. Governor, Reserve Bank of India on 09.04.99 to study the cooperative credit system and suggest measures for revival / restructuring of Cooperative Banks with the following terms of reference (TOR) (1.06).

(i)   To review the functioning of the Cooperative Credit Structure and suggest measures which would make them member-driven professional business enterprises.

(ii)   To study aspects relating to costs, spreads and effectiveness at various tiers of Co-operative Credit Structure and make suitable recommendations for their rationalization and improvement.

(iii)   To study the financial performance of the Coop. Bodies and make recommendations for improving their financial health so that they can become efficient and cost effective instruments for delivery of rural credit.

(iv)   To review the existing supervisory and regulatory mechanism for cooperative credit institutions and suggest measures for strengthening the arrangement.

All the Cooperative Credit Institutions have been eagerly awaiting the recommendations of the Committee as they were supposed to examine the recapitalisation issue. The financial recapitalization requirement for cleansing of Balance Sheets was examined by another Study Group under the chairmanship of Sri J.L.N. Srivastava in 1994 and estimated at Rs. 6600 crores for the ST Coop. Credit Structure to rectify imbalances (Rs. 2800 crore) and to wipe out the unprovided for bad debts and accumulated losses of DCCBs (Rs. 3800 crores). The ST credit structure under the leadership of NAFSCOB has been pressing the Union government to grant one-time assistance of Rs. 6600 crores by way of budgetary allocation. This expectation was justified as the Government had provided Rs. 22400 crores for recapitalization of Nationalized Banks and Regional. Rural Banks (RRBs).

Deliberating on the issue of recapitalisation of the Cooperative Banks and acknowledging the requirement of huge resources for infusion into the system, the Cappoor Committee raised the same problem of "ownership" and ruled out external assistance in shape of grant to the Coop. Banks. The Committee, instead, recommended a rehabilitation package for the ailing SCBS/ DCCBS and PACS with the observation that "viability of member PACS would largely determine the viability of the Central Coop. Banks at the District level in which PACS federate "(6.06).

The National Federation of State Coop.Banks (NAFSCOB) had convened a meeting of the member Banks during August 1999 to examine the recommendation of the Committee. After discussion on each of the points, in the interest of the Coop. Credit Structure, a consénsus was evolved to put forth the views before the competent authorities. The major recommendation of the Committee and the views are outlined below.

1. **Recapitalisation-**

Funding mechanism.One time external assistance to recapitalise the coop credit structure has beenruled out and, instead, a rehabilitation package has been worked out with the following funding mechanism.

ii) 20% should come from the members in shape of cash, after which the rehabilitation process to start.

iii) State Govt. is to contribute @ 40% in shape of bonds which will be extinguished after 3 years of moratorium @ 20% per annum in five equal instalments. The bonds will be issued notionally without involving cash flow to the system. Only interest will be available to the PACS to the adjusted against their dues to the DCCBs.

iv) Central Govt. is to contribute @ 40% in the manner as deserved in (ii) above (6.08 to 6.11).

v) Assistance in shape of Bonds (6.12).

vi) Extinction of bonds in five equal instalments @ 20% P.A. after three years of moratorium (6.12).

vii) Restriction, of the package only 'to potentially viable, units (6.06).

The entre financial assistance of ST structure should not come only from the owners. It is the responsibility of the Government of India to ensure strengthening of farming community as they alone are contributing to the agricultural production in the country. We express our apprehension with regard to the sharing pattern of the financial requirement, which is stated as 40:40:20 by Government of India, State Government in the form of loan and members contributions.

We suggest the sharing pattern as follows :

Government of India: 80 per cent

RBI/NABARD: 15 per cent

Entire Coop. Credit Structure: 5 per cent

This above suggestion is made keeping in view the realities such as the financial status of the State Government etc. and also the fact that it may not be possible to extend 100 per cent grant as a part of revitalization package. Funding through bonds proposed by the committee will not ensure cash flow to the system and therefore, it can not contribute to the viability of the Banks. Hence, the assistance from Govt. of India / Reserve Bank of India/NABARD should come in shape of outright grant.

2.   **Integration of ST and LT structure (3.28, 3.29, 3.30).**

3.   **Re-organization.**
i)   Organization of new societies in areas according to potential and amalgamation / liquidation of existing societies (2.12).
ii)   Amalgamation and liquidation DCCBs and PACS (3:26).

4.   **Duality of control**
i)   Supersession of Board of Directors should not vest with the State Govt. (2.16)
ii)   implementation of Model Coop. Societies Act. (2.19).
iii) Abolition of cadre scheme (2.28)
iv)   Diversification of Business up-to 10% of the deposits of Coo. Banks (2.39).

The recommendation of the committee appears to be paradoxical in as much as it has advocated for merger of Primary Card Banks with DCCB and State CARD Banks with the SCBS when it has explicitly acknowledged the fact that "No institution has a divine right to live if it is not adding any value to the system." If the weak LT structure is merged with the ST structure, both of them would sink together. The SCBS will have no objection, if the CARD Banks are allowed to do the normal banking business. The ST Coop. Structure will gladly accept the responsibility of dispensing investment credit in shape of Medium Term and Long Term Loans.

Reorganization of PACS to transform them, as viable units have been the main focus of recommendation of the all the committees and working groups appointed to study the Coop. Credit System. But, reorganization of primaries have not yet materialized largely due to lack of political will.

Although the Task Force has recommended to complete the reorganization process within a period of one year, it may not be practically possible.

The State Coop. Acts are to be amended suitably to do away with duality of control and to allow the Coop. Banks to be controlled exclusively by the provisions of Banking Regulation. Act.

The State Govt. control over functioning of Coop. Banks can be done away with only by amending the State Coop. Societies Acts to in

v)   Audit of the SCBs and DCCBS by the Firms of Chartered Accountants straight way and for the PACS in a phased manner (5.10 to 5.13).

vi) Nomination of professionals to the Board of Management of the Coop. Banks (2.28).

5.   Audit in Coop. Banks

Since the State Governments are maintaining a large number of staff for audit, Task Force is of the opinion that audit of PACS may be entrusted to the Chartered Accountants in a phased manner. As regards the SCBs/

SCARDBs and DCCBs / PCARDBS, the responsibility should be entrusted to the Chartered Accountants straightaway. (5.12)

6. Costs and margins

i) The PACS should decide on remunerative non-credit business of their own by utilizing the deposits mobilized by them.

Role of Micro Credit

After independence, the major initiative to address the issues of rural indebtedness and poverty was undertaken with appointment of All India Rural Credit Survey Committee in 1952. After conducting a nation wide study on rural indebtedness vis-à-vis role of the credit institutions, the Committee came up with far reaching recommendations. Acknowledging the potential role of cooperative credit organizations as catalysts, it lamented their failure in restricting the exploitation of rural people by moneylenders. The observation of the Committee was "Cooperation has failed in India but it must succeed".

The Committee's recommendations had resulted in innovative steps taken in the country to rebuild the cooperative organisations to come up to the expectations of the people and the economic planner of the country. On its recommendation, State Bank of India Act was enacted in 1955 to extend the banking facilities to the rural area. The process of restructuring of the Rural credit system did not stop there. In 1969, 14 major Commercial Banks were nationalized and in 1975 Regional Rural Banks were organized to provide credit support to the rural population to supplement the efforts of cooperatives.

A number of Committees have been appointed to address the same issue from All India Rural Credit Review

Committee (Venkatppaiah Committee) to Agriculture Rural Credit Review Committee (Khusro Committee) to undertake study of the rural credit system and role of institutional credit in ameliorating the suffering of the rural people. Poverty alleviation programmes from SFDA/MFA, SJSY programme. NABARD has taken over IRDP, ITDA etc. have culminated in to the role of the erstwhile Agriculture Credit Department (ACD) of the Reserve Bank of India. "Service Area Approach" of Commercial Banks have been experimented for grass root planning and the NABARD has prepared Potential Linked Credit Plans (PLP) to bridge the mismatch between credit requirement and flow of institutional credit in rural areas.

The Financial sector reforms, which were introduced in 1991, brought about significant changes in practices and procedures of credit institutions and they aimed at consolidating themselves to become organizationally strong, financially viable and operationally efficient units. The administered interest regime was replenished with liberalized interest rate structure in respect of loans and advances.

The Govt. of India resorted to recapitalisation of Nationalized Banks and Regional Rural Banks. Now the Kapoor Committee has come out with recommendations for revamping the Coop. Credit Institutions through a rehabilitation package. Kissan Credit Cards were launched to provide instant credit to the farmers. All these initiatives helped the Rural Financing Institutions to augment dispensation of credit to the rural areas to counter the age-old dominance of moneylenders.

According to the. All India Debt and Investment Survey, 1991-92, the share of debtbof formal Institutional Credit agencies accounted for only 64% and still 36% of the requirement was met by the money lenders.

It was a fact that, from the share of only 3% in 1954 and 30% in 1969, the achievement of the credit institutions in penetrating the rural areas and catering to the credit requirement to the extent of 64% was praiseworthy. But, the original objective to eliminate the moneylenders and the exorbitant interest rate of the informal credit delivery system could not be achieved. The failure was mainly attributed to the apathy of the Commercial Banks to lend in rural area, large scale over dues of Coop. Credit System, their under-capitalization, weakening of the Regional Rural Banks and the negative attitude of the formal credit delivery system towards the poorest of the poor.

Dynamics of Rural Economy Over the years, due to the initiatives taken by the Government, the rural economy of India has undergone a sea change in respect of production, consumption pattern and occupation of the rural people. Commercialization of agriculture and cultivation of cash crops has given rise to requirement of fertilizer and pesticides in the field. Irrigation has also assumed greater importance in rural area. The diversified activities and cultivation of multiple crops have provided adequate scope to the population to multiply their occupation.

The service sector has also assumed importance with opening of tea stalls, radio, television, cycle, two wheeler repairing shops. Integration of rural market with the urban market has facilitated mobility of labour, capital and products from rural areas still suffer from agonies which include, interalia, lack of road and transport facilities, health, education and access to institutional credit. Even in developed rural area, poorest of the poor are denied institutional credit for want of adequate collateral securities. Exploitation by moneylenders, therefore, continue to exist every where and specifically in tribal areas.

Despite pumping subsidy of thousands of crores of Rupees for poverty alleviation programmes over the years after independence, the desired results have not surfaced in rural economy. One of the major disquieting feature was non-participation and indifference of the target group to the programmes.

It is also a recognized fact that; the poorest of the poor could not get access to credit as the Commercial Banks and the Regional Rural Banks could not assess their actual credit requirement and the cooperatives could not help them on the ground that they did not own any land. Above all, the formal credit delivery system could not identify the economic activities those could be under-taken by the poorest of the poor on the assumption that, "as the basic needs of these people are not fulfilled, they can not mange any economic asset."

To appreciate the credit requirement of the poor, their participation in economic activities and for arrangement of need based informal credit for them, the role of informal micro-credit was thought of as an alternative strategy to address their problems. Organization of Self Help Groups (SHGs) as an experiment proved to be successful in Bangladesh by providing the rural poor the access to credit to improve their standard of living.

The NABARD has taken the lead to replicate the experiment in India through patronization of the strategy. The Reserve Bank of India came out with policy initiatives, which facilitated organization of large number of SHGs and they have been linked to the Commercial Banks, Regional Rural Banks and Cooperative Banks with and without NGOs as intermediaries. The West-Bengal State Cooperative Bank has also patronized the programme for which the District Central Coop. Banks (DCCBs) in West Bengal have coordinated organization and linking-of SHGs by their affiliated PACS with effect from 1996 in a large scale.

From 1904, after enactment of Coop. Societies Act by the then British Govt, The credit cooperatives have been dispensing institutionalized credit in rural areas. Organized on the principles of "Self Help" and "mutual help", the Coop. Credit institutions aim at participation of the members in decisionm making to ameliorate their own sufferings aim at participation of the members in decision making to ameliorate their own sufferings and to improve their standard of living. After independence, during last five decades, these organizations attracted the attention of the economic planners of the country as an indispensable infrastructure to bring about perceptible changes in the rural economy.

The role of the Co-operative Credit institutions and the procedures and practices have undergone changes over the years on the basis of recommendation of various study groups and committees appointed by Govt. of India and Reserve Bank of India. Despite conversion of Imperial Bank of India as State Bank of India (1955), nationalization of major Commercial Banks (1969, establishment f Regional Rural Banks (RRBs) in 1975, the Cooperative Credit Institutions continue to be the single largest purveyor of agricultural credit in the country.

The Short Term Coop. Credit Structure The short term Coop. Credit structure comprises 29 Apex State Coop. Banks at state level, 367 District Central Coop Banks (DCCBS) in the middle rung and 1,00,000 PACS at grass root level. The borrowing membership at the PACS level as on 31st March 1999 was around 440 lakhs with outstanding credit of Rs. 19,586 crores. Only 41 percent of the total membership have availed credit facilities. In Orissa, the number of borrowing member were only 6.67 lakhs as against the total membership of 39.48 lakh agricultural families in the state. It has also been observed that, although the cooperatives were organized and nurtured to take care of the credit requirement of the rural poor, due to procedural difficulties and security oriented lending, the poorest of the poor could not access the credit dispensed by these institutions. Despite being enrolled as members, the landless people could not avail credit from the cooperatives.

As observed by the Capoor Committee (2000), borrowing membership has direct correlation with the level of recovery performance. Unless the borrowing membership is increased by catering to the credit requirement of the enrolled membership, the problem of high level of over dues, imbalance and low level of operation can not be addressed. Financing through Self Help Groups (SHGs) is the best alternative strategy available to cater to the credit requirements of larger membership thereby increasing the level of business.

The Self Help Groups operate on the following principles which are also a part of the principles of cooperation;

i) Propagator of voluntarism.

ii) Practitioner of Cooperative Principles.

iii) Promoter of thrift and savings.

The co-operative philosophy believes in self help and mutual help to achieve common socioeconomic goal. The cooperative credit institutions were organised, to promote self help through participation in socio-economic activities including decision making. But, over the years, the PACS have become large both in geographical coverage and financial and other operations. The objective of increased size of operations aimed at economic viability and financial soundness but in this process, flexibility in operations, cohesiveness, mutual help and trust suffered a serious set back. The operations have also become bureaucratized for which the members do not treat the cooperative societies as their own organizations: The large geographical coverage has created the problems of lack of personal attention, harmony and homogeneity, resulting in lack of cohesiveness.

Although the members in cooperatives are equal in as much as they enjoy "one man one note", in practice, the small/marginal farmers and landless labourers hardly exercise their right and they generally get marginalised in the decision making process. Besides these, most of the landless labourers have remained out of the cooperative fold despite pursuing the principles of universal membership and regular drive for enrolment of new members. All these factors together have proved that PACS / LAMPS / FSS are too large for effective group activities with participation of all the members.

At this juncture, the SHG approach could be used successfully to revitalize the cooperatives and to make them vibrant and viable organizations to come to the expectation of their members. The possibilities, as outlined by Shri Y.Ç. Nanda, Managing Director, NABARD, could be:

i) Revival of thrift and adoption of an approach where credit follows savings and the two are related.

ii) Formation of small groups of 10 to 20 persons. The group could be of :

a) Non members;

b) Dormant Non-borrowing members;

c) Hamlet/Non-borrowing members;

d) Activity - wise.

"The approach has to be to bring the non-members

in to the membership of PACS and activisé the the passive / dormant members by organizing them in 'to groups either on hamlet basis, activity basis or on the basis of any common factor. The formation of groups could give the dormant / passive members a "voice" in the management of the PACS, make it easier for them to organize group activity and reduce / eliminate the necessity of approaching the PACS head quarters each time they have a transaction with the society.

The common thread in all types of groups could be thrift and flexibility, responsiveness and sensitivity in dealing with the individual members by the group. The group could be provided small dosages of assistance linked to the savings mobilized by them, which the group could use for on-lending / group activity on the terms and conditions mutually decided by the groups. The groups would have to be given the flexibility in deciding the terms and conditions for on lending".

The scenario in Orissa

The concept of SHG is not new in the state and also to the short term Coop. Credit structure. The Regional Office, NABARD, Bhubaneswar has been patronizing the SHG programme in all the Districts of Orissa. As on 31.03.2003, around 16,000 SHGs have been organized and 5830 have been linked to the DCCBs and PACS. Rs. 7.90 crores have been advanced to them. The only difference between the strategy adopted by the commercial banks and the RRBs and that of the cooperative banks is involvement of NGOs in organization and linking. In cases of CBs and RRBs, the NGOs are accepted in Orissa as on lending agencies to the groups. NABARD has advocated three patterns for linking Self Help Groups.

- Direct linkage
- Members - SHG-Bank
- Indirect linkage
- Member-SHG-NGO as facilitator Bank
- Member-SHG-NGO as facilitator and on lending agency of Bank.
- Organization of S.H.GS.

Organization S.T. credit structure in Orissa including the O.S.C.B, 17 DCCBs and 2817 PACS / LAMPS/FSS may emulate the experience of West Bengal to establish direct rapport with the SHGs instead of involving NGOs and fully depending on them. The elected Board of Directors, Secretaries of PACS and DCCB branch personnel are sensitized to organize new SHGs by accepting the. Participatory Rural Appraisal method. They may identify the groups on the basis of common economic status, homogeneity and common interest in selected villages. The group size is restricted to minimum 5 and maximum 20.

At the initial stage, the groups already organized by the NGOs are selected for linkage on a selective basis. In some cases, NGOs are working as facilitations only without involving them as financial intermediaries.

The Govt. of Orissa has already modified the provisions of Clause (a) of SubSection (1) of Section 16 of the Orissa Coop Societies Act, 1962 facilitating admission of Self Help Groups as nominal members of PACS /LAMPS (Copy of the Notification is in Annexure). There is no bar in admitting SHGS as nominal members of the DCCBs in the existing law. Only two models are accepted in the state to link SHGS with the PACS/LAMPS and DCCB Branches.

Model - 1 - Members - SHGS - PACS /LAMPS/ DCCBS in the Branches.

Model-II - Members - SHG- NGO as Facilitator - PACS/LAMPS/DCCB Branches.

The PACS / LAMPS are allowed toorganize/link SHGs only in those places, where there is a potential but the primaries are dormant / defunct, the DCCB branches are establishing direct link the SHGs.

Linking for credit support

At the initial stage, only selected PACS/LAMPS/FSS in good working condition are allowed to organize and link SHGs. The DCCBs are selecting the societies for the . purpose. The Branches are also organizing and linking SHGs in those places where the primaries are not in a position to link them for credit support.

The groups organized by NGOs are considered for linkage only after verifying the homogeneity, economic interest and cohesiveness of the group members. Only after six months of organization of the group and mobilization of savings, the groups are considered for credit support.

Conclusion:

At this critical juncture, when the clientele base of the cooperative banks are shying away from the PACS in view of the changing economic policy of the country and the innovative products being offered by the PSU banks and the Private Sector Banks, the reengineering process of the short term cooperative credit structure is largely dependant upon retaining the existing membership and attracting other non user members to come to the fold of cooperatives. The micro credit route is the only solution to enlarge the clientele base by providing avenues to the land less members to use the services and help increasing the turnover of the structure at large.

Farmers Sucide in India

There was nation wide much euphoria about reaching double digit (10%) economic growth in the just concluded Xth five-year plan. The agriculture sector remains as the bottleneck in the path. It shattered the dreams of our policy framers, economists. Our agricultural growth remains at 2.3% instead of much speculated 4% during the last five-year plan. The agricultural production trajectory was most unsustainable i.e. from the minimum 174.8million tons (2002-03) to a maximum of 213.2 million tons (2003-04).

Agriculture sector has a wide array of complex problems and it can be solved in an integrated, systematic manner. Seeing the dismal performance in the sector in the last 2 to 3 years, a number of schemes, packages, proactive approaches were taken by the National government to up lift the sector which remained beyond the LPG umbrella but having a mass of 70% of the Indian population.

The liberalized economic policy, adopted by the nation, during early 90s' failed to have a constructive impact on the rural Indian mass. According to Economic survey report, 2006-07, the contribution of agriculture sector to the GDP of the nation has reduced to 18.5% (2006-07) and it is in a decreasing path. In one side when the share of service, manufacturing, industry sector is increasing in GDP the share of agriculture and allied sector is decreasing. It shows the gradual alienment of rural mass from the mainstream of Indian economy and there lies a great disparity between the urbanites and the rural inhabitants. Taking the above means, the approach paper to the Xith plan states," the plan will aim at putting the economy on a sustainable growth path at a rate of approximately 10% by the end of its period". The agricultural growth rate target has been set at 4.1%.

TENTH PLAN & FARMERS SUICIDE:

Xth plan alerted our policy framers against the much talked wide spread farmers' suicide in the nation. It has left its footmarks in the highly productive northern states like Punjab to southern state of Kerala. A study says about 1 lakh farmers have seen the grim face of suicide after adoption of new economic policy. It may be a factor of assassination of human rights in a democratic nation that could not able to have a check on it. In this new paradigm, certainly, there have been a lot of changes seen in every sector starting from social to agricultural sector. The aspirations of a common farmer have changed. The cropping patterns have changed.

The cropping patterns have changed the unsustained agricultural growth and the dismal rate of agricultural growth is the matter of most concern now-a-days .The National Commission on farmers under the chairmanship of noted scientist, Prof. M.S. Swaminathan has pointed out the five point to check this sector from reverse sliding to avoid a precarious situation ahead. These strategies include a choice of livelihood option given to farmer according to its agro-ecological situation and market demand, soil health enhancement. Water conservation, quality and affordability of inputs, credit and insurance and market tie-up.

CURRENT STATUS OF COOPERATIVES IN INDIA-

Institutional back-up is a major support to I strengthen farmer's base. It has been practically observed in case of introduction of Panchayatiraj system 2.5 lakh of such institutions giving 32lakhs of people's representatives have much influence on the rural social and economic indicators. The subsequent amendments to involve socially downtrodden like SCs, STs and women have shown spectacular achievements in developing leadership amongthe rural mass.

Cooperative is like such an organization that has covered about 100% of rural areas providing basic amenities to the masses. Certainly, there has been a shortfall in achieve- ments. Lack of transparency, democracy as well as politicization of cooperatives has made them a losing soldier standing in favour of farmers. The performance of cooperatives in fertilizer, sugar, cotton, milk and even consumable goods in post-independence era is praise worthy, co- operatives are providing loans to farmers at their doorstep in every comer of India where commercial banks will take some decades more to reach.

They are the peoples' organizations that were established in the principle of for the people of the people and by the people. In the subsequent period, cooperative banks have not been given due importance, they were not modernized, latest technologies were not introduced, professionalism was not given due value human resource development was kept in dark corner, democratic principles were overruled by the subsequent state Governments and people without any banking knowledge were given the charge to rule. All this led to the current sorry state of cooperatives through out the nation.

CO-OPERATIVE CREDIT STRUCTURE FOR FARMERS.

Cooperatives have been demoralized getting step motherly attitude from the government for years. With its existing strength, it has continued its endeavor to help crores of Indian farmers. The farm credit package announced during June 2004 by the Hon,ble Finance Minister stipulated doubling the flow of institutional credit for agriculture in ensuing 3years. The performance of credit flow by cooperative banks t in the Xth five year plan years are mentioned below.

Year Credit	(Rs. In Crores)
2002-03	23,716
2003-04	26,959
2004-05	31,424
2005-06	39,404
2006-07 (till 31 Dec.06)	33,174

Source: (NABARD)

National Commission on farmers (2005-06) has also advised the government to provide institutional support in terms of insurance & credit. Till June 2006, a total of 642.49 lakh kissan credit cards are issued from all the banks to farmers to avail agricultural loans, out of which 319.6 lakh(49.75%) are delivered by the cooperative banks only. Compulsory insurance provision for short-term loanees in primary agricultural cooperative societies in a poor state like Orissa has been praiseworthy. From 2006-07 farmers are getting loans up to principal amount of Rs.3lakh at 7% rate of interest. Concessional rebate to cooperative banks at 2.5% per annum is provided by NABARD for this purpose.

National commission on farmers has strongly recommended for revival and strengthening of cooperative credit structure. It envisaged that state governments should implement Vaidyanathan committee recommendations. According to NABARD directives, cooperative banks are going to involve maximum number of all categories of farmers, share croppers, even old defaulters in its loaning policy providing KCCs which will act as an umbrella against any adverse events.

Conclusion :

In this globalized economy, the laxes in norms for all type of financing institutions have made the availability of loans easy. Divestment and dis investments of government shares have encouraged the business tycoons to give a comparable challenge to cooperatives in rural areas whose only objective is maximization of net profit of the organization. Cooperatives are the institutions that have a collective decision and concern for community principle as started by the character of a true cooperative as per Manchester convention of ICA, 1995. It helps crores of farmers living in rural areas, without any profit motivation. Perhaps it is the only peoples organization that could save the farming community from distress and support them to live.

Mainsteaming Gender

Women constitute half of India's one billion plus population but they continue to be victims of a world view that is predominantly parochial and medievalist. The knowledge revolution of the 21st century has not permited enough to dislodge this deeply entrenched world view. Unhealthy gender view for ages has restricted women from playing their rightful role in family, society and economy at large. This is evident from observations given below-

Women constitute half of the population gand do nearly 60% of the work but their earnings are one-sixtieth that of men and only own 1/100th of assets.

They constitute the large part of disguised unemployment and invisible work force.

They have a marginal role in household and family decision making processes. 10

A Sizeable number of Indian women do not have effective reproductive rights. Many of them even belong to the educated class.

Women's participation in work is basically in supplementary capacity such as part-time, casual, and piece-rated work.

Highest concentration of women work force found to be in informal and agriculture bas sector involving low-skill and drudgery.

Formal sector women participation is low and concentrated in sectors such as Care & Hospitality, primary education, etc.

In nutshell women are not the decision makers either in the sphere of work or family. Stereotypical views foster the belief that "women are incapable of making decisions no matter to what stage they belong, adolescent or adult hood. Since they are incapable, it is the holy responsibility of men folk in the house or workplace to make decision for them."

Women can draw comfort from the examples of Indira Gandhi or Shiela Dixit forgetting that they belong to a different genre of story. By and large our patriarchal society expects women to be docile, submissive, patient and pleasing to the world. These so called feminine traits" enhance work prospect in typical work setup such as care & hospitality. In a chauvinistic world, women like Kiran Bedi.

Tulasi Munda or Suman Jhodia are considered trouble mongers. Their iron-willed integrity anraw courage bites into the nerve of male-dominated decision making circuits .

Slow but steadily the scenario is changing. Mainstreaming gender has started gathering momentum since the fourth world conference on Women held in Beijing in 1995.

This historic conference in a sense has awakened developing countries to the realities of gender issues.

Gender issue relates to problems that Women and men experience as result of society's perception and expectation about feminine and masculine roles, rights and capacities. Women and men are BOXED into situations, which constrain their capacity TO DO and TO BE and hinder their potential to attain a full and satisfying life. (Sylvia H. Guerrero, Ph.D)

This is well recognized in the Beijing conference that empowerment of women is a critical factor in governance of nation, society and family. Beijing platform for action mandates the provision through Convention on the elimination of all forms of Discrimination against women to which India is a signatory. Article 14 of Indian constitution confers equal right opporturnity on men and women. Discriminaton on ground of sex is prohibited in Article 15. But the wide gap between de jure constitutional provision and de facto socio-economic status women continues to be a matter of serious Concern.

Gender bias is deep rooted in culture, custom, traditions and belief systems. It is not easy for women to free themselves as their world view is also shaped by the same environment or trapped in the same vicious mindset. Dowry menace would have vanished a long time ago but for the notorious involvement of women in many cases. As such, elimination of gender discrimination is not enough. It requires "positive Discrimination" to promote gender equity and justice. Article 15(3) empowers state to make "affirmative discrimination" in favour of women.

Interestingly in 1995 UNDP brought out its Human Development Report (HDR) entirely devoted to gender equality. In this report two composite indices were introduced for the first time to articulate gender concern at national and international level. These are Gender Related development Index (GDI) and Gender Empowerment Measures (GEM). HDR 2001 reveals some interesting facts. India's GDP per capita ranks higher than Human Development Index (HDI) and GDI.

However Asian neighbors such as Philippines, Thailand, China, Indonesia and Mongolia have higher GDI ranking than HDR. These are fast growing economies like India. Studies have shown that faster economic growth may not result in better Human Development. Economy may reach new heights but poor may remain as before. Mukesh Ambani, an Indian becoming the richest man of the world may cause cheer but it does not augur well with the fact that as a nation we also have the highest number of poor, highest number of infant mortality, highest number of illiterates and sizeable number of homeless, landless and jobless persons.

How economic growth is shared between rich and poor is a matter of great importance. It is also important to look at how benefits of economic growth and High human development are shared by men and women. International conventions and gender sensitive state policies may not bring overnight change in socially constructed gender perspective. But there is increasing awareness at state level that unless gender issues are addressed in right earnest it will continue to hinder human. social development and sustainable economic growth. What is gender mainstreaming?

It is a systematic integration of gender issues by way of reorganization, improvement and evaluation of political process to ensure that male-female equality is incorporated in all policies at all levels and at all stages normally by those involved in working out policies. (Rabea Naciri, EMHRN, Madrid)

* Institutionalization of gender concern requires a new perspective in managing human resources, new management procedures and inclusion in Budget and evaluations based on gender indicator and programming

led by outcomes. The concept of "Gender Budgeting" and "Gender auditing" has been gaining legitimacy in the India. "Gender budget initiatives analyses how governments raise and spend public money, with the aim of securing gender equality in decision-making about public resource allocation; and gender equality in the distribution of the impact of government budgets, both in their benefits and in their burdens. The impact of government budgets on the most disadvantaged groups of women is a focus of special attention."

The Annual Budget 2007-08 includes an outlay of Rs 8795 crores for 100% women- specific programmes and for schemes where at least 30% allocation is for women. Projects aimed solely at women may not necessarily promote equality. There is need to rethink male-female equality as a transverse axis 3 and not just sector based or specific axis.

Take the instance of a scheme under National Rural Employments Guarantee Act (NREGA) which intends to benefit rural poor and seasonally unemployed. There is no denying that women constitute a sizeable portion of rural poor. To ensure their participation requires sensitiveness towards their role as "triple burden bearer" as mother, wife and worker. NREGA scheme in our state rightly includes the provision that "In case the number of children below the age of six years accompanying the women working at any site are five or more, provisions shall be made to depute one of such women workers to look after such children and she shall be paid the wage rate." It depends on the gender sensitivity of implementing agency to materialize this noble aim. This kind of complementary facility would relieve the hardship of women worker; it will also ensure their better participation.

In contrast to this read following case "three women

in Citibank had miscarriage though none of them had family history of miscarriage. Of the 40 women interviewed, only one had heard that working on computers (VDU) continuously create health could problems including miscarriage.

None of the training sessions had mentioned this problem, though information on health and safety aspects of working with computer is widely available. Employees were ignorant of health hazards due to lack of access to information relevant to women, unwillingness of management to share it and the indifference of employees union to the issues of health & safety of women." There are numerous cases of indifferences. Natural reactions to such story is Let the women not work! This sarcastic view helps no one.

There have been a number of studies to prove that women's access to livelihood and landed assets empowers them in household. It also imparts benefit to children & family in terms of nutrition, health, and education. Above all, works give dignity. Historically Women's work was unrecognized, unpaid, under valued. Even National Sample Survey (NSSO) has failed to consider the economic contribution of rural women. As a result 90% of rural women labour force are termed as "Housewives", thereby excluding their contribution from productive domain. Given opportunity most women would like to work. Unfortunately, bound by family decision and social constraint, many women, particularly unmarried women, are confined to domestic arena. rampant in case of poor Women. Work is indispensable for subsistence of their fanmilies.

Gender mainstreaming is not just fostering beneficiary approach. It seeks to reverse historic injustice.

Think of agriculture operation,. 60% of Marital insecurity is more agriculture operation preparation, seed transplanting, harvesting, winnowing storage, preservation and minor processing done by women. But they are not allowed to

Take credit or farm loan
Take decision regarding farm work
Plough the land
Own agriculture land
Lease in and lease out decision
Buy farm input from market
Large-scale selling of farm output

The phenomenal micro-credit revolution has created vast scope for women to access credit, resources and Iivelihood. Successful approach to gender not only focuses on their vulnerability (domestic violence, sexual abuse, workplace harassment) but also on their capabilities-enhancing their role and agency.

This requires strong commitment on the of the part of the State to address gender gap in terms of- Legal entitlements Women's access to assets, resources and information Involvement and participation in decisiot-making process from household, village levelbinstitutions to state and national legislatiot. Because it is in decision-making forums ald policy-making bodies that women are grossy A change to under represented. As a result, policy Outcome is either gender neutral or blind.

The National Commission on Women reviewed 41 legislative Acts which require accommodate gender issues. force on Empowerment of Women. These Similarly Orissa Government has set up a Task positive steps are headed in the right direction.

NPA Management

(Securitisation and Reconstruction of Financial Assets & Security Interest Act. 2002)This is the usual practice of the Banks in granting loans and credit facilities against different types of securities. Though the banks reserve the right to exercise its legal remedial powers available with the bank for recovery by virtue of deed of hypothecation, deed of agreement and promissory notes etc., the banks never exercised this power without intervention of courts. As financing Bank, the Bank reserves the right to apply legal remedial measures for recovery of dues so financed, taking over of the financed assets securities etc. does not constitute any criminal offence by the bank officials.

As per our prevailing practice, the banks have never exercised this power for recovery of dues by virtues of the core legal power without intervention of the court as because the modus operandi of application / exercising this power is not available at the application point nor the supervisory machineries have ever insisted for its. It may be another factor that even after availability of all such powers the bankers do not like to exercise it perhaps due to non availability of such powers in any form of Act and no statutory locus - standing available to the bankers. The Hon'ble High Court of Krnatak in the case of Basalingaya Vs. Vyasa Bank has upheld that the bank has the right to do so even without intervention of Courts. There are also similar cases like AIR-1976 (Delhi-115) G. Hari Vs. PNB.

Now this enforcement of Securitisation and Reconstruction of Financial Assets & Security Interest Act 2002 which has come in to force with effect from 21st June 2002 is providing the statutory support to the Bankers to exercise the powers for recovery without intervention of the Court. The basic privilege and hidden philosophy provided behind this enactment is that under the prevailing practice system the bankers reserve the absolute right to ask for the money in form of sixty days notice in the manner as prescribed. On the event, any person if aggrieved has to go to the appropriate Court of Law i.e. DRT or High Court etc. to have a stay on the proceedings. According to the prevailing practice the notice of the banker is deemed to be the preliminary step for legal action and a proof of providing opportunity to the borrower for repayment in the process of arbitration.

Now under the new regulation the bankers notice has given with absolute weightage and the bankers book in respect of the dues is recognized as final unless there is objection from the borrowers side through an appropriate Court. Further under this new regulation the rights of the borrower to claim for the compensation and cost has been provided under Section 19 of the Act and therefore it is necessary for the Bankers to take precautionary measures for proper documentation, application of interest accurately and charging of cost reasonably besides the vital documentary precaution like obtaining balance confirmation to establish the liability against the borrower.

Further while giving importance to the security interest in respect of financial assets a very broad boundary has been provided and all types of financial assets including debts and receivable and assets under possession of the third parties are included. So while proceeding for taking possession of such financial assets like debts and receivable, the demand of the secured creditor is absolute and binding on the third party who is in possession of such assets. On the event of non-compliance / deviation by the third party, the penalties and punishments have been prescribed.

In case of Co-operative Banks, the state Co-operative Act. Provides the scope of Arbitration and Execution of awards in the court of the Registrar and for which the Co-operative Banks are enjoying a better scope to have the recovery through the process of law by a little effort.

Even though this scope through departmental courts are available for the Co-operative Banks, the new regulation "Security Interest Act 2002" is applicable for the Co-operative Banks as per notification dated 28th January 2003 of Ministry of Finance and Company Affairs (Banking Division), Govt. of India wherein the Central Government has specified "Co-operative Bank" as defined, in clause (cci) of section 5 of Banking Regulation Act, 1949 (10 of 1949) as "Bank" for the purpose of securitisation and Reconstruction of Financial Assets & Security Interest Act 2002 (54 of 2002). So this new regulation is a blessings to, all the Banking Sectors including Co-operative Banks.

After introduction of prudential norms for assets classification and provisioning for NPAs there was severe shock on the banking industries in maintaining the level of profit as earned earlier due to creation of heavy provisions. On the second stage the concept of CRAR again has been introduced to tune the capital base of the banks in accordance to the risk weighted assets. Thirdly to move towards international standard slowly without one go in maintaining the CRAR at least at 12% and in classifying the assets as per 90 days norms instead of 180 days norms as on 31.03.2004, it has been advised by the regulator to accordingly lay out the road map. All these stringent prudential norms that has been implemented within these few years being on to 2pin is a threat to the profitability of the banks.

Perhaps to minimize the level of NPA the idea for collection in NPA accounts through. OTS/ Compromise ventilates a negative message which tempts the regular borrowers to willfully default in repayment to avail the interest relief through OTS/ Compromise after the account getting bad.

So it will be prudent for the bankers to exercise the recovery process as provided in the new regulation instead of canvassing the borrowers of NPA accounts for the bankers to exercise the recovery process as provided in the new regulation instead of canvassing the borrowers of NPA accounts for close on OTS / Com- promise. Also it will be helpful for the banks to specify the accounts to be considered under OTS in special cases like.

a. Where there is no sufficient security.

b. The borrower is deceased the unit is not function/ sustaining loss for years together.

c. The book outstanding is small and interest amount to be written off is negligible and

d. Other similar types of reasonable reasons if any.

So that the negative attitude in repayment shall not develop with the regular borrowers. Components of Securitisation and Reconstruction of Financial Assets & Security Interest Act. 2002.

It permits the setting of securitisation. A reconstruction companies who can acquire the financial assets (NPAs) of mor Banks. Permits enforcement of securities by the 601 secured creditors without intervention of Court or Tribunal Rights of the secured creditors To take possession / management of the secured assets for transfer, by lease, assignment or sale for realising the........

To appoint any person to manage the secured assets.

Require any person who has acquired visive the secured asset and owes money to the borrower to pay such money directly to the secured creditor.

Who are in and who are out ?

Eligible Categories / Exempted Categories

* Borrowers *All public sector / state level enterprises * Guarantors rehabilitation / OTS is approved NPAs where NPAs where OTS is under process / negotiation and at lest 25% of the offer amount has been deposited been deposited by the borrower / guarantor. Cases where enforcement of security right is not deemed to be effective preconditions to be satisfied.

* The debt (Ledger Balance) must be Rs. 1.00 lakhs & above.
* The amount due must be more than Rabi 20% of the principal amount.
* The security to be enforced must not be agricultural land.
* The security to be enforced must not be under Bank's lien/pledge.
* The account must have been classified to tosas NPA.
* 60 days

Stages leading to realization of security under the Act. Identifying the targeted "accounts and 90002 assigning the recovery target to desinated Authorized officers Issue of notices Seizure of movable property Valuation of movable secured assets Sale of movable secured assets Issue of certificate of sale Taking possession of immovable property Valuation of immovable property Sale of immovable secured assets Delivery of possession Confirmation of sale

Now the option for exercising the powers under the new regulation for recovery is left with the Bankers and we can only say :- "Survival of the Fittest"

Co-operative Education

Cooperation is a movement and a system of life in which persons voluntarily associate themselves to work unitedly adhering to the principles of equity for promotion of their common economic interests and thereby, to liberate them from the exploitation by middlemen. It is a philosophy of life and a moral movement.

Mr. J.J. Worely in "A special philosophy of Cooperation" has said "Cooperative philosophy of a society" must rest on free universal association, democratical toly governed and conditioned by equity and personal liberty." The same thing has been told by many other eminent cooperators and learned persons about cooperation in different languages which in essence, means a movement innovating a system of life for achieving common economic interest in accordance with cooperative principles.

It will be a fallacy of truth to think that the aforesaid objective can be achieved by merely enacting legislations which of course may provide a momentum and direction to the movement. Since last hundred years several legislations right from the cooperative credit societies Act 1904, have been enacted.

So far state of Orissa is concerned, the last enactment on cooperation is the Orissa Cooperative Societies Act 1962 which regulates the activities of a cooperative society. It came into force w.e.f. 1.7.1965. Since then, several amendments to the said act have been brought out, the last being the O.C.S. (Amendment) Act 2002 with the presumption that such amendy ments in the legislation would provide a direction to the cooperative movement in the State for achieving success. But all such attempts proved that legislation alone can not make the cooperative movement a success unless there are put into practice with honesty and sincerity and devotion.

Another piece of legislation namely, "Orissa Self Help Co-operatives Act 2001 has been enacted innovating a cooperative free from any outside interference including the Govt., to be managed by, the members only. But legislation may only supplement to cause or means of success of the movement but it can not supplant such cause or means which essentially, is the promotion of cooperative education and training specifically, among the members, office bearers and employees of societies and the public in general. It's success very much depends upon the acceptability of the cooperative philosophy and ethics by the people.

And for that, it requires untiring effort to propagate cooperative education and training at every level. From the inception of the cooperative movement stress has been placed on promotion of cooperative does not become a reality and it can not be a vital force of self governance. Promotion of education is regarded as a basic principle of the cooperative movement and every society must contribute to promotion of equation not only financially but also by undertaking active programme like dissemination of ideas of cooperation and general literacy on cooperation in country side. The study Team on Cooperative Education 1961, the conference of the

Registrars and Ministers cooperation held at Bombay in 1965, the working group on cooperation.

Administrative Reform commission 1968 and All India, Rural Credit Review Committee 1969 and all others have placed emphasis in education and training as a necessary factor for success of the cooperative movement. On the basis of the report 1957 of the Law committee constituted by Govt. of India, the Orissa Co-operative Societies Act 1962 was enacted. Section 56 (3) of the said Act for the first time, provided for creation of a Cooperative Education Fund which was vested in and to be administered by the Orissa State Cooperative Union. It further provided that contribution of any made by the Government or any institution or society would be credited to that fund.

But section 56 (1) (b) of the act made it mandatory that every society shall out of net profit in any year, credit such portion to the fund as prescribed. In other words, a society was not under any obligation to contribute to the said fund' to it does not earn any net profit. In the course of time, it was found that most of the societies were either making negligible profit or no profit and contribution to the 'Fund' by a few profit earning societies was so meager that it became very difficult for the Union to discharge its obligation of promoting education and training and as a result, this aspect of the job got a setback.

With a view to strengthening the Cooperative Education Fund, section 56 of the Act was amended and a new section as section 56 A was inserted by the O.C.S (Amendment) Act 1983 making it mandatory that every society shall contribute to the 'Fund' annually a sum as the State Govt. may by notification specify or four percent of the net profit earned by it which is more.

Further, rule 45 of the O.C.S. Rules 1965 as amended

by the O.C.S. (Amendment) Rules 1997 providing that the amount specified by the Govt shall be paid by the societies within three months from the date of closer of the cooperative year. In other words, it was made compulsory for every society to contribute to the 'Fund' the sum as specified by the Govt. in the notification within the time stipulated by the statute not with standing the society has earned net profit or not. The said rule further constituted, a committee for administration of the 'Fund' and also prescribed a wide range of purposes for which the funds may be utilized.

The purposes as prescribed are - education of members, office bearers, employees of the societies in coopera-tive principle and practice development of new type of societies, improvement of cooperative societies, development of cooperative movement in general, cooperative publicity, publication of books and journals relating to cooperative movement, conduct of research, case studies and evolution in field of cooperative movement, and award of prizes for rendering meritorious service to the cause of cooperative movement in the state.

The rule also provides that the Auditor General of Cooperative Societies shall audit or caused to be audited the accounts of the Fund annually within a period of six months from the date of closer of each cooperative year and furnish the copies of the audit report to the committee aforesaid, the committee of the union, Registrar and the State Government.

The aforesaid amendments amply demonstrate the significance the legislature have attached to the promotion of cooperative education and training among officers, office bearers and employees of societies and the public as well for success of the cooperative movement. The message of the legislature is clear and loud that the cooperative Education fund has to be got strengthened and propagation of cooperative education has to be taken up seriously to attain the goal. Many cooperative societies do not contribute to the fund within the stipulated period of time and some are also reluctant or even do not contribute to the fund which indicates lack of proper appreciation of the legislative intent behind there provisions that promotion of cooperative education and training is highly essential to the success of the movement.

The Act or Rules does not provide any penal provision against the defaulting society. It also does not provide any mode for early recovery of the dues towards the fund from the defaulting societies except the state cooperative union going for a dispute case u/s for against such defaulting societies. It will really be unfortunate and fallacious as well in as much as when there is no dispute about the amount, which the state Govt. have fixed with the sanction of law.

The State Co-operative Union should raise a dispute case against a defaulting society and be pushed to undergo the lengthy and expensive process of litigation for adjudication and recovery of the said amount, only for the purpose of meeting the expenditure required to discharge a pious obligation of promoting cooperative education and training the union is saddled with, under the scheme of the Act & Rules. A provision should be made in the Act that in case a society fails to remit the sum as specified by the state Govt. u/s 56 (3) of the Act to the Union towards its contribution to the Cooperative Education Fund within the period of timebstipulated in rule 45 (1) of the O.C.S. Rules 1965, the said amount may outrightly be executed by an order of the Registrar of cooperative societies.

It goes without saying that unless the members of

the societies know or are enlightened about their rights, obligations and accountabilities and cooperative principles through education, training, seminars, publications of books and journals etc., success of cooperative will remain a wish only. And therefore all endevour has to be made to strengthen the cooperative education fund and to monitor proper utilization of the fund by the committee constituted in rule 45 of the Rules for the purposes prescribed in sub rule (3) of the aforesaid rules in due compliance of the legislative intent. A portion of the surplus fund of liquidated societies may also be credited to the said fund for application of the same to the cause of development of the cooperative movement as envisaged u/s 76 (d) of the Act.

Co-operative Education Fund

In section 56(1) (b) of the OCS Act 1962 which provides for crediting 4% of its net profit by a Co-operative Society to the Cooperative education fund has been amended by the Orissa Co-operative societies (amendment) Ordinance 2007 to the effect that the aforesaid provision shall not be applicable to a Co-operative Credit society.

The words "Co-operative credit Societies" as has been defined in section 2 of the Ordinance 2007 which means "The Orissa State Cooperative Bank, Central Co-operative Bank Primary Agricultural Credit Co-operative Societies Largesized Advise Multipurpose Co-operative Society, Service Co-operative Society and farmers, service Co-operative Society by whatever name they are called and registered under this Act" 2. In other words the aforesaid Co-operative Credit Societies henceforth, will not credit 4% at their respective net profit earned in a Co-operative year to the Co-operative Education Fund.

Here an attempt has been made to see the relevance of amending section 56(1) (b) of the Act excluding cooperative credit societies from the preview of the aforesaid section. At the out set it may be pointed out that the objectives of amending section 56(1)(b) by the ordinance 2007 could have been achieved merly by an order of the State Govt. under provision to section 56(3) of the Act which empowers Govt. to exempt a society or a class of societies from payment of contribution to the Co-operative Education Fund instead of undergoing troublesome exercise of the amendment and unnecessary burdening the Act.

Let it be as it may the amendments including the one section 56(1) (b) has been brought out by the ordinance 2007 on the basis of the Memorandam of Understanding in short (MOU) between the State Govt. and NABARD so as to make the Cooperative Credit Societies eligible to avail financial assistance of about Rs1080 crore or so under the financial package to revamp the deteriorated financial condition of cooperative credit societies in the state as well as to improve their working condition as per the recommendations in the report of the Task Force constituted by the Reserve Bank of India under the chairmanship of Shri Baidyanathan in 2004 to suggest an action plan for Rural Cooperative credit Institutions and as well as the legal measures required for facilitating the operation.

One of the eligibility conditions for getting the financial assistance under the aforesaid package as it appears in clause 9.10 of the M.O.U is that there shall be no compulsion on cooperative credit societies on contribution to funds other than those required for improving the networth/ own fund of societies. In other words the MOU in clause 9.10 means that contribution to funds may be made by a cooperative credit society if such contribution improves the net worth of the society. To be more clear and precise, clause 9.10 does not place any embargo against any mandatory contribution to funds by cooperative credit societies if such contribution contemplates or is intended to improving net worth of societies.

The word net worth has not been defined precisely

any where. It carries different meanings with reference to the context. The ordinary meaning of the word net worth is value in return of money to earn or yield. It also denotes the excess of book value of all assets over liabilities. With reference the context it also carries the meaning of quality, credibility, efficiency which is helpful in earning more. This the words "improve the net worth of societies" means not only in terms of money but also any thing which improves the quality efficiency of credibility of value of the society of value of the society and enables it to earn more and reduces expenditure.

Cooperation is a movement with an endeavour to establish a system of life for achieving common economic interest of persons who voluntarily associate them selves and function in a democratic manner for achieving the objects free of any exploitation by middlemen. In order to giving a direction to the movement in the above line several legislative measures were taken and are being taken from time to time on the basis of the reports of expert committees consisting of learned persons having rich experience in rural economy, the cooperatives are concerned with.

But those could not yield the desired results and Co-operative remained far from goal in fulfilling aspiration of the people particularly, the functional societies like marketing, consumer's, cold storage, processing societies etc. which were organized under the Co-operative Societies Act 1912 and onwards failed to achieve the objectives.

Some of them have disappeared and some are facing obliteration Co-operative Credit Societies have become feeble to carry with it the burden of meeting credit requirement of the rural masses of their own strength. One of the important factors of such failure as has been pointed out in different reports of the expert committees is that those who are associated with Co-operative have not conceived the philosophy of cooperation embodied in Co-operative principles in right perspective and could not develop the culture to accept the institution as their own.

As a matter of fact, from the very inception of the movement stress has been placed on dissemination and propagation of dale Co-operative education among the people and for proper training to the functionaries of Co-operative for success of the movement. Rock Pioneers suggested that cooperatives should set aside a part of their surplus fund for education.

The International observe that all Co-operative societies should make provision for education of their members office bearers employees and general public so as to realize the cooperative philosophy and principles and to put those into practice in real sense to achieve the common economic interests free from any outside or inside exploitation. Saraiya committee in their report "Co-operative planning committee 1951" also placed much emphasis on imparting training as an essential factor for success of the movement so also the report of the committee.

All India Rural Credit survey 1951-52 constituted by Reserve Bank of India consisting of eminent persons Shri A.D. Gorwala (Chairman) Prof D.R. Gadgil Shri Venkatappia and Shri N.S.R. Sastri (Member secretary) placed much significance on training to the Co-operative functionaries and observed it highly essential for improving efficiency of the employees and profitable management of institutions. The Committee observed that revamping of rural credit structure alone would not bring success to the movement. Integrated development of cooperatives as a whole is necessary for achieving fruitful results. Mirdha committee in their report 1956 observed that the strength of the movement depends on existence of a vast enlightened membership and that without promotion of education and training enlightened membership does not become a reality and it can not be a vital force of self governance.

Propaganda of education is one of the basic coop principles and essential for functioning of cooperative successfully and that every society must contribute to the promotion of education and training not only financially but also by undertaking active programme like dissemination of ideas of cooperatives and general literacy on cooperation in countryside.

The study team on cooperative education 1961, the conference of Registrar and ministers held at Bombay 1965 the working group on cooperation, the Administrative commission reform 1968 The Ardhanariswaran committee report for Democratization and professionalisation management in of cooperatives and many other have placed emphasis in education training and expertise manpower for achieving integrated success in cooperatives expertise man power provides good governance which helps in getting more return and improving return of societies.

The Orissa State Cooperative Union was organized in the year 1948 as spokesman of the Cooperative movement in Orissa with the main object to impart cooperative training and education to employees office bearers and numbers to establish and manage training classes in cooperation and allied subjects connected with rural development for officials and non officials to function focusing centres for non official opinion in Cooperation to hold seminars and study circles, to promote field studies and and abresearches connected with cooperation and to take up ;the common cause of cooperatives related to the above matters.

As a matter of fact the purpose of spreading cooperative education a statutory status was assigned to a fund called as "Cooperative Development Fund" in the Orissa Cooperative societies ACT 1951 (the first cooperative statute for the state of Orissa) Rule 67(1) (a) (b) of the O.C.S. Rules 1953 framed under the said Act provided as follows:- "Rule 67 contribution made by a society under section 45 of the Act for any Cooperative of public purposes shall be credited to a fund to be called" The cooperative Development Fund" Such fund may be utilized for the following purposes :-

a) The education of numbers of Cooperative societies in cooperative principles and practices.

b) The propagation of cooperation through conferences publication of magazines pamphlets etc of any other suitable methods or the task of Propaganda of Cooperative education and training functionaries was entrusted cooperative Union which is a non trading society established for the common cause of the Cooperative societies and it depended upon subscriptions contribution from other societies to discharge the aforesaid task. In the Directorate of Registrar a separate wing was functioning as education and propaganda for the above purpose.

On the basis of the recommendation of the Law committee Report 1957, the Orissa cooperative societies Act 1962 was enacted replacing the O.C.S. Act. 1951 and in section 56 of the Act-62 provision was made for a fund called as Co-operative education fund to be appropriated for propagation of Co-operative education and training to cooperative functionaries about the new technology and methods of administration and management which was thought as an essential factor for efficient working and improving net worth of societies contribution by societies and the above fund our of their net profit was made compulsory under section 56 of the ACT-1962 read with rule 45 of the OCS Rules 1965 but it was conditioned with distribution of devident to the members.

As such the amount of contribution by societies to the Fund was very negligible. Gradudly, it became increasingly difficult on the part of the Union to meet the expenditure required for maintenance of the infrastructure at Gopalpur-on-sea, Baripada, Koraput and Bargarh and to sustain the training activities out of the Cooperative Education Fund, Govt. Grants were also slashed.

Considering the significance of the Coop. Education fund and its role in improving the net worth of societies it was made mandatory by a legislative measure measure for every cooperative society (except those exempted by Govt.) to contribute to the Fund 4% of its net profit or the amount as specified by Govt. which ever was more by amending the Act. in 1983. Again in order to ensure proper administration of the Fund a statutory committee was provided under role 45(2) The objects for which the fund shall be utilized were well defired in rule 45(3) and as well as statutory arrangement were made for timely audit of the fund by the Auditor General of coop. Societies.

Above statutory provisions demonstrate the significance attached to the training of cooperative personnel and propaganda of cooperative education undertaken by the Union as an important weapon to improve the networth of the societies specially, in the era of liberal economy where keen competition is faced for achieve the target. In this back ground the relevance of the cooperative Education Fund in improving the net worth of societies increased many fold and It would be merely a misnomer and fallacy of the truth to suggest that contribution by societies to the Cooperative education fund does not improve net worth of societies.

It was experienced that it was not practicable on the part of each society some of which including the Cooperative credit Societies are very small to have an infrastructure of its own and to undertake the task of propaganda in cooperative education training to their own employees, office bearers and members with their meagre income.

There fore as told earlier this task was centralized and entrusted to the state cooperative Union which has been established by Co-operative societies for the primary purpose of imparting training and propaganda of Co-operative education the common causal of societies including the Cooperative credit societies. It has infrastructure for imparting training at grass root level trough their training centre in the state in respect of the new methods and technology as and when warranted under the reports of the expert committees like the present one the task force for achieving result.

The MOU between the state Govt. and NABARD at clause 9.10 does not prohibits compulsory contribution of funds which the amendment to section amendment improves of in other words helps to improve the networth of societies as it appears, this has not been taken in right prospective while effecting section 56(1)(b).

The brought out keeping the cooperative Credit societies out of preview of the section 56(1) (b) will undoubtedly create paucity of funds required by the Union to I discharge its statutory obligation of propagation of cooperative education research work case studies apart from training to personnel which I will be a great setback to the cooperative movement.

Even if the M.O.U meant Co-operative credit societies not to contribute to the Cooperative Education Fund it has to be persuaded to see the reason and to reconsider the same in as much as spreading cooperative education and philosophy among the people and proper training of Co-operative personel are the life line to the success of the Co-operative movement. That apart revamping of cooperative Credit societies in isolation of other non credit Cooperative societies will be a be a counter productive unless attempt is made for integrated development of cooperatives irrespective of the class they belong to .

In the draft model Co-operative societies Act. drafted by the planning Commission provision has also been made for contribution up to 3% of the net profit to the cooperative Education fund with the Union and up to 5% for any purpose connected with the development of the cooperative movement.

In the background discussed in proceeding pares contribution to cooperative Education Fund by Coop. Credit societies for improving net worth of societies has more relevance. It should be rethought by all concerned and position of section 56(1) (b) of the Act ante to the amendment by the said Ordinance 2007, should be restored which will be a great great service to the Cooperative movement.

Deprived Children-
A New Horizon

Dedicated and enlightened membership is the essential requirement for success of Co-operative Movement. But the Indian Co-operative movement lacks much in this respect .Co-operative Societies are usually sponsored by the Govt. and without understanding the basic principles of Cooperation.

People come up for membership and take leaderships. Of course it is not required that the members should know all the principles of Co-operation, but one thing they should have i.e. desire to co-operate amongst one another, the sub structure upon which the other principles such as democratic management etc. can be developed. Leadership has also to play a very important part in leading fellow Cooperators. So the leader of a Co- operative should be transparent, committed and socially conscious person of high moral standard having no bias as this is a socio-economic moral movement.

So in order to prepare sincere, responsible and committed Co-operators, for the suture, Co-operative attitude should be developed in the mind of the youngsters from the very beginning. It will be very easy to show the seeds of cooperation in the mind of the children as they are fresh and inquisitive. This will also help them in becoming better and socially conscious citizens in future.

The Problem-As per International Labour Organization (ILO) "a total of 152 million children- 64 million girls and 88 million boys - are in child labour globally, accounting for almost one in ten of all children worldwide.1 Nearly half of all those in child labour-73 million children in absolute terms- are in hazardous work that directly endangers their health, safety and moral development.

The agricultural sector accounts for 71 per cent of all those in child labour and for 108 million children in absolute terms, representing the sector with the largest share of child labour. Most of them have not gone to schools and live in unhygienic condition and suffer from malnutrition. The ILO has further viewed that the solution lies in an integrated approach to dealing with different root causes of child labour.

Co-operatives are naturally well placed to directly influence these root causes, because they combine a social and economic mission to meet their members' needs. We see those children performing strenuous works in tea shops, cycle shops, engineering works and many other places. These poor children are exploited in many ways. The child labourers are offered low wages and asked to work for longer hours at an age in which they require care and facilities for their mental and physical development.

We also know that about sixty percent of boys and girls drop out of school even before completing high School education. In most of the cases the reason is economic and utter poverty compel them to drop out of school, to help parents in field, traditional occupations or seek even hazardous employment in urban places.

So if these children can be engaged in a Co-operative

way of production in low cost projects, they can supplement their family income and keep their study continuing. In some cases this may also help them for self employment in future.

Younger persons within School/College going age who are now have resorted to beggary can be rehabilitated in this way. Minor boys and girls who have now are going to other States or hazardous sector inside the State can also be rehabilitated in this way. The problem has been further magnified in the Post COVID era.

Here the question comes what kind of co-operation can way be organized for the children? How such societies will be managed? Can such societies be economically viable? Can the existing legal provisions permit for organization of such Co- operatives? Whether the present Labor Laws permit for engagement of these deprived children as Apprentices? In brief we are going to discuss about formation of Co-operatives for children within the age group of seven to fifteen with these objectives.

a) To inculcate the spirit of cooperation in the minds of young boys and girls.

b) To help the children in earning some money while continuing their study by working in spare time.

c) To engage the children who are now working as child labourers, in a Co-operative way of production and simultaneously imparting them education and looking after their overall development.

As per Rule 16 of the Orissa Co-operative Societies Act only an individual competent to enter into contract under Indian Contract Act can become a member of a Co-operative Societies. The relevant section of this Indian Contract Act denies minors to enter into any contract. But a special provision has been made under this rule which permits students of a recognized educational institution to form Co- operative Societies for their benefit.

But keeping with this special provision of the Act, in very few Schools (a good number of Colleges have Co-op. Consumer Stores) only Co-operative Consumer Stores have been organized to supply essential commodities and study materials to students but no other kind of society has been organized.

The performance of these student Co-operative Consumer Stores need a detailed study. Even though there is no legal bar to form any other kind of Society for the benefit of minor students of an educational institution no attempt has been made of scheme has been formulated for organizing any other kind of society. Under the present legal position discussed above Co-operatives for minors outside the School cannot be organized. So to form such Co-operatives a further relaxation in the O.C.S. Act is necessary.

The labour law may not stand on the way of forming such Co-operatives for the deprived children as this move for organizing the child labourers who are victims of poverty in a Co-operative way of production and simultaneously imparting them education will not exploit but emancipate them. Moreover they will work in these Co-operatives as apprentices which may also help them for self employment in future.

Management :

Doubts may be expressed regarding the ability of the young boys and girls in managing a Co-operative Society. To some extent this is true. But no sweeping remark should be given on this. In High Schools we see with help form the teachers the minor boys and girls manage cultural functions successfully. No study of course till now has been made what extent the students are participating in the management of School-Co-operative Consumer Stores. Boys in some tea shops and pan shops also keep accounts and perform the other duties with responsibility.

For a better and efficient management guardians and teachers should be given place in the Managing Committee of Cooperatives in Schools. Similarly in the managing committee of Cooperatives outside Schools parents, social workers and teachers of nearby schools should be retained as Directors. The aims of retaining these people in the management is to guide the young people in the right path.

Types of Projects -

Broadly the Cooperative Societies for children can be classified in two kinds, (a) Economic cum Educative (b) Educative. Besides Co-operative Consumer Store, following projects can be taken up by children which can pay them economic benefit. In these Cooperative Societies they may Earn While Learn like Apprentices.

a) Thrift activities only with a Bank approved under Banking Regulation Act

b) Bee-keeping (Loans should be given for purchasing materials)

c) Knitting (for girls), Pickle production

d) Gardening

e) Dairy,Poultry

f) Pisciculture, Dry Fish processing

g) Handicraft and traditional Cottage Industries.

h) Domestic Processing and Storage activities

i) Horticultural Crop Production and Marketing

j) Floriculture

k) Organic Manure production

l) Mulberry

m) Pottery and other activities related to earth
n) Cow dung Products
o) Vending and Doorstep Marketing
p) Tourist Guide Other Co-operatives which will have only educative aim may not pay any material advantage but will mainly inculcate the spirit of Co-operation, mutual help and adjustment can also be organizedbin some sectors as mentioned below. Following projects can be taken up under this Scheme.

+ Philately
+ Gardening
+ Sanitation
+ First aid
+ Library
+ Debating and literary works.
+ Other cultural functions.

The items are only indicative. These societies can be registered as single purpose or multipurpose societies. The Schemes discussed in (A) are no doubt economically viable and management cost of such Societies shall be much less as they will be managed by teachers and parents on voluntary basic. This will create an atmosphere where the Children will learn the supreme co-operative principle each for all and all for each.

Sources of Capital :

Members Savings under Strict Supervision : These Societies can raise capital from its members and simultaneously encourage the habit of saving. We see that the small saving campaign is running with good success in schools.

Loan : The projects discussed above are low cost

projects so giving such small loan to children will not be risky and financing institutions should finance these projects by taking the parents as security.

Grants in Aid : In relevant cases Government should give aid to these Societies, wherever necessary aid in kinds should be given. The Co-operatives doing sanitation and first aid works can be supplied with the required materials by Blocks and Health Centers. Gardening and pisciculture societies can be given demonstration facility by Agriculture / Fisheries Department. These Children can be tagged to existing Women Self Help Groups (WSHGS) who are engaged in this sector under "Mission Shakti" initiative of Government of Odisha.

For developing Co-operative attitude among the children a State level organization in the line of "Boys Scouts" can be organized for coordinating the programme throughout the state and to decide policy matters. The Children Welfare Board may also have a corner for these activities. Issues for Discussion-However the points of consideration can broadly be classified into four sections:-

Analysis of the abject poverty and the condition of Indian Children in different professions along with their food and living condition. The Economic necessity being organizing coops for children to improve their Socio Economic Moral Standard and so also prepare socially conscious and committed leadership for co-operative movement.

The Economics of such societies.

The problem of Management and legal construction in organizing such societies.

Co-operative in Tamilnadu

The meaning of co-operation has got wider sense of its application in our practical life. If there will be no co-operative Administration or Institutions still the concept of co-operation will be existed and we must have to feel its existence in our day to day life. Co-operation is a nature of an human being, without which he cannot live in a society. The peoples of Tamilnadu as well as the Government has been selecting the path of co-operation as the instrument of progress and prosperity and they determined that co-operation is the only way for the success of economic and social development of their state.

I got an opportunity to acquire some knowledge regarding the function of co-operatives in Tamilnadu during my fourteen days long study tour in Tamilnadu state as a trainee of XV Session of H.D.C.M. along with my colleagues under the Institute of co-operative management, Bhubaneswar.

Tamilnadu is a land of temples along with rich heritage and ancient culture and full of religious activities. The people have accepted the co-operative movement in their heart and soul.Where ever we visited we could find the presenceof a co-operative society dealing with multipurpose activities according to the day to day need of the people.

We visited a primary co-operative Agricultural Society (PACS) at Madurai in Tamilnadu, the Primary Society is designated as Primary. Agricultural co-operative Bank (PACB) instead of society. The PACBS are dealing with the business of public distribution system. They are providing Rice, Sugar, Wheat, Kerosene, Salt, Maida, Suji, Tea and even detergents and medicine as well as S.T., M.T. loan to its members and simultaneously working as Mini Banks to transact Banking business. Civil supply and consumer welfare department has got no role in the state when each primary co-operative society is holding Kerosene volts, issuing Ration cards and operating fair price shops in each villages and Gram Panchayats. About 25000 PDS centers are operating in Tamilnadu under the control of PACBs.

Every PACBS are seems to be market complex or the center of economic activities where every essential commodities are readily available. So the people think that, the co-operative society is their Government and the services rendered by the societies are so systematic and transparent & time bound that any question of curruption or misutilisation does not arise and the peoples do not bother whether the management is political or non-political.

Throughout Tamilnadu each and every society from Apex to Primaries all are managed by nominated official management where the co-operative principle is violated for absence of elected democratic management. Election has not been conducted since 7 to 10 years in the co-operative institutions.

When I asked the Secretary of the society regarding the cause he responded state forwardly that, election provision is a loss item for the progress of co-operatives if the elected management will be formed more political and unlawful activities, more political interference, corruption and misutilisation will be taken place in the service sector which the peoples do not like and so also government do not desire when all the co-operative institutions are incurring profit.

There may be some political ground for non-conducting elections by the State Govt. but in reality we do not want to put more burden on the co-operative institutions as stated by a departmental officer as his personal opinion. We visited one snake catcher co-operative society at Chennai which is a rare thing I could observe in my life. The society has been registered society and obtained permission from the under the category of industrial co-operative concerned departments to catch poisonous snakes to procure poisons for preparation of snake bite injections.

Secretary of the society described before us that, the Society purchases four kinds polsons shakes from the licence holding snake catchers in exchange of Rs.1000/- to Rs. 1200 per each snake. After procuring poisons four times from a partiuclar snake the reptiles will be left out. In the reserve forest without causing any damage to its body. The cost of the poison is Rs.10,000/- to Rs 30,000/- for one gram which are exporting to other states and foreign countries for preparation at snake bite injection and medicine. This seems to be very wonderful thing that such type of co-operative society is existing in Tamilnadu which has got a great significance in the global market.

We visited the Tamilnadu Apex Handloom weavers co-operative Society at Chennai which is an eye witness of progressive co-operative movement in Tamilnadu. The Apex society has got 205 show rooms in allover India. The share capital of the society is 25 crores and Government share capital is 24 crores its annual turnover business is 300 to 350 crores about five thousands weavers societies are its member. A magnificient market complex is functioning inside the boundary of the society where about four hundreds stall sare operating. But management is a nominated official body headed by an 1.A.S. officer. The Apex Society as well as the Government is very conscious towards the payment of dues to the weavers in time. Due to proper management and guidance and modern out look and concentrated approach the society never incure any loss.

We visited the state co-operative Bank of Tamilnadu which is the biggest investor of agricultural credit sector of the state and a model of progressive co-operative credit movement of the state. 80% the people of Tamilnadu depends upon the co-operative Bank for their livelihood and existence as well as sustainable financial and social improvement. It is providing ATM facilities at all its Branches and providing higher interests on deposits to the people in comparison to other Banks.

We visited the state co-operative union which is started functioning in the year 1914 the guardian of the co-operating institutions in Tamilnadu. The Union is managed by an Add Registrar of co-operative societies as to special officer. The union is publishing three journals in both Tamil and English languages in order to propagate the ideals of co-operative movement in the state. There are 20 Institutes of co-operative management, three co-operative industrial Training Institutes, one co-operative polytechnic college having the subject of computer Engineering Mechanical Engineering. Electrical & Electronic Engineering are functioning under the control of Co-operative Union.

We visited the Central Co-operative Bank which has got 10 lakhs customers having 63 branches and a deposits of 1100 crores. The working capital of DCCB's is 1600 crores and its net profit is 47 to 50 crores in each year.

We visited the Madurai Co-operative Printing Press at Madurai which has been started functioning in the year 1951. It is supplying Books, statutory and other forms, and stationeries to the co-operative institutions, Government departments local bodies and to all Govt. undertakings. The co-operative printing works ltd. is incurring net profit of Rs.5 to Rs.6 lakhs in each year on its annual sales, turnover of 70 to 75 lakhs. The management is controlled by a special officer in the rank of A.R.C.S. designated as co-operative sub-registrar in Tamilnadu.

The Registrar of co-operative societies is the most powerful authority and dignified person of the state. All departments are co-ordinating him for the cause of social & economical development of the state. The office of the R.C.S is a big set up like a Mini Secretariat. Four Additional Registrars, Four joint Registrars, Nine Deputy Registrars, three co-operative sub-registrars (ARCS) Four Sr. Inspectors, Four Jr. Inspectors, one Chief Engineer, One deputy Labour Commissioner, One Executive Engineer, one Financial Advisor and Chief Accounts officer, One Asst. Engineer and under them about three hundreds employees of different categories working in the office of R.C.S. All constructions works in co-operative institutions of the state are executed under the direct control and supervision of R.C.S. and all labour disputes are disposed off by the labour department attached to the office of the R.C.S.

Further in addition to the power and function of R.C.S. there are 14 functional Registrars having charges of various sectors under the co-operation department and all are I.A.S. officers equal to the rank of R.C.S. as stated below.

1) Registrar of Co operative societies - In charge of

Agriculture, Banking, Consumer welfare, Public Distribution System (PDS) and other sector.

2) Director of Handlooms and Textiles - In charge of all weavers co-operatives and spinning Mills.

3) Commissioner of Dairy development - For milk production and Dairy development co- operatives.

4) Director of veterinary and Animal Husbandry.

5) Registrar of C.S. for housing sector.

6) Director of Industries & Commerce and Tea production.

7) Chief Executive officer - Khadi co- operatives, cottage and village industries.

8) Chief Executive Officer - Palmgur production co-operatives.

9) Director of Fisheries co-operatives (Inland and River dept.)

10) Director of Co-operative Sugar Industries.

11) Commissioner - Sericulture.

12) Director - Oils seeds.

13) Director - Food, Health and social development.

14) Director - Agro Engineering Co-operative activities have been entering into every sectors of the state and has been rendering tremendous services at the peoples doorstep.

Government has decided in principle that any co-operative officer managing any particular co-operative institution as the Chief Executive Office will be continued for a stipulated period without any disturbances. The efficiency and sincerity as well as service attiude towards the public is the main criteria for selection of a Govt. officer to be deputed to the co-operative institutions. The right person for the right job is the best way for any orgnisation to ensure success is the motto of the Government.

The three remarkable things we could observe in Tamilnadu that is, (i) Co-operation is a subject in college and university courses. (ii) Diploma in co-operative management is an eligibility criteria to entre into co-operative services. Any officer as well as employees must have to obtain diploma before getting a job in co-operative department. (iii) In each co-operative Institutions photograph of both previous and present chief minister is hanging on the wall of each room side by side in order to maintain neutrality and ensure faith & trust in the minds of the members.

There has been a substantial growth of co-operative sector in diverse areas of the economy during the past few decades with co-operatives operating in various areas of the economy of the state such as credit, production, processing. marketing, input distribution, housing, dairying, textiles and other service sectors. Although the co-operative institutions are now functioning under the direct control and patronage of the state Government still the ultimate objectives of the co-operative movement has been achieved in reality. The ideas which we have been learned from our observation study will definitely help us for the growth of co-operative movement in our state.

■

"It is good to have goodwill,
It is good to have enthusiasm.
But it is essential to have training."
– Jawaharlal Nehru

The Connotation 'Representative'

What is the true appreciation of the exact connotation of the expression "representative". When a man is a representative, he represents not his wishes, but the wishes of those, the wants of those, the rights of those who elected him as their representative.

Very often people when they get a representation in local bodies or even in a Council Chamber seem to lose sight of the fact that as soon as they accept the representative position, their self is annihilated. They must fight for the rights of others. That is the beginning of self-government. When a man comes in as a representative, first of all he has to govern himself. He must say to himself : "my wish is nothing; my wants are nothing, my demands are nothing, first of all, all that is mine must be postponed to what belongs to my electors, my rights must yield to what is within the rights of those whom I represent".

It is on account of the want of proper appreciation of this character that very often we find some men, who occupy influential position in society or an influential position which is accorded to them on account of their official position, sometimes enforce their own will and begin to think what they consider right that must be the that things to do.

I am sure these institutions will progress as time advances and people begin to appreciate the real meaning of these terms. There will be a complete cessation of this self assertion and the wishes and demands of the people will assert themselves in a most conspicuous and most prominent manner. I am sorry people do not properly realize the meaning of the term "Local Self-Government".

I do really attach a great importance to the term and consider that the success of the Local Self-Government depends on a right appreciation of this simple term. Self-Government means governing oneself. We should remember that these members of municipal bodies, members of these district and local boards are creatures of Statutes. Take away the Bengal Municipal Act from the Statute Book What is a Municipal Commissioner? Nobody understands that word. They take their birth from a Statute and so does a member of the District Board. Now being a child of the Statute, his duty, his obligation and his rights are defined in that Statute. What his rights are, how these rights he can exercise - all these are detailed in the Statute.

If he assumes a right which infringes the provisions of the Statute, he commits suicide. He takes a suicidal position. As a Minister of Local Self-Government while I am prepared to give them any latitude of discretion where they do not infringe.the law - I am jealous of the law and shall with zeal maintain the provisions of the law. I believe there can be no true freedom except by obeying the law. Disobedience of law is not freedom. Such a definition reminds me of the line of Milton :-

"License they mean when they cry for liberty." It is only by obeying the law that you canfreely move. Take the law of gravitation. The law of gravitation governs us all and yet if we do not obey the law and jump about, or if you were to suspend the law for a few minutes, what will be the result ? Hon'ble members will not be in their seats; this House will not be a building standing as it is; everything will be flying about, each one of us will be knocking his head against the other. Because there is the law of gravitation to keep each one in his place, we have the freedom of moving as we wish.

Govt of Odisha Coop dept. Circular

Whereas Elections to the Managing Committees of all primary Co-operative Societies in the State have not been completed as yet; And whereas, elections to the Managing Committees of Central and Apex Co-operative Societies have been scheduled to be completed by the September and December end respectively in the circumstances.

And whereas State Elections to the Municipal Bodies have to be held round about the same time as the elections of the Central & Apex Societies would be held, making men, materials and almost every thing including especially the law & order machinery, non-available for the Co-operative Elections.

Whereas the objectives of the Orissa Co- operative Societies (Amendment)Ordinance 2001, later on substituted by the Orissa Co-operative Societies (Amendment) Act 2001 does not appear to have been fulfilled as yet in regard to empowerment of the weaker sections to participate in the elections and through that in the management of the affairs of the Co-operative Societies which are an effective instrument of state action for amelioration of the conditions of the poor in the state..

Whereas the objectives of earlier amendments to the Orissa Co-operative Societies Act, regarding enrolment of individuals, especially professionals, as members of higher societies like the Central and Apex Co-operative Societies in a Bid to processionalise the management of Co-operative Societies in the, State have not been fulfilled as yet and therefore elections if-held now, will return the same set of. non-professional personnel as members of the Managing Committees of higher societies as before.

Now, therefore, the State Government, in exercise of the powers conferred by Section 123 of the Orissa Co-operative Societies Act, 1962, do hereby exempt the Urban Co-operative Banks & District Central Co-operative Banks in the State other than the Co-operative Societies which have already been exempted from the provisions of Section 28-A of the Act, prior to issue of this order, from the provisions of Section 28 excluding sub-section (1) and (3-b), Sec. 28-A of the Act and direct that the provisions of Sec. 28-B and Sub-Sec (1) of Sec. 31 of the said Act shall apply to those Central Co-operative Banks and Urban Co-operative Banks in the manner as specified below for a period of 18 months from the date of issue of this order :

MODIFICATION :

28-B. election process not to be held up - Not withstanding anything contained in this Act and Rules, election process of a Society, once started, shall not be held up, and no matter relating to election of the President or members of the Committee shall be called in question before any authority under this Act until the declaration of the result of such election.

Provided that Government shall have powers to

withhold the election process of any Co-operative Societies at any stage with reasons to be recorded in writing.

31 (1). All the members, Vice-presidents & President of the Managing Committees of the Urban Co-operative Banks and the Central Co-operative Banks, other than the Co-operative Societies which have already been exempted from the provisions of Section 28-A of the Act prior to the date of issue of this order, shall be nominated by the Government. Provided that the existing Managing Committees nominated by the Registrar in pursuance of the provisions of Sub-Clause (ii) of clause (g) of sub-section (2) of Sec-28 of the Act shall continue in office till a Committee is nominated by the State Government.

Policy on Co-operative in Odisha

U tkal Gourav Madhusudan Das was the founder of modern Odisha. He was anepoch-making legendary figure not only in Odisha but also in India. His novelist personality is reflected in ex-ordinarily patriotism and multifarious talents after his higher education and working as a lawyer in Calcutta for some years hereturned to Odisha in 1881 in worked day and night for Odisha's economic development. His contribution to co-operative movement is unparallel. "Madhusudan organized the workers and daily labourers and sowed the seed of organized co-operative movements. In 1898 he established the first co-operative known as "Cuttack Co-operative Store". Hence he is ever remember as the pioneer co-operative movement in Odisha.

Influence by Madhu Babu late Bidyadhar Panda, Headmaster, Subarnapur Middle M.E. School formed a Rural Co-operative Society at Banki in 1903. Another four village Co-operatives were set up in 1907.In 1910 Banki Dampada Central Co-operative Association consisting of 50 Co-operative Society was established which in crores of times was named as Banki Central Co-operative Bank. This is was the glorist istory of Co-operative Movement of our state and un forgettable contribution of Utkal Gourav

Madhusudan Das. Utkal Gourav Madhusudan Das established the Utkan tennery and Odisha Arts on Co-operative Principle.

Co-operative was a socio-economic life. The Principle of cooperation is as old as human civilization itself. Co-operative have been playing a vital role all over the world irrespective of the tight of economy follow. Co-operative Movement is adistinct segment of Indian economy and in acts as an effective mechanism of Socio-economic transformation of rural community. Wherever Co-operatives have worked they have become a part of their members lives and a source of strengthen to their family to the Nation.

Co-operative Movement flourist in all parts of the country during the last 100 years and the growth of the Co-operative Movement in Odisha is unique and fenominal.

Odisha is one among very few states which is taking a lead role to frame a comprehensive Co-operative Policy. The policy is a focused development of the State. The policy documents bring out approse of the state towards further development of the Co-operatives.

Co-operative movement has played a vital role in the development of rural sector in Odisha. Its role was significant in relieving the rural poor from the clutches of private money lenders and thereby creating developmental opportunities. Co-operative movement is a movement which function byintervening in various sectors. It spreads over almost all sectors such as credit, procurement, production, construction, marketing, agriculturally processing, consumer sector, traditional industries, public health, education, Insurance and development of basic infrastructure sector. In this way Co-operative movement is intervening in various ways in the development of Odisha.

During 1962 a uniform law was enacted known as the Odisha Co-operative Societies Act 1962 : Co-operative Societies were established covering all activities concerned with the day to day life of the common man which played a significant role in the socio-economic development of Odisha. At present Co-operative movement has spread over to all sectors of our state. There is not even a single sector in Odisha where Co-operative movement has not reached.

Near about Nine thousands Co-operative societies in different sectors were registered under the Registrar of Co-operative societies and societies were also working under Functional Registrars, dairy, handloom, fisheries, industries and coir are the different sectors in which these societies are working : Primary Agricultural Credit Societies are the most significant among the Co-operatives inour state. Sixty five percentage of total crop loan of farmers disbursed by Co-operative sector in Odisha are dealt by Agricultural Co-operative societies in Odisha.

Co-operative sector in Odisha not only work for public welfare but also functions as a job provider to the society. They have not only gained the confidence of more than one crore members of Co-operative institutions but also as a livelihood for more than 1 lakh employees in Co-operative sector. Co-operative banks are not working with profit motive. Shares are linked with the loans taken by the members. In this way, the working of Co-operative banks is district from commercial banks.

Weakness of three tier Co-operative credit structure, fall in agricultural loans, weak linkage with local self-government institutions, mounting NPAs and slow progress of the modernization measures are some of the problems which still persist in the sector. The government considers it important to move forward by solving these problems. Considering all this, the government is trying to formulate a comprehensive Co-operative policy which can accelerate the future growth of the Co-operative movement in the state. Co-operative policy is putting forward the perspective of sustainable development of Odisha state through the development of Co-operative movement.

General approach of Co-operative policy

Co-operative movement which has spread over worldwide is going forward by undertaking activities for welfare of people in different countries. International Co-operative Alliance (ICA) in a critical study conducted 12 years ago on Co-operative legislation and policy reforms pointed out a clear distinction between Co-operative policy and legislation in India.

Co-operative policy was further expanded by making changes in tune with the Liberalizations, Privatization, Globalization (LPG) policies of the central government. Support given by the government to the co-operative sector was reduced substantially and was left open to the cut throat competition of the market forces. It badly affected the growth and development of lot of small co-operatives which could not attain equivalent competiveness in a market driven economy. Many programmes which were brought out in the name of making the regulatory frame work fault less in the co-operative sector were not beneficial to the co-operatives. Methods adopted in these were in such way to minimize the control of the state government and at the same tie trengthening the contro of Reserve Bank of India. Many criticisms have come up in this regard that these initiatives were directed to reform the co-operative credit sector like new generation banks. The general approach which has come up including in the legislative assembly was that some of the recommendation of Vaidyanathan Committee report will weaken the co-operative sector in the state. Mean while discussions have also come up in line that the constitutional amendment aimed to transfer a sector which was hitherto under the control of the state government to the central government is in fact a challenge to the federalism. However the verdict given by the Gujarat high court against this amendment allowed the sector to remain as state subject even now.

It is essential to frame co-operative policy considering the uniqueness of the state. Only then the movement can go ahead by overcoming the challenges. The policy which considers the experiences and specialities of Odisha is putting forward certain view points. This policy document brings out approach of the state towards further development of co-operatives. It discusses the global perspetive, vision and mission, specific policies with regards to various sectors, it is relationship with Local Self Governments (LSGs) and issues with regard to the existing legal frame work and proposed changes thereon.

Vision :-

To stream line and build a robust, vibrant and sustainable co-operative movement in the state so as to enable the society to reach greater heights byensuring equitable socio-economic development working in accordance with the government.

Mission :-

Develop the co-operative movement to function effectively, efficiently and economically for the benefit of its members and the society.

To utilize the movement for mobilizing the people

on a voluntary basis to ensure maximum participation in governance by involving in planning, organizing and implementing various schemes formulated for the overall growth of society and local economic development.

United Nations perspective and the co-operative sector in Odisha

United Nationas have put forward five sustainable development goals with respect to co-operatives. They are as follows

Poverty Eradication and Zero Hunger (Zero Poverty)

Food Security

Gender Equality

Decent Work and Economic Growth

Combating Climate Change

If we can understand how far the co-operative sector in Odisha have internalized the above said development goals, it will be clear how far we have aligned with the global perspectives of co-operatives. Through that we can understand the growth of our co-operative movement and it will be clear how we can make them stronger and take them forward.

Co-operative Policy Perspective

Co-operative movement in Odisha has carved out a niche for itself in important sectors like credit (both Rural and Urban) banking, diary, agriculture marketing, consumers, handloom and handicrafts, fisheries, labour and housing activities. The indelible imprint made by co-operative is identified by the government and hense the co-operative policy address the twin objectives of ensuring autonomy, independence and strengthening of the movement on the one hand and identifying it as a launch vehicle to implement various socio-economic security programmes of the government, on the other.

The State Government is propounding a perspective plan for development which pro-poor, environment friendly and proposes an alternate development model. The policy envisage strengthening and development of Co-operatives as a tool for local economic development.

NABARD and Co-operative Sector

During 1980s, Co-operative societies in the agricultural sector of Odisha were functioning with the financial support of NABARD. The funds are primarily used for agricultural production and infrastructural development. In agricultural production credit sector around 35 to 40 percentage of the agricultural credit disbursed as refinance are given at a subsidized interest rate. Along with that interest subsidy given by the Central Govt. from time to time is also available. In order to use the above said credit facilities effectively and thereby strengthen the agricultural sector, pressurizing for getting a higher share to the state is "also very important to the co-operative sector."

Some of the existing weaknesses

Co-operative sector which has given very significant contribution to the development of Odisha has to be taken forward aligning to the requirements of the new era. For that we have to examine the weakness and take necessary initiatives for correcting those weaknesses of the three tier credit structure, decline in agricultural loans, mounting NPAs should be looked into seriously.

Weakness of three their credit structure

Primary Agricultural Credit Societies (PACS) were

unable to provide modern banking facilities to the members/account holders. Their area of operation was very limited. This geographical limitation drives away the customers from co-operative banks. Other than that those co-operative banks functioning at different level, different places using different software's are unable to provide technology based banking services to the young generations.

Main responsibility of three tir credit structure is to provide agricultural credit. By the time the refinance facility received at a lower interest rate from NABARD which passes through three tiers of State Co-operative Banks and District Co-operative Banks and reaches the former through Primary Agricultural Credit Society, the actual beneficiary has to give higher rate of interest due to the interest margin imposed by different three tiers.

Professional approach from employees as well as Board of Directors of three tier co-operative banking system as per the desires of the customers are lacking.

Severe imbalances can be seen in the resource availability and use of co-operative banks working in different areas. These imbalances in the credit deposit scenario curtail the development of co-operative banking sector.

Another weakness is that the isolated co-operative banks are not able to deal with NRI deposits and foreign exchange transactions.

Decline in Agricultural Credit

Primary Co-operative Societies
1.	The Primary Agricultural Credit Societies shall continue to function as a multi service society for its members and general public.

2. To develop the existing long term credit structure offered by PCARDBs as an institution for promoting rural development.

Co-operative Education

Co-operative education plays a vital role in modernizing, professionalizing and making it people friendly. Efforts will be taken to revise the syllabus and academic programme. Interventions for the capacity building programmes for the existing persons working in this field may be given more importance.

Other changes

To establish an Apex Co-operative Federation for miscellaneous type co-operative societies.

Conclusion

In the context of rising inequalities due to the neo-liberal policies, the basis of the co-operative policy is to equip the co-operatie movement for effective interventions in shaping the overal development of the state and also reduging the inequalities in the society.

Co-operative Policy prospective :

Co-operative movement in Odisha has carved out a riche for itself in important sector like Credit, Banking, Diary, Agricultural, Marketing, Consumers & Handlooms & Handicrafts, Fisheries, Labour and Housing activities. The indelible imprint made by Co-operatives is identified by the Govt. and hence the Co-operative Policy addresses the twin objectives of ensuring autonomy, independence and strengthening of the movement on the one hand and identifying it as a lunch vehicle to implement various socio-economic security programme of the Govt. on the other hand.

The Govt. of Odisha is propounding a prospective plan for development which is proper environment friendly and proposes an alternate development model. The policy envisages strengthening and development of co-operatives as a tool for local economic development NABARD and Co-operative sector.

During 1980s Co-operative Societies in the agricultural sector of Odisha were functioning with the financial support of NABARD. The funds are pre-use for development in agricultural production. Credit sector around 62 to 70% of the agricultural credit disbursed as refinance are given at a subsidized interest rate along with that interest subsidy on agricultural production and infrastructural given by the central Govt. from time to time is also available.

"The idea of cooperation is something much more than emerely an efficient and economic way of doing things. It is economic, it is fair, it is equalizes and prevents disparities from growing. But it is something even deeper than at, it is really way of life." — **Jawaharlal Nehru**

O.C.S. Act 1962 and Rules for Performance

All India Rural redit Survey Report was a landmark in giving a signficant direction to the cooperative movement. With the background that "Cooperative has failed, but it must succeed", the Committee in their report recommended valuable policies to effect a new orientation and far-reaching changes in actual working of cooperative societies. One of the important recommendations among others in the report, was for state partnership in societies. In other words, according to the committee, direct assistance and participation of Government in societies was necessary for success of the cooperative movement.

Sir Malcon Darling K.C.LE. also suggested similarly in his report. The Committee on Cooperative Law constituted in the year 1956 for suggesting legislative amendments also recommended for State partnership in societies. Almost all the State Government in the Federal structure including Orissa accepted these recommendations and enacted legislation for their respective States. State of Orissa enacted "The Orissa Cooperative Societies Act 1962", as a follow- up action replacing the OCS Act 1951. In the new enactment 1962 a separate chapter (Chapter V) was provided as "State aid to Societies", containing section 40 to 54. In section 40 of the Act the mandate was as below-

"It shall be the duty of the State Government to encourage and promote the Cooperative Movement and to take such step in this direction as may be necessary."

With a view to strengthening the financial base of societies, provisions were made in the said Act enabling Government to extend financial and other aids to societies by way of subscribing directly or indirectly to the share capital of societies, lending loan and advances to societies, guarantee the repayment of principal and payment of interest on debentures issued, guarantee the repayment of share capital of a society and dividend thereon, guarantee the repayment of principal and interest on loan and advances to and deposit with a society and to give financial assistance in any other form including subsidies to any society.

While envisaging financial aid and assistance to societies in such a big way simultaneously, statutory foras with a system or mechanism were also provided in the Act and Rules to review effectively, the performance and expenditure of societies particularly, those aided by Government in order to preventing any misuse of the funds and properties of societies which are discussed below.

1. Under Section 31 of the Act 1962 the Government have the right to nominate one-third of the total number of members of Committee not exceeding four in respect of a society assisted by the Government. The object behind the aforesaid system of Government nominees on the Committee is to provide an effective instrument in monitoring the performance and expenditure of the societies by Government aided.

2. Sec. (2) of Sub Rule (5) of Rule 36 of the O.C.S. Rules 1965 envisages a system whereunder difference of opinion if any, between Government nomineesb and others

in the Committee of a society aided by the Government, in any matter, it shall be referred to the Government whose decision thereon, shall be final. The object behind this system is to provide an effective instrument to ensure proper and productive utilisation of the funds and properties of such societies and to run the society in confirmation with the provisions of Act and Rules.

3. Section 12 (5) of the Act provides for effecting amendments of bye-laws by the Registrar to incorporate the same in the bye-laws of an Apex Central Society, Cooperative Bank or financing Bank and other aided societies in order to achieving better financial performance.

4. The definition of the "Financing Bank" was widened u/s2(e) of the OCS Act 1962 so as to embrace within its bounds the scheduled Banks, NABARD, RBI, IDBI or any similar Bank and also non-Banking Financing Institutions by the OCS (Amendment) Act 1991 so as to enable those institutions to frequently inspect and look into working of societies financed by it and to safeguard their money. It was also made mandatory to consult the financing Bank in the event of super session of the committee of a society for mismanagement.

5. Under Section 32 of the Act, Registrar is empowered to supersede the committee of a society in case of mismanagement, non-performance or indulgence in financial irregularities and likewise by the committee, and to appoint 5 administrator to manage and run the society on right tracks.

6. In Section 33 A of the Act, a system exists for the Registrar to control the financial performance and expenditure in the form of determination of the conditions of service including salaries and other allowances of the employees of societies and as such, enabling to prevent

overstaffing and to set an uniform standard of expenditure in that regard and curb unnecessary expenditure.

7. Section 64 of the Act 1962 provides a mechanism empowering Registrar to inspect records of a society at least once in every cooperative year either on his own motion or on application of any creditor of the society including the financing Bank. Besides, a financing Bank is also empowered to inspect the records of a society indebted to it. Under this mechanism the performance, non-performance of the society can be surfaced and imporvement if any there on, suggested for effecting safeguards of the money and properties of societies.

8. Similarly, Section 65 the Act contemplates enquiry into the constitution, working and financial condition of a society by the Registrar to ensure that the society functions adhering to the provisions of the Act, Rules and bye-laws.

9. A system of a independent audit of the books of accounts of every society for every cooperative year exists under section 62 of the Act. The scope of audit has since been enlarged so as to include within its purview apart from purely financial matter, "an examination of the irregularities in term of the Act, Rules and bye-laws if any, in respect of constitution, financing and business of the society effecting the financial position or otherwise of the society."

10. Audit has been segregated from administration and vested with a new insitution designated as, "Auditor General of Cooperative Societies" which has been created to function independently from administration with a view to lending more independence to audit and ensuremore free and fair audit of accounts of societies.

11. That apart, a system has been provided in Section 62 for compulsory concurrent audit of the accounts of societies with annual turnover of Rs.25 lakhs or more, on

day to day basis to ensure early detection of irregular expenditure if any and to ensure that the norms and quality in financial and account matters in such societies are observed.

12. Under Section 63 A of the Act, the Auditor General of CS is under obligation to furnish to the State Government an annual report for every cooperative year within nine months of the closure of the year in incorporating therein a classfication of societies in the State on the basis of audit findings for the year which shall be laid before the State Legislature. This system will ensure accountability of societies.

13. Under Section 28 and 29 of the Act, more frequent meetings of the Committee and General Body have been made compulsory and non-convening of G.B. meeting by the committee has been made to attract penalties like automatic supersession of the Committee and as well as, disqualification of an absentee member in such meeting from contesting election with a view to ensuring active participation by the members in the affairs of the society, Section 29 (2) also empowers G.B. to review the operational deficit if any, and to allocate liabilites on members therefor.

14. Under Section 67 of the Act a mechanism has been provided which empowers the Auditor General of C.G. to initiate surcharge proceeding against an officer, officer bearer or an employee of the society whose indulgence into the act of any misfeasance like breach of trust, wilful negligence or misappropriation of funds and properties etc. has caused any deficit in the assets of the society and to recover the same from such delinquent officer, office-bearer or employee as the case may be, with a view to safeguarding the funds and properties of the society and prevent any unlawful expenditure in societies.

15. A system has been established u/s 123 A of the Act providing for inspection of the records of any society and enquiry into the affairs of the society directly by the Government.

Not withstanding existence of so many foras aforesaid in the Act and Rules for reviewing the performance and expenditure of societies and to prevent unlawful expenditure, a large number of cases of unlawful expenditure, mal-performance, non performance and misappropriation depleting the funds and properties of societies could not be prevented and functioning of societies could not be streamlined in right direcion to the desired extent. The echo of the observation made five decades back that "Cooperative has failed but it must succeed," still resounds with an increasing and alarming vibration in the domain of cooperatives, of course, with few isolated cares of success which may serve as a silver lining igniting hope for success of the movement.

In undoubtedly, demonstrates that the statutory authorities established and functionaries created under the above mentioned foras, have failed to effectively discharge their respective obligation they are saddled with thereunder - may be due to variant factors, either tagged with personal comforts discomforts or situation beyond control arising out of administrative compulsions which more often than not, are based upon political considerations.

In the fifth Indian Cooperative Congress 1967, the then Prime Minister, Smt. Indira Gandhi observed, "...there is also a widely prevalent feeling that cooperatives are too mixed up with politics. I wish you would also discuss how to depoliticalise it." The Ardhanareswarn Committee on "Cooperative Law for democratisation and preofessionalisation of management in cooperatives", constituted by Government of India 1985 in their report observed that politicisation of cooperatives had led to certain undesirable developments such as "induction of political workers on the Board of Cooperatives and in some cases ministers holding offices as chairman, and suggested that to distinguish" non-political character, it would be appropriate to avoid holding political and cooperative offices simultaneously by the same person.

There was also a growing feeling that due to lot of legislative, administrative and Government control or interference in the functioning of cooperatives, the movement got a set back and therefore, cooperatives be made free from those clutches and be allowed to function, controlled and governed by the members themselves. Accordingly, with due honour to such feelings, "The Orissa Self Help Cooperative Act 2001" was enacted envisaging therein a cooperative of self governance by the members and free from any outside interference. A few number of cooperatives have come up under the aforesaid Act. Reports are also surfacing that such cooperatives with few exceptions, have also become victim of one man show and devoid of any actual active member participation in the manner intended under the said Act, postulating attention of the Government for remedial measures.

Be that as it may, legislative manoeuvres or legal jugglery of any magnitude alone, will not be able to energise the cooperative movement unless it is coupled with will power and strong determination of sensitised cooperators dedicated to cooperative principles and active participation by members in the affairs of the cooperatives.

Yes, cooperative has not achieved the objectives to the desired extent. But let us wish, "it must succeed"; for it is a very strong and powerful weapon in the armoury of the weaker section the cooperatives stand for, to uplift their economic conditions and social status as well.

■

"The secret of successful Co-operative efforts it that members must be honest and know the great merit of Co-operation and it must have definite progressive goal".
– Mahatma Gandhi

Housing Movement

Introduction :

Cities are growing at an exponential rate. Scores of people head towards developed cities with the hope of making it big in life. Existence in cities is becoming very complex because of rising expectations and aspirations beyond the available means. This is a phenomenon found in most developing societies. Unemployment, rising prices, frustration contributing to corruption, delinquency, theft, crime and other heinous activities are the prominent causes that make people feel insecure particularly in big cities.

URBANISATION ACROSS THE WORLD

About one third of world's population lived in urban areas in the year 1975. The urban population is expected to double by 2025. Further growth in urbanization is expected to take place only in developing countries, as in the developed countries, this growth has already taken place to a large extent. During the period 1990 95, the urban growth rate in the countries like Burkina Faso, Mozambique, Nepal, Afghanistan, etc. was around 7 per cent per annum, which created a heavy burden on the local Governments, for development of basic infrastructure.

Due to rapid urban growth rates in many cities in the developing countries, these cities are horizontally expanding. A commonly used term for measuring urban growth is the 'mega city' i.e. a city with a population exceeding 8 million. According to UN, in 1950, there were two mega-cities with 10 million or more inhabitants. By 2005, their number had increased to 20 and it is projected that there will be 22 mega-cities in 2015. Developing countries will have 17 of these 22 mega cities in 2015.

Many of the intermediate size cities may actually be growing faster i.e. at rates over 5 per cent per annum on an average than the big cities. As a result, there is a proliferation of 'million cities' (with population between one million to 10 million).

ROLE OF HOUSING COOPERATIVES

The main objective of housing cooperative is to provide its members with suitable housing accommodation at a reasonable cost and on easy terms of payment. The modern concept of housing does not limit the scope of housing to provision of housing alone, but a comfortable shelter with such surroundings and services as would keep a man healthy and cheerful throughout his life. A housing Cooperative, therefore, after providing decent houses to its members also strives to create an environment that is conducive to the fulfilment of the physical, social, economic and spiritual needs of its members. The key role of housing cooperatives is "to establish and carry on its own account or jointly with individuals, educational, physical, social and recreative activities particularly for the benefit of its members". A cooperative also provides services for basic amenities like water, electricity, sanitary services, etc. to its members. Its efforts are further directed towards building up a community life within the cooperative, based on good neighbourhood andbfellow feelings and it transforms itself into a new community wherein "each is for all and all are for each.

SOCIAL ACHIEVEMENT OF HOUSING COOPERATIVES

The social achievements of housing cooperatives can be summarised as under :

(a) Social Activities and Services:

Besides, developing housing estates, the housing cooperatives have also built schools, libraries, parks, etc. for the community thereby improving literacy rate.

(b) Social Functions

Housing cooperatives organise special programmes for their members on occasions like New Year Day, Labour Day, and Cooperative Week etc. They also organise tours and excursions on holidays. These functions bring people together and provide opportunity to understand each other.

(c) Health Services

Many housing cooperatives have arranged health services for the benefit of their members. They have opened dispensaries, first aid, family planning and welfare centres.

(d) Youth Development

A number of housing cooperatives have organised youth clubs and sports centres. Some cooperatives have opened gymnasiums and even play grounds. Others have organised debating clubs, published newsletters, conducted essay writing competitions, etc. to encourage young people to participate in literary pursuits.

(e) Ecological Improvement

A significant contribution of housing cooperatives is the improvement of the ecology of the concerned area. Housing cooperatives pay special attention to the disposal of garbage and to keep the surroundings dean. They plant trees and maintain gardens. In India, for instance, it is generally a housing cooperative that wins the prize for the best garden.

(f) Women's Organisations

Housing cooperatives have been especially helpful in promoting women's organisations. Special associations of women get formed in many housing cooperatives which, often take up activities to economically benefit the female members.

(g) Transport Operations

Some housing cooperatives have arranged special transport services for their members.

(h) Promotion of other Cooperatives

Many housing cooperatives have promoted other types of cooperatives e.g. Consumer Stores, Thrift and Credit Cooperatives for the benefit of their members.

(1) Influence on Human Behaviour – One of the outstanding merits of housing cooperatives is the healthy influence they exercise on human relations. On account of better social and emotional interaction, the members of housing cooperatives generally display improved social behaviour and mental health. The incidence of addiction to drinking and juvenile delinquency are lower in housing cooperatives when compared with areas where people live in isolation, and are devoid of social activities.

(2) Emotional Integration – Housing cooperatives have been instrumental in bringing about desired emotional and social integration amongst people belonging to different religions, castes and sects etc. In housing cooperatives, people of diverse religions, castes etc. voluntarily choose to come closer and live as one large family true to Aristotle's dictum that "man is a social animal". In housing cooperatives one does not come across cases of conflicts on account of differences in castes, languages or religions of their members.

CONCLUSIONS

The various Governments must address their priorities towards overall social development so as to remove various disparities and thereby help crime prevention programmes. They must find ways to help communities to deal with underlying factors such as poverty, inequality, family stress, unemployment, absence of educational and vocational opportunities that undermine safety of community and result in increased crime. The prevention policies at the city level should include forging partnerships between municipal authorities, community based organisations like cooperatives, police and judicial system.

There is also an emergent need on the part of particularly developing countries to discourage migration and reverse the existing trend through speedy development of rural areas and creation of small cities. Instead of forcing people to migrate and settle where the infrastructure is available, such an infrastructure providing for employment opportunities, better sanitation & hygienic conditions should be created in rural areas. The improved facilities of health and family welfare, affordable housing, access to safe drinking water, transport and communication facilities, education etc. if made available to the needy people in rural areas, would discourage their migration to cities.

Through the afore said achievements, housing

cooperatives have demonstrated their ability to remove the accompanying evils and thereby build up an ideal social life within themselves. When our social fabric is threatened, in present times, by conflicts and tensions rooted in differences in language, religion or caste, housing cooperatives can certainly play a positive role to check the malady. With the members voluntarily choosing to live in association with others, conflicts and social tensions can be substantially reduced to create conditions for an ideal homogenous living. Even in developed countries, housing cooperatives have been quite active. In USA, particularly in New York City, where former slum areas were cooperativised, a large number of workers living in conditions well below modern standard were re-housed. Studies made by the International Cooperative Alliance (ICA) in South Asian countries like Malaysia, have revealed that houses constructed by cooperatives, besides being cheaper in cost and need based, have contributed to the development of a community spirit and co-operation.

The Odisha Self Help Co-operative Ordinance-2013 (Repeal)

Government of Odisha in exercise of powers conferred by Clause (1) of the article - 213 of the Constitution of India have been pleased to promulgate this Ordinance No. 1/2013-namely The Odisha Self Help Co- operative (Repeal) Ordinance, 2013 published in the Odisha Gazette Law Department Notification No. 1068 dtd. 6th June, 2013.

2. Section 2 (1) of the aforesaid Ordinance repeals the Self Help Co-operative Act, 2001 Sub-section (2) thereof, provides that any investigation, proceeding or remedy in relation to any right privilege, obligation, and liability claim or demand, penalty forfeiture or punishment under the Act so repealed shall continue or be enforced.

3. Section 3 of the Ordinance mandates is that :-

(a) any Co-operative registered under the said repealed Act existing immediately before commencement of the Ordinance, shall be deemed to be registered under the corrosponding provision of the OCS Act, 1962. In other words, all the existing Cooperatives came within the purview of the OCS Act, 1962 w.e.f. 6.6. 2013 the date, the Ordinance came into force; and

(b) the said Cooperatives shall amend their respective byelaws or the article of association by Whatever name called, so far they are inconsistent with the provisions of the OCS Act, 1962, following the procedure laid down there for in the said Act and reconstitute their Board of Directors within three months from the date of coming into force of the Ordinance i.e. by 5.9: 2013, and

(c) In case any Cooperative fails to complete the aforesaid exercise within three months from the date of commencement of the Ordinance, the Board of Directors of that Cooperative shall stand dissolved on expiration of the said period for three months and

(d) upon such dissolution of the Board of Directors the management of the said Cooperative shall vest in the Registrar who shall within a period of two months, there from take steps for amendment of this bye laws and reconstitution of the Board of such Cooperative in accordance with provision of the O.C.S. Act, 1962 and bye-laws.

4. On a careful reading of the Section 3 of the Ordinance it transpires that :-

(a) the mandate to the cooperatives is that they shall amend their bye-laws and reconstitute the Board of Directors within a period of three months from the date of commencement of the Ordinance, and that non compliance thereof by any cooperative would result is dissolution of its respective Boards and vesting of the management in the Registrar on expiration of the said period of three months. But the mandate to the Registrar who upon vesting of the management in him also acquires the status of the Management-in-Change of such Co-operative as well, is that he shall take steps for such amendment of the Bye-laws and reconstitution of the Board of Directors within a period of two months from the date of vesting of the Management in him.

"Shall amend the byelaws and reconstitute the Board of Directors" and "To take steps for amendment of the Bye-law and reconstitution of the Board of Directors" are not synonymous to each other. The former denotes completion of registration of the Bye laws and reconstitution of the Board within the stipulated period whereas, the later means only initiation of the action of amendment of Bye laws and reconstitution of the Board. That means, it would be a sufficient compliance of the mandate by the Registrar if he merely takes steps (initiate action) for amendment of the Bye-laws and reconstitution of the Board at his level, either as Management-In-Charge of the Cooperative or as the statutory authority under the Act; and non-amendment of the byelaw or non-reconstitution of the Board of Directors within the said period of two months and continuance of vesting of the management of the Cooperative with him beyond the said stipulated period of two months would not amount to violation of the mandate by him or illegal. But in the case of a cooperative any such non amendment of the bye-laws and reconstitution of the Board within the said stipulated period of three months would amount to breach of the mandate; and dissolution of its Board; and vesting of the management in the Registrar will be inevitable under the legislative compulsion even if, the Cooperative has taken steps in that regard within the stipulated period.

(b) The existing Bye laws of the Cooperatives have been framed under the repealed Act which had basic and contrasting differences from the OCS Act, 1962 under which now the Cooperatives have come. To amend the existing bye-laws, therefore, would postulate several major amendments and may be En-Bloc amendment, which would require immense and time consuming exercise; and it would not be practicable for the Cooperatives to amend their bye laws and thereafter, to reconstitute the Board within the stipulated period of three months, more so, when the Election rules U/s. 28 A(9) of the OCS Act, 1962 which has a significant bearing on the amendment of the Bye-laws particularly, matters relating to the constitution of the Board of Directors, had not come up by the date, the Ordinance came into force, as understood.

That apart, completion of amendment of the bye-laws statutorily needs the cap of a registration certificate to be granted by the Registrar U/s. 12 of the Act after meticulous examination of each clause of the proposed bye-law at his level for which section 12 (4-a) of the Act allows him sixty days time, Similarly, the Election Officer subject to the direction of the State Cooperative Election Commission is the authority to conduct election of the office bearers and to grant declaration certificate of their having been so elected which is necessary for constitution of the Board. Both the above authorities are not within the purview of the cooperatives yet, the cooperatives have been directed to amend their bye-laws and reconstitute the Board or to face dissolution of their Board and vesting of the management in the Registrar under the ordinance on expiration of the stipulated period of three months.

(c) Mandate U/s. 3 of the ordinance so far it relates to dissolution of the Board and vesting of the management in Registrar is that it shall be applicable to such of the Cooperative who do not amend their Byelaws and reconstitute the Board within the stipulated period of three months. But none of Cooperative would be able to comply with the said mandate for the reason discussed in earlier paras. As such, exclusion of the any Cooperative from the aforesaid mandate of Section 3 of the Ordinance appears to be fallacious and unreal one. In effect, all the Cooperatives would come to the fold of the Ordinance and their Board of Directors dissolved under legislative compulsion on expiry of the stipulated period of three months.

5. The point what is being driven at is that under the Ordinance the Cooperative would suffer with dissolution of their respective Bounds and vesting of the management in the Registrar not for their own default but also for non performance or mis performance of someone who is/are not within their authority or are beyond their control of course, Co-operatives can take steps or initiate the process for amendment of the Bye laws and reconstitution of the Board like the one Registrar has been mandated to do. The Cooperative can neither amend the Bye-law nor can reconstitution the Board by itself for reason discussed at para 4(b).

6. In this background, allegation of the kind that providing the Cooperatives with an opportunity to amend their byelaws and reconstitute the Board of Directors within a periodof three months from the date of coming into force of the Ordinance in the given facts and circumstances, is illusory, merely a guise of natural justice and tainted with ulterior motive may not be ruled out which as it seems may render the ordinance shady.

■

"Look back and get experience"
Dr. Abdul Kalam

Quality Programme in Co-operatives

Every body agrees that quality is a good think. Whether you talk of quality of product, quality of service or quality of suppliers, everybody agrees that it should be of the highest standard. This applies within organizations from the highest level. It applies to suppliers, to customers, to users of services - in fact to anyone you may care to ask. And yet, despite this rare unanimity, there is much talk and little action.

Organizations grow continuously only through quality or perish when there is diminishing quality in its approach. Cooperatives like IFFCO, Amul, Kribhco, OMFED and many other organizations have reached where they are today only through imbibing quality culture. If they fail to keep up that vital ingredient ie. quality, then they will be no where. So it is high time all cooperatives shoud accept total quality as the main norm for its future survival.

Achieving quality standards within organizations is about attitude at all levels. Quality is not just about systems, is not just about using specific techniques, and tools. Quality is about the attitude of mind of all the individuals within the organization it is about winning the hearts and minds not only of them but also of customers who must come to believe that the organization produces goods or services which meet their specific requirenent.

Creating an environment and implementing a programme which recognizes the crucia! mportance of attitudes in an organization is the key to the long term success and profitability of that organization. Management has the key responsibility in any total quality programme. Quality involves every body within an organization. It is not the specific responsibility of any particular individual or group of individuals. A steady commitment to continuous improvement and total quality can revolutionize organizations and bring enhanced competitiveness and profitability in the long term.

Training and devefopment play a key role at all levels in the organization and this should be continuous. In helping organizations to implement total quality programmes, training has certainly been regarded as a key factor for better output by its human resources. It is essential that all levels understand not oniy the programme as a whole but the various techniques and tools associated with the programme. Otherwise defensiveness can creep in if the lower levels seem more knowledgeable about such things. Investment in training is a critical factor in the success of total quality programme, it requires all levels to be involved and to attend, compulsorily, without excuse.

A successful total quality programme must be based on certain basic principles. We shall discuss in detail how to approach its implementation. Underlying the whole approach are six fundamental requirements, based on the concept that people are at the heart of a successful programme.These are - Top Management Commitment Attitude change Continuous improvement Strengthened supervision Extensive training Recognition of performance.These are considered in detail below. Top Management should continuously rein force a total quality programme by what they do.

We have to recognize that changing management attitudes is the key to success within an organization and that must start at the very top. The future success of the organization is dependent on the commitment of top management. To show commitment, top management should make sure that everybody within the organization from top to bottom is clear about the long term goals this affects management the quality of communications, indeed everything that is done within an organization.

Total quality requires a complete change in the attitude and culture prevailing in the organizations. Originally quality control was designed to restrict the occurrence of inferior products within a certain tolerance range.

In Japan, however it bas been changed into a movement for total elimination of inferior products through creative cooperation by all quarters concerned. When inferior goods are producted Japanese workers consider it a shame and even weep. Achieving this type of attitude change is critical to the long term success of a total quality programme.

Linked to attitude change is the need to create a climate of continuous improvement quality improvement should always be at the forefront of everything that is done, continuously reinforced and developed by management through the systems, processes and organizations which make such improvements possible.

Any suggestion, hovwever small, should be recorded on the chart and at the end of the year there should be prizes for those who put forward the most Suggestions. Every step needs to be taken to encourage individuals within an Organization to be part of the improvement process and to look for opportunities to make changes.

Top management needs to provide opportunities and the investment in training to ensure the quality of supervision improves. Motivation theory and practice emphasize strongly the importance of recognizing performance and achievement. Recognition is generally given through prizes and competitions for either the most or the best proposals and projects. The emphasis is very much on recognition of contribution and achievement, with no direct monetary rewards.

The organization climate survey provides a good foundation in helping to understand attitudes and possible resistance to change. Equally important is to review effectiveness by carrying out an organizational effectiveness by carrying out an organizational effectiveness audit. The issues which require addressing in such an audit would include:

A) a review of the work environment which would take account of :

Organization structure: Looking at the hi-erarchy within the organization, the extent to which responsibilities are divided üp, the separation between direct and indirect departments, possible overlaps and duplication.

Work organization : Looking within departments, particularly at how work is divided and organized.

Decision making processes and the extent :

He to which decision making is delegated or 1high level bureaucratic processes whereby sl decision making is centralized in a few key areas.

Communications- The effectiveness of communications both within and between departments and whether the existing vehicles really work, the extent to which top management actually promotes good communication, whether employees feel well informed.

Physical conditions - The general environment in which people work.

Pay structure It is likely to promote or inhibit commitment to quality standards or is there an incentive oriented style where production rather than quality is important ?

Trade union relations : Looking at the present state of industrial relations within the organization and the extent to which the trade unions are likely to Cooperate with a total quality programme.

B) Technology and techniques which apply with the organization and which may affect the implementation of a total quality programme include.

Cost control - Methods and systems of controlling costs within the organization.

Production planning – The extent to which there is an effective production panning process within the organization.

Marketing – Particularly the structure of the marketing department and how it relates to the external and internal contacts essential to successful marketing.

Technology- The extent to which technology has been introduced and possible future plans.

C) The individual - Looking in particular at how individuals within the organization are considered with particular reference to recruitment and selection techniques and the extent to which positive efforts are made to try to generate proper fits between new employees and the skills required.

Training and management development with particular reference to skills training, growth of knowledge and emphasis on development of positive attitudes.The purpose of training in concepts or quality is to ensure that there is a thorough understanding within the organization both of quality and the specific company objectives. in introducing total quality it should be emphasized that it consists of- a philosophy of getting things right first time' or "zero defects".

A systematic approach to improving the overall quality performance of the organization based on a body of principles and methods.

A central strategy of the organization based on an integrated system involving all processes and all people.

A found on customer requirements In explaining the approach to total quality it is important to emphasize the particular focus of the strategy. For instance, a number of alternative strategies can be considered where the emphasis may be on : increasing efficiency and productivity.

Creating a better product or service.

Improving performance of people within the organization.

Getting the most out of the existing organizational structure. Transforming work process. Maximizing customer satisfaction.

The key to success in introducing total quality within an organization, involving task groups and quality circles in seeking ways of continuous improvement to quality is based on a systematic approach to joint problem solving.

The principles are based on depersonalizing conflicts by diluting emotions and adopting a systematic approach Providing a logical framework which encourages the facts to come to surface so that the facts rather than the individuals determine the solution.Integrating the objectives of the organization and of the people working in it.

Brain storming is a way of getting as many ideas as possible on a problem or a solution in the shortest possible time. Brain storming works most effectively when there is a group of people responding within the following framework don't discuss - Just concentrate on writing up ideas as quickly as possible without criticizing anything that is said.

Build on other's suggestion - by using the thoughts of others to trigger one's own thought processes - the classic lateral thinking approach. Go for quantity - by trying to write up as many ideas as possible within a period of time, say five or ten minutes. Be imaginative - quite often the most creative solutions come from initially daft ideas, avoid creating on environment where people are inhibited from putting forward ideas because others criticize or laugh at them.

Brainstorming is based on the principle that discussion can be helpful not only in solving problems but in changing attitudes, obtaining commitment and perhaps most important, in developing ideas.

Total quality is recognized by all as being the key to the future of individual organizations.It is recognized that total quality is about management and in particular about participative management. Without participation, without dialogue within organizations, without listening to clients and customers, total quality will never by achieved. Total quality is all about changes in the way of thinking, the behaviour and the culture within organizations.

As the Japanese have so successfully demonstrated, total quality is about shared values and motivating everybody in the organization from top to bottom to maintain and keep the highest quality standards. In simple terms total quality is about attitudes, a way of life, achieving excellence It is about success through people.

Co-operatives are organizations by the people, for the people and of the people. They can fight with private entrepreneurs and corporate only through the significant instrument that is quality. If they overlook the quality aspect, then they will meet the fate or innumerable organizations that have met their natural end. Therefore from Primary Co-operatives to apex organizations, all should adopt total quality programees and shed their collective inertia in order improve their performance and achieve their organizational goals. Quality is the only mantra that can save us in this would of cut-throat competition.

पूर्णतः सहकारी स्वामित्व
Wholly owned by Cooperatives

IFFCO'S NANO FERTILISER – GATEWAY FOR REVOLUTIONIZING AGRICULTURE

INDIAN FARMERS FERTILISER COOPERATIVE LIMITED (IFFCO)

Indian Farmers Fertiliser Cooperative Limited (IFFCO) is a leading cooperative society in India, established in 1967 to empower farmers and promote sustainable agriculture. It is one of the largest fertilizer manufacturers in the country and plays a crucial role in ensuring the availability of quality fertilizers at affordable prices. IFFCO's commitment extends beyond fertilizer production to encompass farmer training, financial assistance, and leveraging technology for agricultural advancement.

Fertilizers havebeen long the backbone of agricultural productivity, ensuring that crop receive the essential nutrients needed for healthy growth and high yields. Due to excessive use of Chemical Fertilisers, Indian agriculture is facing numerous challenges such as nutrient inefficiency, declining soil health and increasing food demand. IFFCO's focus is now exploring on various options, including organic fertilizers, biofertilizersand precision farming techniques to reduce reliance on chemical fertilizers. By supporting research and innovation in this field, IFFCO aims to empower farmers with sustainable solutions that enhance soil health, increase crop yield, and protect the environment. Hence, the potential of innovative Nano Fertilisers in Indian agriculture highlights the transition from conventional fertilisers to more sustainable practices.Nano Fertilisers offer precise nutrient delivery, reduced environmental impact, and improved efficiency.

RISK OF OVERUSE OF CHEMICAL FERTILISERS

1. **Risktoenvironment:** Volatilisation, leaching and denitrification losses from fertiliser leads to pollution, NOx, CO2, CH4 emission leads to global warming, temperature variation, rainfall variability etc.

2. **Risktosoil:** Acidity, Nitrate Toxicity, less availability of other nutrients, Impacts soil microbial population, flora and fauna.

3. **Risktocrops:** Seedling injury, Crop lodging, Succulency & susceptibility to insect, pests and diseases; higher weed infestation, Delayed crop maturity; Imbalance in availability of other nutrients; Reduction in crop yield & quality.

4. **Risktowater:** Hypoxia (lack of Oxygen), Algal Blooms, Eutrophication, Pollution of Aquifers.

5. **Risktohealth:** Blue Baby Syndrome (Methemoglobinemia); Nitrate Toxicity, Particulate matter (PM) affects Lungs.

In this connection, to reduce the use of chemical Fertilisers,IFFCO continues to expand its portfolio of Nano fertilizers with the development of 2nd generation Nano Urea Plus Liquid and Nano DAP Liquid aims to provide added benefits and more nutrition to crops in a climate smart manner.

INNOVATIVE NOVEL NANO FERTILISER BY IFFCO
BENEFITS OF USING IFFCO NANO FERTILISERS

	IFFCO NANO FERTILISERS NOTIFIED UNDER FERTILISER CONTROL ORDER (FCO), 1985		
Sl. No.	Product	Nutrient Concentration	Date of Gazette Notification
1	Nano Urea Liquid	4% N	S.O. 885 (E), 24th February, 2021
2	Nano Urea Plus Liquid	16 % N	S.O. 1718 (E), 15th April 2024
3	Nano DAP Liquid	8% N, 16% P2O5	S.O. 1025 (E), 2nd March, 2023

1. **Enhanced Crop Productivity:** Nano fertilizers offer superior nutrient delivery, resulting in higher yields, improved quality, and greater resistance to diseases and pests. This translates to increased farmer incomes and greater food security.

2. **Resource Efficiency:** Nano fertilizers are designed for targeted delivery, minimizing nutrient loss through leaching or runoff. This conserves valuable resources like water and reduces environmental pollution.

3. **Sustainable Agriculture:** By promoting efficient nutrient use, nano fertilizers contribute to sustainable agricultural practices. They can help reduce reliance on chemical fertilizers, mitigating their negative impacts on soil health and the environment.

4. **Promotes PM-PRANAM Scheme:** Use of Nano Fertiliser in Agriculture is promoting PM-PRANAM Scheme by protecting the health of Mother Earth by incentivising the states/UTs with reduced use of

chemical fertilisers and promoting use of alternative efficient fertilisers.

5. **Helps in Govt's Subsidy saving:** Nano fertilizers are highly efficient, meaning farmers can use less of them to achieve the same results as traditional fertilizers. This reduced usage directly translates to lower fertilizer costs for farmers and, consequently, lower subsidy burdens for the government.

6. **Reduction in Transportation Cost:** Nano fertilizers are highly concentrated, meaning farmers need to apply much smaller amounts compared to conventional fertilizers. One 500 ml Nano fertiliser pack is equivalent to one bag of granular urea / DAP bags and it is sufficient to spray in one acre of crop. Hence reduces farmers input cost of storage and transportation.

7. **Economic Growth:** Increased crop yields and improved agricultural productivity drive economic growth, benefiting both farmers and the wider economy.

8. **Technological Advancement:** Investing in nano fertilizer research and development fosters innovation in the agricultural sector and positions the country at the forefront of agricultural technology.

NANO FERTILISER PLANTS

IFFCO has established the first ever Nano Urea &Nano DAP fertiliser production facilities at IFFCO Kalol unit, Gujurat. Further the production unit expanded and production started at Phulpur and Aonla unit, Uttar Pradesh.

Products	Plant Location	Annual capacity (Lakh bottles of 500 ml each)	Date of Commercial Production
Nano Urea Plus	Kalol, Gujurat	495	01.08.2021
	Phulpur, Uttar Pradesh	600	01.03.2023
	Aonla, Uttar Pradesh	600	01.03.2023
Nano DAP	Kalol, Gujurat	600	01.10.2023

Further establishment of Nano Urea Plus plants at Bengaluru(Karnataka) & Deogarh(Jharkhand) and Nano DAP plants at Kandla (Gujurat) &Paradeep (Odisha) is under progress.

RESEARCH/FARMERS FIELD TRIALS&STATE GOVT/SAU'S RECOMMENDATIONS

At IFFCO, they have done more than 2.15 lakh field demonstrations till date to promote usage of Nano Fertilisers among farmers. IFFCO also led the field trials across the 15 Agro Climatic zones (ACZ) of the country in which 1270 Nano DAP (120 ACZ trials in Odisha) and 200 Nano Urea Plus (8 ACZ trials in Odisha)trials were conductedunder the guidance of Department of Fertilisers(DOF). Over 411 ICAR-KVKs monitored these trials on various crops, including paddy, Maize, Cotton, Groundnut, Chilli, Cabbage, Cauliflower, Onion, Brinjal, Tomato, Potato, Green Gram, Black Gram, Sugarcane etc. These results demonstrated an increase in yields, marking a positive step towards promoting sustainable agriculture through Nano Fertiliser in India.

- Based on these research and findings of Nano Fertiliser trials, Odisha University of Agriculture Technology (OUAT), Bhubaneswar has recommended *"Substitution of 25% nitrogen of soil test dose with spraying of Nano Urea Plus @ 4ml/lit of water in paddy at active tillering and PI stage can produce at par yield as per soil test dose with saving of granular urea fertiliser".*

- Department of Agriculture and Farmers Empowerment, Govt. of Odisha has also stated that *recommended dose of Nitrogen for paddy can be replaced up to 25% by Nano Urea Plus with an application rate of 2-4ml/lit of water and spray volume of 125 litres per acre.*

- Government of Odisha has also been included Nano DAP in Comprehensive Project on Rice Fallow Management (CPRFM) Scheme, where in 18 districts of Odisha has been supplied with Nano DAP for sustainable management of Rice crop.

PRODUCTION AND SALES ACHIEVEMENT DURING FY-2024-25

With high spirit of innovation and excellence, IFFCO was able to accomplish a *total all India sale of 365 Lakh Bottles of Nano Fertilisers (9.27 Lakh Bottles in Odisha).* This included 268 Lakh Bottles IFFCO Nano Urea Plus Liquid (5.55 Lakh Bottles in Odisha) and 97 Lakh bottles of IFFCO Nano DAP Liquid (3.72 Lakh Bottles in Odisha) during FY-2024-25. This sale of IFFCO Nano Urea Plus Liquid is 31%, Nano DAP is 118% and overall, 47% higher than the sales of last FY-2023-24.

Further, the *total production of IFFCO Nano Fertiliser during FY-2024-25 was 456.38 Lakh Bottles* in which Nano Urea Plus Liquid was 371.24 Lakh Bottles and Nano DAP was 85.14 Lakh Bottles.

CONCLUSION

Application of Nanotechnology is increasing in every sphere of human life. In crop production, through Nano Agri-inputs nutritional requirements of crops can effectively be met through targeted, stage-wise and slow-release application without disturbing the Agri-ecology. IFFCO's efforts to continuously provide farmers with the best quality Agri-inputs for better crop production by keeping in pace with the latest technologies globally has led to the upgradation of Nano Urea Liquid to Nano Urea Plus Liquid. The invention of Nano Fertiliser clearly indicates that applied nanotechnology is evolving fast due to better understanding of nano systems and Nano Urea Plus gives more flexibility to farmers for providing effective nutrition to crops without leaving any environmental footprint.

ଆସିକା ସମବାୟ ଚିନିଶିଳ୍ପ ଲିଃ, ଆସିକା

ଆସିକା ସମବାୟ ଚିନିଶିଳ୍ପ ଲିଃ ଦୀର୍ଘ ଛଅ ଦଶନ୍ଧି ଧରି ଗଞ୍ଜାମ ଜିଲ୍ଲାର ବିଭିନ୍ନ ବ୍ଲକ୍ ରେ ଆଖୁଚାଷ କରିବା ନିମନ୍ତେ ଚାଷୀମାନଙ୍କୁ ରଣ ସୂତ୍ରରେ ଅଧିକ ଅମଳକ୍ଷମ ଓ ଅଧିକ ଶର୍କରାଯୁକ୍ତ ନୂତନ କିସମର ବିହନ, ରାସାୟନିକ ସାର, ଜୈବିକ ସାର, କାରଖାନାର ମଳିଖତ, କୀଟନାଶକ ଓ ତୃଣନାଶକ ଇତ୍ୟାଦି ଯୋଗାଇ ଆସୁଛି । ଚାଷୀ ଆଖୁ କାରଖାନାକୁ ଯୋଗାଣ ସମୟରେ ପରିବହନ ଭତା ବାବଦକୁ ରିହାତି ଯୋଗାଇ ଦିଆଯାଉଅଛି । ଚିନିଶିଳ୍ପର କ୍ଷେତ୍ର ଅଧିକାରୀ ଓ କର୍ମଚାରୀଙ୍କ ଦ୍ୱାରା ବୈଜ୍ଞାନିକ ପ୍ରଣାଳୀରେ ଆଖୁଚାଷ କରିବା ନିମନ୍ତେ ବୈଷୟିକ ଜ୍ଞାନକୌଶଳ ଯୋଗାଇ ଦିଆଯାଇ ଅଛି। ରାଜ୍ୟ ସରକାରଙ୍କ କୃଷିବିଭାଗ ଓ ଚିନିଶିଳ୍ପର ମିଳିତ ସହଯୋଗରେ "ଆଖୁ ଉନ୍ନୟନ ପ୍ରଯୁକ୍ତି ମିଶନ୍" ଜରିଆରେ ଆଖୁଚାଷୀମାନଙ୍କୁ ବିଭିନ୍ନ ପ୍ରକାର ପ୍ରୋତ୍ସାହନ ଓ ବୈଷୟିକ ତାଲିମ ପ୍ରଦାନ କରାଯାଉଛି । ଉକ୍ତ ପ୍ରୋତ୍ସାହନ ନୂତନ ଆଖୁଚାଷ, ମୂଳି ଆଖୁଚାଷ, ବିହନ ଉତ୍ପାଦନ ଓ ଉତ୍ପାଦକତା ବୃଦ୍ଧି ନିମନ୍ତେ ଏକର ପ୍ରତି ଯଥାକ୍ରମେ ୯୦୦୦ ଟଙ୍କା, ୬୦୦୦ ଟଙ୍କା, ୧୦୦୦୦ ଟଙ୍କା ଓ ୪୦୦୦ଟଙ୍କା ହିସାବରେ ଯୋଗାଇ ଦିଆଯାଉଅଛି । ଆଖୁଚାଷୀ ମାନଙ୍କୁ ବିଭିନ୍ନ ଡାଟୀୟ କରଣ ବ୍ୟାଙ୍କ, ଆସ୍କା କେନ୍ଦ୍ରୀୟ ସମବାୟ ବ୍ୟାଙ୍କ, ବ୍ରହ୍ମପୁର କେନ୍ଦ୍ରୀୟ ସମବାୟ ବ୍ୟାଙ୍କ ଓ ଉତ୍କଳ ଗ୍ରାମୀଣ ବ୍ୟାଙ୍କ ଜରିଆରେ ଫସଲ ରଣ ଯୋଗାଇ ଦିଆଯାଉଅଛି ।

ଏଣୁ ଚିନିଶିଳ୍ପର ସଂରକ୍ଷିତ ଅଞ୍ଚଳ ଯଥା ଗଞ୍ଜାମ ଜିଲ୍ଲା, ନୟାଗଡ ଜିଲ୍ଲାର ଓଡଗାଁ, ରଣପୁର, ନୟାଗଡ, ନୂଆଗାଁ ବ୍ଲକ୍ ଓ ଖୋର୍ଧା ଜିଲ୍ଲାର ବାଣପୁର ଓ ଚିଲିକା ବ୍ଲକ୍ର ଚାଷୀ ଭାଇ ମାନଙ୍କୁ ଅନୁରୋଧ ସେମାନେ ଅଧିକ ପରିମାଣର ଆଖୁଚାଷ କରି ନିଜର ଆର୍ଥିକ ଅଭିବୃଦ୍ଧି ସହିତ ଚିନିଶିଳ୍ପର ଉତ୍ତରୋତ୍ତର ଉନ୍ନତି ତଥା ସମୃଦ୍ଧିରେ ସହାୟକ ହୁଅନ୍ତୁ ।

ଡ. ସୁଶାନ୍ତ କୁମାର ପଣ୍ଡା
ପରିଚାଳନା ନିର୍ଦ୍ଦେଶକ

ଶ୍ରୀ ରବିନ୍ଦ୍ର ପଣ୍ଡା
ସଭାପତି

ODISHA CONSUMERS' CO-OPERATIVE FEDERATION

ଓଡ଼ିଶା ଖାଉଟୀ ସମବାୟ ମହାସଂଘ ଲିঃ.

PLOT NO- A/31, POST BOX NO. 125, OPP. SHRIYA TALKIES, UNIT - III, BHUBANESWAR - 1

Email:occfbbsr@gmail.com

OUR FEATURES:

✓ To provide all types of quality consumer goods in reasonable price.

✓ To provide better service & timely supply

✓ We have supplied all quality materials to ITDA, DWO, DSWO, DFO, Horticulture, Agriculture, Schools, Hostels, & other Deptt.

OUR BRANCHES AT:

❖ OCCF LTD.,BARIPADA

❖ OCCF LTD.,JEYPORE

❖ OCCF LTD., MALGODOWN, CUTTACK

❖ OCCF LTD., ROURKELA

❖ OCCF LTD., DHENKANAL

❖ OCCF LTD., PHULABANI

❖ OCCF LTD., SAMBALPUR

❖ OCCF LTD., KESINGA

❖ OCCF LTD. BHANJAPRABHA (H.O.), BRANCH, BBSR

❖ OCCF LTD.,BHANJAPRABHA-I.D. MARKET BRANCH

❖ OCCF LTD.,BHANJAPRABHA, CUTTACK BRANCH

❖ OCCF LTD., BERHAMPUR BR

❖ OCCF LTD., PURI BRANCH

"Buy Well, Buy Better and always Buy from Co-operatives"

: ଜୟ ତୁ ସମବାୟ :

Sd/-	Sd/-
Dr. Sushanta Kuamar Panda, OCS	SRI PRATAP CHANDRA DHAL
Addl. Registrar of Coop. Societies &	PRESIDENT
Managing Director, OCCF Ltd.	Managing Director, OCCF Ltd.

ଓଡ଼ିଶା ରାଜ୍ୟ ପଣ୍ୟାଗାର ନିଗମ, ଭୁବନେଶ୍ବର

ପ୍ଲଟ ନଂ-୨, କଟକ ରୋଡ଼,ଭୁବନେଶ୍ବର ୭୫୧୦୦୬

> ତାର୍ଗ ୨୬ ବର୍ଷ ଧରି ରାଜ୍ୟରେ ଖାଦ୍ୟଶସ୍ୟ, କୃଷିଜାତଦ୍ରବ୍ୟ,ସାର,ସିମେଣ୍ଟ, ରିଲିଫସାମଗ୍ରୀ, କୀଟନାଶକ, କାଗଜକିଲ ,କାର୍ପାସ,ଟାୟାର, ବିଭିନ୍ନ ଯନ୍ତ୍ରପାତି ତଥା ଅନ୍ୟାନ୍ୟ ସାମଗ୍ରୀର ବୈଜ୍ଞାନିକ ପଦ୍ଧତିରେ ସଂରକ୍ଷଣ କାର୍ଯ୍ୟରେ ନିୟୋଜିତ ।

> ରାଜ୍ୟରେ ୩୦ଟି ଜିଲ୍ଲାର ୮୮ଟି ସ୍ଥାନରେ ୫.୨୧ ଲକ୍ଷ ମେଟ୍ରିକଟନ କ୍ଷମତାବିଶିଷ୍ଟ ଗୋଦାମଘର ପରିଚାଳନା ମାଧ୍ୟମରେ ସେବା ପ୍ରଦାନ ।

> ପଣ୍ୟାଗାରରେ ଜମାକାରୀଙ୍କର ରକ୍ଷିତ ସାମଗ୍ରୀ ବନ୍ୟା, ବାତ୍ୟା, ଭୂମିକମ୍ପ ଆଦି ପ୍ରାକୃତିକ ବିପର୍ଯ୍ୟୟ ତଥା ନିଆଁ ଓ ଚୋରିଜନିତ କ୍ଷତିରୁ ସୁରକ୍ଷିତ ରଖିବା ପାଇଁ ବୀମାଭୁକ୍ତ ଅଟେ ।

> ରାଜ୍ୟ ଯୋଗାଣ ନିଗମ ଓ ଭାରତୀୟ ଖାଦ୍ୟ ନିଗମକୁ ଯଥାକ୍ରମେ ୨,୫୪,୩୩୬ ଓ ୧,୫୧,୨୩୪ ମେଟ୍ରିକଟନ ଗୋଦାମ ଘର ଯୋଗାଇଦେଇ ରାଜ୍ୟରେ ଖାଦ୍ୟଶସ୍ୟର ସଂରକ୍ଷଣ ଓ ଯୋଗାଣ ନିମନ୍ତେ ସେବା ପ୍ରଦାନକରି ପଣ୍ୟାଗାର ନିଗମ ଏକ ପ୍ରମୁଖ ଭୂମିକା ଗ୍ରହଣ କରିଆସୁଛି ।

> ଏହି ସଂସ୍ଥା ୧୯୮୪-୮୫ ଆର୍ଥିକ ବର୍ଷ ଠାରୁ କ୍ରମାଗତ ଭାବେ ଲାଭ ପ୍ରଦାନ କରୁଅଛି ଏବଂ ଉଭୟ ରାଜ୍ୟସରକାର ଓ କେନ୍ଦ୍ରୀୟ ପଣ୍ୟାଗାର ନିଗମକୁ ନିୟମିତ ଭାବରେ ଲାଭାଂଶ ପ୍ରଦାନ କରୁଅଛି ।

> ନିଗମର ୪୮ଟି ପଣ୍ୟାଗାର WDRA କତ୍ତୃପକ୍ଷ ଦ୍ବାରା ପଞ୍ଜୀକୃତ ହୋଇଥିବାରୁ କୃଷକ ଓ ଜମାକାରୀ ମାନେ ଗୋଦାମରେ ରକ୍ଷିତ ଦ୍ରବ୍ୟ ପାଇଁ ହସ୍ତାନ୍ତର ଯୋଗ୍ୟ ରସିଦ ମାଧ୍ୟମରେ ବ୍ୟାଙ୍କ ରଣର ସୁବିଧା ପାଇପାରିବେ ।

> ପଣ୍ୟାଗାର ଗୁଡ଼ିକର ପରିଚାଳନା ଓ ଆନୁଷଙ୍ଗିକ କାର୍ଯ୍ୟକୁ କମ୍ପ୍ୟୁଟରୀକରଣ ମାଧ୍ୟମରେ ସୁଦୃଢ଼ ଓ କ୍ରିୟାଶୀଳ କରିବାପାଇଁ ୱେରହାଉସ ମ୍ୟାନେଜମେଣ୍ଟ ସଲ୍ୟୁସନ କାର୍ଯ୍ୟକାରୀ କରାଯାଇଛି ।

> ରାଜ୍ୟ ଓ କେନ୍ଦ୍ର ସରକାର ସଂସ୍ଥା, ଘରୋଇ ଅନୁଷ୍ଠାନ ତଥା ବ୍ୟକ୍ତି ବିଶେଷ ନିଜର କୃଷିଜାତ ଦ୍ରବ୍ୟ ଓ ଅନ୍ୟାନ୍ୟ ସାମଗ୍ରୀ ପଣ୍ୟାଗାର ଗୁଡ଼ିକରେ ସଂରକ୍ଷଣ କରିବା ନିମନ୍ତେ ସବିଶେଷ ତଥ୍ୟପାଇଁ ନିଗମର ମୁଖ୍ୟ କାର୍ଯ୍ୟାଳୟ ସହିତ ଯୋଗାଯୋଗ କରନ୍ତୁ । (ମୋ- ୯୯୨୭୦୦୪୨୫୦)

ଏକ ଶସ୍ୟଦାନା ସଂରକ୍ଷଣ , ଏକ ଶସ୍ୟଦାନା ଉତ୍ପାଦନ ସଙ୍ଗେ ସମାନ ।

ପରିଚାଳନା ନିର୍ଦ୍ଦେଶକ
ଓଡ଼ିଶା ରାଜ୍ୟ ପଣ୍ୟାଗାର ନିଗମ

With Best Compliments

State Bank of India Staff Association

Co-operative Society Odisha Ltd. Cuttack – 753 002

PHONE : 0671-2368125, 2368294

E-mail:sbisacs@gmail.com / sbisac@rediffmail.com

Website : www.sbisac.in

SBI

ESTD. : 16TH JUNE, 1976

ଖୋର୍ଦ୍ଧା କେନ୍ଦ୍ର ସମବାୟ ବ୍ୟାଙ୍କ ଲିଃ.,ଖୋର୍ଦ୍ଧା।

Regn.No.95 PU Dt.22.03.1912,RBI Licence No. RPCD/BBSR/15/2011-12 Dt.02.05.2012

E -mail ID-khordhaccbank@gmail.com ,ceo@khordhaccbank.com

ରିଜର୍ଭ ବ୍ୟାଙ୍କ ଦ୍ୱାରା ଲାଇସେନ୍ସ ପ୍ରାପ୍ତ   ୧୧୩ ବର୍ଷର ଅଗ୍ରଣୀ ବ୍ୟାଙ୍କ

ବ୍ୟାଙ୍କରେ ଉପଲବ୍ଧ ସୁବିଧା ଓ ସୁଯୋଗ

୧. CBS ଦ୍ୱାରା ୯୮ ଗୋଟି ଶାଖା,୭୩ ଗୋଟି ସମ୍ପ୍ରସାରିତ ଶାଖା ଓ ଅନୁବନ୍ଧିତ ୧୧୭୬ଗୋଟି PACS ରେ କୃଷି ଓ ବ୍ୟାଙ୍କିଙ୍ଗ ସେବା ପ୍ରଦାନ ।

୨. ୧,୦୦,୦୦୦/- ଟଙ୍କା ପର୍ଯ୍ୟନ୍ତ ସମିତିରୁ କୃଷି ରଣ ନେଇ ଠିକ ସମୟରେ ପରିଶୋଧ କଲେ ସୁଧ ଦେୟ ମୁକ୍ତ ଅଟେ ।

୩. ୧,୦୦,୦୦୧/- ଟଙ୍କାରୁ ୩, ୦୦,୦୦୦/- ଟଙ୍କା ରଣ ଉପରେ ମାତ୍ର ୨ ପ୍ରତିଶତ ହାରରେ ସୁଧ, ଝାଡଗାଡ଼ା ଓ ଲୁମିହୀନ ଚାଷୀଙ୍କୁ ବଳରାମ ଯୋଜନା ମାଧ୍ୟମରେ କୃଷି ରଣ ପ୍ରଦାନ ।

୪. କୃଷକମାନଙ୍କ ପାଇଁ ପ୍ରଧାନମନ୍ତ୍ରୀ ଫସଲବୀମା , ଦୁର୍ଘଟଣାଜନିତ ବୀମା ଓ ଜୀବନ ବୀମା ଉପଲବ୍ଧ ।

୫.ସରକାରୀ ମୂଲ୍ୟରେ ସମିତି ରେ ବିହନ,ରାସାୟନିକ ସାର ଓ ଜୈବିକ ସାର ଓ କୀଟନାଶକ ଔଷଧ ଯୋଗାଣ ବ୍ୟବସ୍ଥା ।

୬.କୃଷି ଆନୁସଙ୍ଗିକ ମିଆଦୀ ରଣ ଯଥା ଗାଈ,ଛେଳି , ମେଣ୍ଢା ପାଳନ, କୃଷି ଯନ୍ତ୍ରପାତି ,ପୋଷଣା ଖୋଲା,ମାଛ ଚାଷ ,ଫଲ ,କୁଟ ଚାଷ ,ପାନବରଜ ଓ ଜଳସେଚନ ନିମିତ୍ତ ରଣର କିସ୍ତି ଠିକ ସମୟରେ ପରିଶୋଧ କଲେ ଶତକଡା ୩ ଟଙ୍କା ସୁଧ ରିହାତି ବ୍ୟବସ୍ଥା ।

୭.ସମସ୍ତ ପ୍ରକାର ବ୍ୟବସାୟିକ ଭିତ୍ତିକ ରଣ,ଗୃହ ଉପକରଣ କ୍ରୟ ରଣ ,ଚତୁର୍ୱୀୟ ରଣ ଓ ସମିତି ବନ୍ଧକ ରଣ ଅତି କମ ସୁଧ ରେ ଉପଲବ୍ଧ ।

୮. ଅତି ସହଜ ,ସରଳୀକୃତ କାଗଜାତ ଓ କମ ସୁଧ ରେ ୨୪ଦିନିଆ ଓ ୪ ଚକିଆ ଯାନ ପାଇଁ ରଣ ଉପଲବ୍ଧ ।

୯.ସ୍ୱର୍ଣ୍ଣ ବନ୍ଧକ ରଣ ଅନ୍ୟ ବ୍ୟାଙ୍କ ତୁଳନାରେ ସ୍ୱଳ୍ପ ଶତକଡା ମାସିକ ୮.୧ ହାରରେ ପ୍ରଦାନ ।

୧୦.ମିଶନ ଶକ୍ତି ମାଧ୍ୟମରେ ମହିଳା ସ୍ୱୟଂ ସହାୟକ ଗୋଷ୍ଠୀଙ୍କୁ ₹,୦୦,୦୦୦/- ଟଙ୍କା ପର୍ଯ୍ୟନ୍ତ ବିନା ସୁଧରେ ରଣ ।

୧୧. ଆର୍ଥିକ ସ୍ୱାବଲମ୍ବନ ପାଇଁ କ୍ଷୁଦ୍ର ବ୍ୟବସାୟ ରଣ ବିନା ବନ୍ଧକରେ ୧,୦୦,୦୦୦ /-ଟଙ୍କା ପର୍ଯ୍ୟନ୍ତ ରଣ ଉପଲବ୍ଧ ।

୧୨.IMPS ,NEFT ,RTGS ,AEPS ,PoS ,CTS Clearing ,ATM, Micro ATM ଓ RuPay କାର୍ଡ ମାଧ୍ୟମରେ ଉନ୍ନତ ବ୍ୟାଙ୍କିଙ୍ଗ ସେବା ଉପଲବ୍ଧ ।

୧୩. ସଦର ଶାଖା, ଭୁବନେଶ୍ୱର ମହିଳା ଶାଖା ଓ ଖୋର୍ଦ୍ଧା ମହିଳା ଶାଖା ୦ିରେ Safe Deposit Locker ଉପଲବ୍ଧ ।

୧୪.ସର୍ବନିମ୍ନ ସହାୟକ ମୂଲ୍ୟ (MSP) ରେ ସମିତି ମାନକ ଦ୍ୱାରା ଖରିଫ ଓ ରବି ଫସଲ କ୍ରୟ କରି DBT ଦ୍ୱାରା ଅର୍ଥ ପ୍ରଦାନ ।

୧୫.ମିଆଦୀ ଜମା (Fixed Deposit) ଓ ସଞ୍ଚୟ ଜମା(Saving Deposit) ଉପରେ ଅନ୍ୟାନ୍ୟ ବାଣିଜ୍ୟିକ ଓ ଗ୍ରାମ୍ୟ ବ୍ୟାଙ୍କ ଠାରୁ ଅଧିକ ସୁଧ ଦେବା ସହିତ ଜମା ରାଶି ବୀମା ଦ୍ୱାରା ସୁରକ୍ଷିତ(DICGC) ଓ ବରିଷ୍ଠ ନାଗରିକମାନଙ୍କ ପାଇଁ ମିଆଦୀ ଜମା ଉପରେ ୦.୫ ପ୍ରତିଶତ ଅଧିକ ସୁଧ ପ୍ରଦାନ କରାଯାଏ ।

ଅଧିକ ବିବରଣୀ ନିମନ୍ତେ ନିକଟସ୍ଥ ଶାଖା / ବ୍ୟାଙ୍କ ମୁଖ୍ୟ କାର୍ଯ୍ୟାଳୟ ସହ ଯୋଗାଯୋଗ କରନ୍ତୁ ।

ଶ୍ରୀ ସାରଥୀ ଶତପଥୀ

ମୁଖ୍ୟ କାର୍ଯ୍ୟ ନିର୍ବାହୀ ଅଧିକାରୀ

ଖୋର୍ଦ୍ଧା କେନ୍ଦ୍ର ସମବାୟ ବ୍ୟାଙ୍କ ଲିଃ.

ଶ୍ରୀଯୁକ୍ତ ଅଭିଷେକ ସିଂହ ସାମନ୍ତ

ସଭାପତି

ଖୋର୍ଦ୍ଧା କେନ୍ଦ୍ର ସମବାୟ ବ୍ୟାଙ୍କ ଲିଃ.

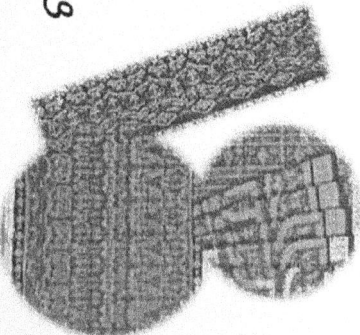

Amlan

https://goswadeshi.in/collections/serifed

www.amlanodisha.com

INDIAN FARMERS FERTILISER COPERATIVE LTD.

State Office : Acharya Vihar, Commercial Complex, Ground Floor, Bhubaneswar
H.O. : IFFCO Sadan, C-1, District Centre, Saket Place, New Delhi

କୃଷି ଓ କୃଷକର ସାମଗ୍ରିକ ବିକାଶ ଲକ୍ଷ୍ୟରେ ସମବାୟର ଅବିରତ ପ୍ରୟାସ

⓵ ରାଜ୍ୟରେ ଯୋଗାଇ ଦିଆଯାଇଥିବା ସମୂଦାୟ କୃଷି ରଣର ୫୦% ରଣ ସମବାୟ ବ୍ୟାଙ୍କ / ସମିତି ଜରିଆରେ ପ୍ରଦାନ

⓶ ସରକାରଙ୍କର ସୁଧ ରିହାତି ଯୋଜନା ମାଧ୍ୟମରେ ୧ ଲକ୍ଷ ଟଙ୍କା ପର୍ଯ୍ୟନ୍ତ ବିନା ସୁଧରେ ଏବଂ ୧ ଲକ୍ଷରୁ ଉର୍ଦ୍ଧ ୩ ଲକ୍ଷ ଟଙ୍କା ପର୍ଯ୍ୟନ୍ତ ୨% ସୁଧରେ ଫସଲ ରଣ ଯୋଗାଣ

⓷ ପ୍ରତ୍ୟେକ ଚାଷୀଙ୍କ ପାଇଁ କୃଷି ବୀମା

⓸ ଯୁଗ୍ମ ଦେୟ ଗୋଷ୍ଠୀ (JLG) ମାଧ୍ୟମରେ ଭୂମିହୀନ ଋଷୀ, ପ୍ରକୃତ ଋଷୀ, କ୍ଷୁଦ୍ର ଓ ନାମମାତ୍ର ଋଷୀଙ୍କୁ ଫସଲ ରଣ ଯୋଗାଣର ବ୍ୟବସ୍ଥା

⓹ ରୁପେ କିସାନ କାର୍ଡ ଦ୍ୱାରା ଏ.ଟି.ଏମ୍ ରୁ କୃଷି ରଣ ଉଠାଣ

⓺ ମିୟାଦୀ ରଣରେ ଆବଶ୍ୟକ ହେଉଥିବା ଅଂଶଧନରେ ବ୍ୟାପକ ରିହାତି

⓻ ରୁପେ ଡେବିଟ୍ କାର୍ଡ ଗ୍ରାହକମାନଙ୍କ ପାଇଁ ବିନା ମୂଲ୍ୟରେ ଏକ ଲକ୍ଷ ଟଙ୍କା ପର୍ଯ୍ୟନ୍ତ ଦୁର୍ଘଟଣା ବୀମା

⓼ ସମସ୍ତ ସଭ୍ୟ /ସଭ୍ୟାମାନଙ୍କର ଆର୍ଥିକ ଅନ୍ତର୍ଭୁକ୍ତି ନିମନ୍ତେ ଆକାଉଣ୍ଟରେ ଆଧାର (Aadhaar) ସଂଯୋଗୀକରଣର ସୁବିଧା(PACS/FSCS/LAMPCS)

⓽ ଜମାକାରୀ ମାନଙ୍କ ପାଇଁ ପ୍ରଧାନମନ୍ତ୍ରୀ ସୁରକ୍ଷା ବୀମା (PMSBY) ଏବଂ ଜୀବନଜ୍ୟୋତି ବୀମା ଯୋଜନା (PMJBY) ର ପ୍ରଚଳନ (OSCB/DCCB)

⓵⓪ ସରକାରଙ୍କର ଆର୍ଥିକ ସହାୟତାରେ PACS ମାନଙ୍କର କମ୍ପ୍ୟୁଟରୀକରଣ

ଓଡ଼ିଶା ରାଜ୍ୟ ସମବାୟ ବ୍ୟାଙ୍କ
www.odishascb.com

ଆମେ ବଢ଼ାଉ ସମ୍ପର୍କ

ODISHA RAJYA TALGUR SAMABAYA SANGH LTD.
PALM CRAFT
Accreditation No.under NPOP
NPOP/NAB/0025
Date Palm
Jaggery Product
ଖଜୁରୀ ଗୁଡ
Block
Granules
Liquid
Talgur Bhawan, Udyogpuri
Khandagiri, Bhubaneswar
Odisha-751030
India
Website: www.ortss.org
Email:
ortssbbsrl959@gmail.com
info@palmodisha.com
Contact: +91 9178507264,